Western Americana

Planned in connection with

CALIFORNIA'S
CENTENARY CELEBRATIONS
1946–50

✿

EDITED BY

ROBERT GLASS CLELAND *AND* OSCAR LEWIS

ALREADY PUBLISHED

THE BIG BONANZA. "DAN DE QUILLE" (William Wright). *Introduction by* Oscar Lewis.

MINING CAMPS; A STUDY IN AMERICAN FRONTIER GOVERNMENT. CHARLES HOWARD SHINN. *Introduction by* Joseph Henry Jackson.

IN PREPARATION

CALIFORNIA, FROM THE CONQUEST IN 1846 TO THE SECOND VIGILANCE COMMITTEE IN SAN FRANCISCO; A STUDY OF AMERICAN CHARACTER. JOSIAH ROYCE. *Introduction by* Robert Glass Cleland.

THE SHIRLEY LETTERS: CALIFORNIA IN 1851 AND 1852; A SERIES OF TWENTY-THREE LETTERS FROM THE CALIFORNIA MINES. "DAME SHIRLEY." *Introduction by* Carl I. Wheat.

ELDORADO, OR, ADVENTURES IN THE PATH OF EMPIRE. BAYARD TAYLOR. *Introduction by* Robert Glass Cleland.

OTHER VOLUMES TO BE ANNOUNCED

These are BORZOI BOOKS, *published in New York by* Alfred A. Knopf

MINING CAMPS

A STUDY IN AMERICAN FRONTIER
GOVERNMENT

MINING CAMPS

A STUDY IN

AMERICAN FRONTIER GOVERNMENT

BY

Charles Howard Shinn

INTRODUCTION BY JOSEPH HENRY JACKSON

NEW YORK
ALFRED A. KNOPF
1948

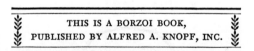

THIS IS A BORZOI BOOK,
PUBLISHED BY ALFRED A. KNOPF, INC.

FIRST BORZOI EDITION

Dedication

TO MY FRIENDS IN CALIFORNIA

INTRODUCTION

THE California mining camp in the golden prime of '49 was flush with money and energy, vigorously and roaringly alive. Its streets sprawled up hills and down canyons; its citizens worked like galley-slaves all day, laboring hip-deep in icy water with pick, shovel, and rocker so that they might spend like drunken sailors half the night. Many kinds of men made up those mushroom camps, from every corner of the United States and most of the countries of Europe, Asia, and South America. They paid a dollar apiece for eggs, and fifty dollars a barrel for their flour; whisky sold for fifty cents a drink, and a butcher-knife with which to pick leaf-gold from crevices in the rock sometimes brought as high as thirty dollars. These miners dug and fought and gambled; they drank heavily, wrote long letters home, wept easily over the picture of a child or a bride, went armed day and night. They were a hardy, generous, careless, brawling, courageous lot, heroes after their fashion.

Yet they were not a lawless group. The leadership went with the majority, which was made up of men from the States. And these Americans had a passion for regulation. Like their forebears in the Anglo-Saxon tradition, they wanted everything to be orderly, clear, correct. Independently of one another, groups of men scattered throughout the California gold country came together and set down the outlines of their schemes of self-government. It was perhaps the most impressive demonstration ever conducted of the peculiar genius of the American people for retaining individual independence yet having the rules understood.

Charles Howard Shinn's *Mining Camps,* subtitled

[v

A Study in American Frontier Government, was written
some thirty years after the gold rush because Shinn,
then a student in political science at Johns Hopkins
University, felt this record of a hitherto neglected phase
in American development to be a contribution to the
practical political experience of the race. He puts it just
this way in his text and he proves his point fully before
he is through. For the growth of law in the gold regions
of California was not a phenomenon isolated in space
and time; far from it. The habit of law and regulation
was planted in these Argonauts before they reached the
diggings, and the influence of their understanding of
the need for law, won through hard experience, was felt
far beyond the period and the place. These men who
had worked out practical methods of self-government
the hard way moved out to new communities following
the discoveries of precious metals in other places. Wherever they went they remembered the discipline of their
Sierra camps. Up on the Fraser River, on the great
Comstock Lode, in Idaho and the Black Hills, in Montana and Colorado and down in the Panamints and the
rugged ranges of Arizona, men turned to the precedent
established in the California foothills, ordered their
camps by the law of the miner as the gold-rush settlements had built it up. American miners wandered to
the Australian placers; they traveled to Central America, to Peru, Chile, Ecuador, Brazil, and Patagonia; they
shipped to the Transvaal to try their luck, and to Tibet,
Assam, Abyssinia, and Siberia and the rivers of the
Guinea Coast; long before the days of the Yukon rush
they prospected in the South Seas, in Madagascar, in
Venezuela. With them they took their principles of law
and order, the accretions, layer upon layer, of their
gold-rush experience in the California Sierra. As Shinn
writes, "Everywhere we find men long trained in the

lessons of the mining camps walking as calm conquerors through the midst of this world of tumult, action, and desperate struggle, ruling railroad systems, laying ocean cables, planning isthmus canals, aiding in a thousand enterprises." Everywhere the men of the mining camps proceeded to extend, into new regions, local institutions that were in the highest sense their own. The California gold-rush era, as Shinn demonstrates in this study, was much more than a brief and brilliant period characterized by vigorous impetus and splendor, and therefore by its nature romantic. It was a period, as he notes, "of great historical importance, closely connected with a curious past and an influential fact in forms of local organization even yet incomplete." Shinn wrote in 1884 (Scribner's published his *Mining Camps* in 1885), but it would be perfectly reasonable to say now, a long century after the California gold rush, that the "influential fact" of the American frontiersman working out his own law as he went along still has significance. It is the purpose of Shinn's book to examine the historical importance of miners' law everywhere, but particularly the significance of the rules set up by the California gold-rush miners, who were to spread their habit of thought, reflected in the laws they made, throughout their own country and much of the world.

Law in the mining camp began, actually, before the camp itself. The discovery of gold at Sutter's Mill was made in January 1848, and the news reached the East in time for hundreds of societies, associations, and companies to organize in that pre-gold-rush year. The beginning of such an organization was a set of rules and procedures; the surviving records show with almost monotonous regularity that any group of Americans setting out to get some of California's riches commenced

operations by putting on paper a list of laws. Under
these, captains were elected, treasurers were appointed,
commissary heads were chosen to take care of provisions
for the trip. Members of an association agreed to obey
their captain — usually providing a method of electing
another leader if they saw fit — and signed their names
to such agreements as a matter of course. There was trouble sometimes, in spite of the rules, but that was to be
expected. The laws were there. Invariably the gold-
seekers saw the necessity for some scheme of government,
and invariably they put together some sort of organiza-
tional code.

After the Argonauts arrived in California, their laws
expanded as new situations developed. First the law applied to the gold itself. A man might take up so many
square feet as his claim. If he left his tools on his claim,
that was enough to keep it inviolate for a certain number of days. Penalties were provided for theft, for claim-
jumping, for other infringements upon the individual's
rights, which were the rights of all. Doubtless the miners
did not stop to reflect upon why they thought as they
did, why they took it for granted that a man had rights
that must be respected. Shinn suggests that these miners
of '49 were merely repeating the experience of other
men of their trade for thousands of years — the under-
ground toilers of north Wales and Cornwall, of the
Black Forest and the Harz Mountains, of Moravia and
Styria and northern Spain, the workers in the Greek
placers of Pactolus and the Roman gold-fields of Etru-
ria and Lombardy, in Hannibal's mines at Carthage, in
the Midianitish hills, whose wealth furnished the might
of a hundred and thirty-five thousand Bedouin warriors
who overran Palestine. At any rate, the miners of those
earlier centuries did think in the same patterns, as the
fragmentary record proves. Mining law, frequently in-

dependent of ordinary civil law and operating coordinately with it, more than once led the way in the ever broadening concept of man's right to govern himself.

In the California Sierra, moreover, a wide variety of questions needed to be settled almost immediately. The forty-niner could and did limit a man's right to hold river footage or grass-roots pay-dirt on a hillside — even, later, the extent of his claim on a quartz ledge that went no one knew how deep. From the beginning, behavior was restricted in such matters as horse-stealing and murder, and legal machinery was set up to enforce whatever the members of a group or camp or town decided to be fair and right. But there was water, for instance. A plentiful supply of water was an essential in placer mining. What about the miner's rights here? Or a man might conclude that he had had enough of mining and decide to farm or to run cattle in the hills. How about his rights in land, in grazing privileges? Problems like these had to be met, and the men who had been trained in the mining community's methods met them with the same common sense they had shown in their approach to the gold itself. Borrowing liberally from the Spanish land laws and principles, adapting these to their own special needs and combining them with what they already knew of Anglo-Saxon common law, they worked out a body of precedent which has profoundly influenced American jurisprudence and upon which much of our law concerning water-rights, grazing privileges, and land tenure rests today. All knew that the land they worked was government land and that it belonged to all alike. Out of this knowledge arose the form in which mining-camp law was first cast. As Shinn observes, this form was the flowering of an "unconscious socialism," and the later law that grew out of that body of attitudes and rules and decisions was colored for all time by the assumption that all men had equal rights in the pursuit of fortune. The California mining camp, so to say, informed by a spirit consciously or unconsciously socialistic, watered and tended the early shoots of our democratic process a good deal more significantly than most of us realize. Indeed, some of the offshoots of that carefully nurtured seedling have developed into full-grown plants in our own time. For instance, many companies of miners forbade their members to use ardent spirits, and it was common for such organizations to require members to set aside a certain percentage of gains as a security fund to be drawn upon when any man fell ill or found that his claim had petered out.

"The historian of the future," Shinn wrote, in a paper not included in this volume, "will consider the mining camp as an episode of institutional importance, casting light upon the national character." Now, half a century later, it is clear that he was right. And the fact that Shinn understood this and developed his point in detail — in addition to providing an admirably detailed picture of early California mining-camp life — is reason enough for reissuing his book now.

Charles Shinn was only incidentally a writer in the field of government. Moreover — like many of the state's citizens — he was a Californian only by accident.

His father, James Shinn, was descended from the early Quaker proprietors of southern New Jersey; his mother, Lucy E. Clark, came of a New England family rooted there since the middle of the seventeenth century. But James Shinn caught the itch of the age; the forties and fifties were years of unrest; there was a common urge to move on to the new West. He followed the trail southward, first into Texas, and Charles was born in the spring of 1852 in Austin, a frontier town then barely sixteen years old. James Shinn stayed in Texas only until his son was old enough to travel and then headed westward again, this time to the continent's end. A nurseryman and orchardist, he found California's climate what he had been looking for all his life. He bought land in Niles, across the bay from the thriving city of San Francisco, laid out his farm, and settled down to grow the best nursery stock he could.

The boy, Charles, grew up in the quiet atmosphere of rural Alameda County, learned his father's business, absorbed a knowledge of trees and plants, which later stood him in good stead. Even before he reached his teens the gold rush was over; gold continued to be enormously important in the state's economy, but the Comstock had been discovered by the time Charles was eight years old, and thousands of Sierra miners had been drawn over the mountains into Washoe to the new bonanza. Many remained, of course, the lucky ones developing the deep quartz mines when the grass-roots gold was gone, others coming down into the flourishing cities and towns in California's great central valley and on the coast. Any boys of Charles's generation knew hundreds of these men and heard them talk; after all, the gold rush had been the great adventure of the century. Much that Shinn later used in his *Mining Camps* and in *The Story of the Mine* must have soaked into his mind as he listened to ex-prospectors yarning about the great days.

James Shinn was an educated man, and Charles came naturally by his proper respect for books. On his father's farm the boy learned to work hard, and the College School, afterward the University of California, was not too far away. When he was ready he put himself through two years there, earning the diploma that gave him the right to teach in the state schools. For the next few years he moved about, teaching in Alameda, San

Luis Obispo, Monterey, and Shasta counties. This experience gave him material for many articles he was to write. The history of California interested him from the beginning, and when he wrote about Spanish pioneer houses in California, for instance, his knowledge was evident; in one county he discovered and listed twenty-nine such adobe relics when the official county historian had found only two. When he helped Harry N. Morse, one of the notable bandit-catchers of the 1870's and 1880's, write his memoirs, he was intimately acquainted with the geography of every region in which that officer of the law had ever pursued a stage-robber.

All this, though, was to come. But young Shinn began early to try out his talent. At eighteen he was selling poetry to California newspapers and magazines. In his early twenties he was continuing with his verse and turning out factual pieces on farming, fruit-growing, and home gardens. It was characteristic of the young man that he wrote only about matters upon which he was thoroughly informed, and editors, recognizing this reliability in their new contributor, asked for more. It was also characteristic of Shinn — not merely in those years but all his life — that he knew a surprising amount about a great many things. These qualities led him with irresistible logic into a newspaper office, and for five years, from the age of twenty-five until he was thirty, he worked for the San Francisco Bulletin, going out on regular assignments, frequently contributing graceful verse to the editorial page, ranging the state to write articles that would help the paper's circulation in what was then called "the back country." Much of this traveling was done in the foothill mining region, and Shinn talked with miners now growing older, visited settlements that were already ghost towns, dug into the records of California's past. Doubtless he also talked of the advantages of fruit-growing in that area, whose rich red soil was so admirably suited to the purpose; at any rate, much of the foothill country, now predominantly given over to orchards, developed in that direction during those years.

Teaching and newspaper writing, however, confirmed the young man in his belief that he still had a lot to learn. At the College School he had studied under a teacher he greatly admired — Daniel Coit Gilman, who became president of the University of California when it grew out of the school. Gilman had gone to Johns Hopkins University in Baltimore to be its first president, and when Shinn made up his mind to acquire more formal education he followed his old teacher to the East. He was thirty now, but what was the difference when a man wanted schooling? Gilman welcomed him, directed his study, imbued him with his own enthusiasm for original work. This stimulus led Shinn to think of the subject he knew best — the story of California's mining camps. And because he was studying history and government, he chose to do his research in a field he knew. In 1884 he was given his A.B. degree, and shortly after graduation he sent to the editor at Scribner's the manuscript of a book he had put together from his college papers. Its subject was the significance of the mining camp as a phase of the development of frontier government in America. Shinn wrote easily and well; his newspaper experience had given him fluency and the ability to organize his material. Better, he knew exactly what he was talking about; he had laid the foundation in his California youth, and he had built well and truly upon this foundation through his work at Johns Hopkins. Scribner's accepted the book immediately, and published it in 1885.

Mining Camps had a modest success. The general

public, which had begun to look back with nostalgia to the days of '49, may have preferred the still-popular romances of Bret Harte, but serious readers found *Mining Camps* a genuine contribution to the study of government. Shinn might well have remained in the East, a budding author who knew his trade. But he had spent his formative years in California and it had become his country. He did stay for a few months in New York, writing verse and articles for newspapers and magazines, the *Atlantic Monthly* and the *Century Magazine* among them. Then in San Francisco the *Overland Monthly,* which Harte had made famous twenty years before, was newly brought to life, and Shinn's sister, Millicent, an able writer and critic in her own right, was made editor. This seemed a good opportunity for Charles. He came back to California and joined the *Overland* as business manager.

The difficulty here was that Charles Shinn was a writer and not a financial expert. If he was anything else he was an outdoor man. He had grown up as a farm boy, had roamed over most of northern California, learned much of its history, more about its trees and plants. His true interests were in these directions. Nevertheless he stayed with the *Overland* for almost five years, though he was at least as interested in contributing to its columns as in managing its none too prosperous affairs. He went on writing for other magazines; the files of the *Century* and *Lippincott's* in the East and of the *Argonaut* in San Francisco contain articles, verse, and even stories written during this period. Because he had learned his trade, Shinn could write an acceptable piece of short fiction, at any rate for the editors of that day. Fiction, however, was not his best talent. He turned out pleasant and competent little poems; indeed, he continued to write verse as long as he lived.

But his strong points were his talent for writing simply
and informatively, and his knowledge of practical agriculture, horticulture, and forestry. There was still something of the teacher in him too. And none of these interests could find the scope it required in the kind of
job he now had. Still, a man thinks twice about free-
lancing when he has a wife, and Shinn had married
Julia Tyler of Oakland in 1888. He stayed with his sister's magazine for another two years. But when, in
1890, he had a chance to combine his interests by join-
ing the Agricultural Department of the University of
California, he took it. In that year he became Inspector
of Experiment Stations for the university, a post he occupied for the next eleven years.

As far as writing went, these were the most productive years of Shinn's life. He kept up his connection
with the *Century,* and contributed to Western magazines steadily. He turned out more verse for the newspapers and weeklies, and wrote *The Story of the Mine*
for Appleton's "Story of the West" series. Ripley Hitch-
cock, editor for Appleton, called this authentic yet pop-
ularly done account of Nevada's incredible Comstock
Lode "a contribution of lasting value to American history," and the reviewers of the day agreed. At the university his work called for constant writing, and he produced dozens of pamphlets and reports related to his
work — monographs on such subjects as Australian salt
bushes, acacias in California, deciduous fruits, the Russian thistle, and the like. He had already written his
Pacific Rural Handbook, and regularly sold historical
articles on the missions of California, pioneer families
of the state, and similar topics to periodicals in the East,
whose editors at this period were actively interested in
California lore. Now he began writing for Western magazines such as *Sunset, Land of Sunshine,* and *Out West,*

which were part literary magazines and part boom-and-boost sheets in the fashion of the time. His university job was in a field he knew and liked. He worked hard at writing, which had always been his favorite occupation. And he had a baby daughter and a wife who supported him warmly in such enthusiasms as camping in the foothill forests when the baby was only two years old — and of course writing an article about the experience. Life moved along serenely.

It was about this time that the word "conservation" came into the public vocabulary. Gifford Pinchot was spreading his gospel everywhere, and in the middle 1890's Shinn was made a member of the National Forest Commission. His knowledge of the California forests was broad, and he had long preached conservation. Now the idea was gaining headway in Washington, and Shinn energetically set himself to promoting the doctrine in California. He wrote verses about the noble *Sequoia sempervirens* of the coastal regions; he lost no chance to remind the public that indiscriminate waste of the national resources would lead to national bankruptcy. In magazine articles of any description he usually managed to insert a paragraph or two on this question that was so close to his heart. A *Lippincott's* piece, for example, which was supposed to inform the reader on the products and opportunities of California, accomplishes this goal to be sure; but it concludes: "If wise and strongly enforced legislation protects the great Californian forests that clothe the upper Sierra and the Coast Range and keep the secret springs of all the streams, there will be no more happy and prosperous commonwealth in all the land. The loss of our woods is the most immediate danger that threatens the material growth of California." The idea became a crusade with Shinn, as it did with Pinchot himself, with Theodore

Roosevelt and many another intelligent American. And Shinn liked crusades. They matched his idealistic approach to life.

It was not surprising that this, one of the really important crusades in his nation's life, should draw Shinn more and more into its orbit. His wife saw eye to eye with him, encouraged him in his unaffected desire to help the people of his state in the battle most of them did not fully understand in spite of its significance to them — the battle against the ruthless type of private industry which fought the conservation idea so that it might retain the privilege of exploiting what, in the mind of the conservationist, should be the property of all the people. It is easy to see why, when the position was offered him in the summer of 1901, Shinn became Forest Examiner and then Head Ranger in the Forest Reserve, which later became the responsibility of the Forest Service. His area was what was then known as the Sierra Forest Reserve; afterward it was broken up into several parts, one of which became the Sierra National Forest.

This was something Charles Shinn liked even better than his university work, and he threw himself into it with fervor. He continued to write; his verse was always a sort of release for his spirit. There were reports to be made, of course, and he kept up his contacts with magazine editors, giving them the California material they always seemed to want. Sometimes it was in the form of articles on the need for conserving the forests, often it was something to do with California's history. Shinn had begun to broaden his field and to examine the older Spanish period and its legendry. His writing had to be done between times; he was chasing off to Washington on forestry business; he was serving as California's delegate to the American Forestry Congress;

he was taking on all comers in the righteous struggle to hold the forest lands against encroachment by private interests. Perhaps the best reflection of his views — especially significant in the light of events to come — is found in a letter from him to Governor Pardee of California, a former schoolmate. From Washington, where he was "looking out for western interests," Shinn wrote, early in 1905:

"The great needs are: Better regulations about grazing in the Reserves, so as to help our foothill settlers; opening the Parks to limited grazing; restoration of Yosemite Valley to the Federal Government; laws by which the great water and power privileges in the Reserves, now given away, are sold under a sinking fund arrangement and made to produce to the Nation and the State some revenue." Shinn was well aware that the real fight would be on this final point. Indeed, it is quite evident that he had already been attacked as the 1905 equivalent of a Red, for he concludes: "One English company that secured, under present laws, rights in a Reserve worth $5,000,000 and invests $3,000,000 in plant, simply gets the power for nothing. It *isn't* socialism to remark that they should pay the Government annual rental on something like $2,000,000!" What the Governor thought about it remains anyone's guess. He replied cagily: "What you say about the primary needs in the forests and foothills interests me," and let it go at that.

Shinn stuck to his beliefs throughout his decade of service to the government. So wrapped up was he in his beloved forests that he and his wife moved to Northfork in Madera County, a spot on the banks of Willow Creek some two thousand feet up in the hills. In the house he built there — Peace Cabin, he called it — Shinn made his headquarters, writing when he could, keeping up

the good fight for the thing he believed in. Though he
was no longer a young man, he might have continued
his good work for many more years if he had not been
doing so thorough a job of it. But his good friend Pinchot was dismissed from the Forest Service by President
Taft, and it seemed to those on whose toes Shinn had
stepped in his constant advocacy of the people's rights a
good time to get this annoyingly sincere man out of the
way. Shinn was arbitrarily charged with dealing unfairly
in some matter of grazing permits, and the Forest Service was ordered to investigate. It is pleasant to record
Forester Olmstead's statement to the press: "Following
charges by citizens of Mariposa County reflecting upon
the integrity of Charles H. Shinn, Supervisor of the Sierra National Forest, District Forester Olmstead an-
nounces that a thorough investigation has been made
by the Forest Service and that Shinn has been com-
pletely exonerated. . . . He is now considering the pro-
motion of Shinn to an even more useful sphere of
work."

But the dismissal of Pinchot had been one sign of the
pendulum-swing in the new direction, away from the
Roosevelt-Pinchot-sponsored effort to set aside forest
lands for all the people. There was corruption in high
places; many will remember Pinchot's blistering attacks
upon the administration, and the split that resulted in
the Progressive Party. And Shinn felt that his usefulness
here was at an end. He left the Forest Service in 1911,
still vigorous as he neared sixty, in no way discouraged
about mankind, content to keep up with his writing and
his friends.

The last fourteen years of his life were spent in that
same Peace Cabin at Northfork from which he had
helped to guard the forests that had become so large a
part of his life. He wrote almost as much as ever, re-

viewing books for the Fresno *Republican,* contributing
to *Sunset,* the *Overland* (now revived once more), and
to newspapers up and down the state, writing to his
friends letters into which he would slip sprigs of the
fragrant incense-cedar beside his door.

As he had been all his life, he was interested in everything. In 1914 he was writing to the California State
Library to inquire about any existing records of an ex-
perimental colony called Icaria-Speranza, founded in
1881 on the Russian River near Cloverdale. Evidently
he was projecting some account of such ventures in co-
operative living, for he added that he would like any
information available on other colonies of the sort in
the West. In another letter he observes that though he
is not rich and does not pretend to be a collector in the
full sense, he has enjoyed himself finding early letters
and documents where he can. He adds: "My own idea is
that in ten or twenty years I shall write a one-volume
history of California and its people, about 800 or 900
pages. I had such a thing blocked out once, but never
knew enough." Later he refers again to the Icarian colony and its failure: "Funny, isn't it, how hard it is for
dead-in-earnest reformers to endure each other! Bless
them all, anyhow!"

Even from such fragments it is easy enough to see the
kind of man Shinn was, growing older without losing
any of his humor or balance, never weakening in his
lifelong conviction that the upright and sincere man
would prevail — but that even if he didn't, no proper
man could be otherwise. A brief excerpt from an article
of his about books and reading illuminates his nature
as well as anything he ever put on paper. Wrote Shinn:
"I wish continually to maintain the doctrine that literature is but handmaid and servant of the good, the pure
and the serene. Only the wise and gentle should dare to

analyze the lives of men; it is only such whose words can really increase the value of life." In this considered opinion it is possible to see mirrored the man himself, a modest, gentle, transparently good human being who was satisfied to make his life one happy adventure after another and to regard living as the greatest adventure of all. When he died, at the home of his daughter in Ukiah in 1924, at the age of seventy-two, the Forest Service hastened to name a Sierra peak for him — Mount Shinn, which rises more than eleven thousand feet to overlook the San Joaquin River, into which empties Willow Creek, on whose north fork Shinn lived out the last years of his life. It was the Forest Service, too, that printed the best tribute to his memory, privately in its *District Bulletin*. Noting that the Shinn place at Northfork was for sale, the editor wrote: "That hits, doesn't it? A great deal can be crowded into a small sentence — respect, and love, and a tightening of the throat. Peace Cabin is for sale. But the highmindedness, the fine courage, the inspiration that have come from Peace Cabin are not for sale. We own the real Peace Cabin."

Mining Camps, then, is an important study in its own right for its original contribution to our knowledge of ourselves and our method of self-government — our American character, as Shinn puts it. The book is also the reflection of a man who, because he was himself a fine example of the American character, understood that it was rooted in a tradition of sturdy independence that is practical, essentially realistic, and, for all that has yet been proved to the contrary, ineradicable. It is peculiarly appropriate that this reissue should come at a time when California is on the threshold of its three centenary years: 1948, which marks the hundredth anniversary of the gold-discovery at Sutter's Mill; 1949, when the state will remember the Argonauts of the gold rush; 1950, when California will celebrate a century of statehood. It would be difficult to suggest a better time to make generally available a work long recognized by the student as a classic in its field, or a better time to remind Americans of a man who represented the best of America in character and its fulfillment.

JOSEPH HENRY JACKSON

Berkeley, California
April 1946

PREFACE

Few undertakings of my busy life have brought me more pleasure than the group of studies linked together in this volume. They were begun and carried to completion while I was a student at this university; and if they possess any value, it is chiefly because of the spirit of original investigation fostered here in every department of knowledge.

Since I am about to send this volume to the press, I desire, with sincere respect and affection, to place on record my sense of personal obligations to President D. C. Gilman, Professor Gildersleeve, Professor Paul Haupt, Dr. H. B. Adams, and Dr. Richard Ely, of Johns Hopkins; to President W. T. Reid and Professor Cook of the University of California; and to Dr. Josiah Royce of Harvard — all of whom have helped me by the loan of pamphlets, by advice, and by their cordial interest in the undertaking.

CHARLES HOWARD SHINN, A.B.

Johns Hopkins University, Baltimore
December 1884

CONTENTS

MINING CAMPS

A STUDY IN AMERICAN FRONTIER
GOVERNMENT

Chapter I. SCOPE OF THE PRESENT INVESTIGATION

The following pages deal largely with ancient, medieval, and modern mining laws and with the life of mining camps; but this is solely for their value as contributions to American political science and American institutional history. The proposed investigation is as far removed, on the one hand, from a technical history of mining as it is removed, on the other hand, from a digest of mining decisions. It is primarily a study of the mining-camp commonwealths; that is, of those states and territories in the remote West whose development has been under conditions widely different from those that prevailed on the Atlantic slope and in the Mississippi Valley. It is also a study of the Spanish land system in Mexico and in California, and of the relations of priest, alcalde, and commandante, in mission, pueblo, and presidio; for otherwise the place of the true mining camp, as a nucleus of most effective organization, cannot be fully understood. It is an attempt to break ground in a comparatively new field and to examine the laws and customs, not of primitive pastoral nor of primitive agricultural communities, but of the workers in ores and the toilers in auriferous river-sands.

The best thoughts of such writers as Maine, Seebohm, Nasse, the Von Maurers, Laveleye, Kovalevsky, have been devoted to studies of early land-tenure. Patiently they have examined the traces of village communities; of common lands, *"Wald, Weide,* and *Wiese";* of the prehistoric "three-field system," whose rude crop-rotation the Teutonic farmers have followed, with various

[3

modifications, since the days of village moot assemblies by the Frisian sea and on the Swabian mountains; and of the Russian mir, Swiss *Landesgemeinde,* and old Teutonic field meetings — all of them primitive social organizations, and sources of such institutions as Saxon territorial tithings, English parish assemblies, and New England town meetings. For men of our Germanic race this line of investigation is, doubtless, the widest and most important one that institutional history offers; but we shall do well to remember that all beginnings of government and society are valuable to the student, and that, since the days of Tubal Cain, the arts of mining have fostered peculiar independence and developed a most distinctive organization.

Thoughtful Americans feel that they cannot too thoroughly understand our early civic communities, our towns, parishes, and counties, the germs of state and national growth, so firmly rooted in the past of our race. As Green, the "historian of the English people," wrote: "in the village moots of Friesland or Sleswick . . . England learned to be a mother of parliaments." Freeman, historian of the Norman Conquest, looking beyond our political and geographical separation, holds that "the English-speaking commonwealth on the American mainland is simply a part of the great English folk," and urges that the members of this mighty kindred should be to each other "at least as much as were the members of the scattered Hellenic settlements" — these all Englishmen, as those were all Greeks. In studying American colonial life, this sense of noble unity increases; and we are inevitably brought to studies of the European sources of that life. Virginia and Massachusetts lead us not only to the England of Shakspeare and Cromwell, but also to that older England of the Continent.

But if our institutional studies cease at the summits

of the Alleghanies, we have learned only a part of the lesson that America has to teach. In that New West beyond the rocky borders of Nebraska and the remote sources of the Missouri, American pioneers have shown their hereditary fitness for self-government under exceptionally trying conditions. They have wrought out, and are still extending into new regions, local institutions in the highest sense their own. Their state life, growth of law, crystallization of society, largely came from small settlements known as mining camps and from a social organization presenting remarkable political and economic features. So strong, natural, and impressive has been the display in these camps of a capacity for organization of the highest order that the episode known in the West as "the mining era" deserves to be called a stanza in the political epic of the Germanic race to which we belong.

The influence of the Atlantic colonies prevailed without opposition in the early settlements of the Mississippi Valley; but there came a time when American frontiersmen of the third generation found a new environment, adopted a new occupation, and met alien influences from Moor and Saracen, from Spaniard and Mexican. Problems more difficult were nowhere else presented on the continent: nowhere else were they more triumphantly solved. Today, over the western third of the United States, institutional life traces its beginnings to the mining camp: that is the original contribution of the American pioneer to the art of self-government. Boone and his foresters, Carson and his trappers, Bent, Bridger, Beckwourth, and their "mountain men," all melted away before the tides of civilization, without being forced by imperious necessity to the creation of any code of local laws or to the organization of any form of permanent government; but the early miners of the Far

West showed large and noble capacities for bringing order out of chaos, strength out of weakness, because they were a picked body of men, and also because the life they led fostered friendship, encouraged individuality, and compelled the closest social union.

Thirty-seven years ago the discovery of gold in California caused thousands of miners to assemble in the canyons of the Sierra Nevada; and soon they were forced, by lack of territorial and state government, to organize for self-protection and to enact and execute their own civil and criminal codes. The previous history of this region had been such that many foreign influences continued to act either directly or indirectly upon the rude but efficient system of the early mining camps, until, with the formation of permanent government under a state constitution, all necessity for this local camp law of the mountains of California appeared to have suddenly ended. Nevertheless, a large portion of this local law, created thus rapidly and under such unique social conditions, exhibited surprising vitality. It persistently kept its place, persistently extended itself to other territories, persistently influenced township and county government. It found ample recognition from territorial and state legislatures, from Congress, and from the Supreme Court of the United States; and it ultimately developed into what can safely be called the "American system of mining law" — a system that is honored throughout the civilized world, and forms the basis of mining jurisprudence in many of the newer gold regions of other countries.

At the present time in the United States, over nine states and territories, and throughout a rapidly developing region already peopled by more than three million persons, and extending from the silver ledges of southern New Mexico to the frozen placers [1] of Cœur d'Alene, and even beyond, mining property is still held in the main by customs of tenure originated by the early placer- and quartz-miners of California. Although the present laws allow mineral lands to be "patented," and purchased from the government, it is still true that only the well-developed mining properties are so purchased, and that the vast majority of claims are held by simple possessory rights under the "land laws" of the camp or district. Often the early "camp" grew into a "district," embracing several camps; and this district ultimately developed into a township of a county; while the original "camp" in many cases became a "county seat," though still retaining strong evidence in local customs of its growth and previous history. The free, strong life of the mining camp has been a factor of prime importance in the social, literary, and institutional development of large and prosperous American communities. The laws of the mining camp, in modified form, still influence many of the newer states and territories. Nothing that is likely to happen will ever take from the civilization of this imperial domain of Pacific coast and Rocky Mountain region certain characteristics due to the mining-camp era. Even when, a century hence, it is, perhaps, divided into twenty states, with a population of twice as many millions, the atmosphere and traditions of the mining camp will yet linger in the mountain gorges, and fragments of the miner's jurisprudence will yet remain firmly embedded in local and state law.

In order to better understand these camps of the Far West, it has seemed proper, and indeed necessary, to

---

[1] The word "placer" is from the Spanish. It means "content," "satisfaction." "Placers are superficial deposits of gold which occupy the beds of ancient rivers" (decision in case of Moxon *vs.* Wilkinson, 2d Montana Reports).

first investigate, though briefly, the ancient and medieval mining systems. Through legal sources and by means of history, chiefly Spanish, English, and German, we must connect the mining experiences of the New World with those of the Old, sufficiently, at least, to serve for purposes of illustration. We shall everywhere discover that, as Professor Stubbs says in his *Constitutional History,* "the roots of the present lie deep in the past," and that "nothing in the past is dead to the man who would learn how the present comes to be what it is." The very kind of local law and self-government known to the miners of California has existed in some degree among the miners of many other lands. The mining tribes of ancient Siberia, the mining cities of desert-guarded Midian, the Grecian "companies" that "drifted" in the hill of Laurium, the Carthaginian "prospectors" who "panned out" gold from the sands of Tagus and Guadalquivir — each and all contribute precious material to our investigation. Above all, the customs of Cornwall and Thuringia serve to define, illustrate, and explain the workings of primitive law on the Pacific coast. We must also study the Spanish civil and mining code as developed under Mexican skies and as transplanted to the soil of Alta California. In California itself we must trace Spanish-American forces from the days of saintly Padre Serra and bluff Governor Portalá to the advent of the bold, restless Anglo-Saxon trappers, farmers, and miners, with their capacity for work and their faculty for organization.

At the point of time when the military governors of newly conquered California began to rule along the coast, and when the eager, energetic miners first pitched their tents beside the foaming Feather and Yuba, and swung their mighty picks against the splintering bowlders, and hewed their "rockers" from the giant mountain pines, century-old, overhead, our investigation, pursued through so many preliminaries, broadens at last into the study of American miners' courts, their officials, their criminal and civil codes, their land system, their forms of procedure and government. Some of these forms were adopted from Spanish law, some from primitive forms familiar to the Germanic races from the times of Tacitus, some were peculiarly a product of the men and the emergency, but all are historically interesting and important. From this point our studies are properly confined to an examination into the growth of these forces, and of their abiding influence upon later society and government. We must not look upon this period as merely a brilliant episode full of impetus and splendor, dear to the heart of the Western pioneer, and crowded with precious accumulations of material for coming poet and novelist, but as including elements of permanent historical value, judged by a standard of utility, and as, in reality, an episode of great institutional importance, closely connected with a curious past, and still an influential fact in forms of local organization as yet incomplete.

One result of our labors will, perhaps, be that we shall more clearly comprehend the capabilities of our Germanic race for swift adaptation of the means to the end; for readiness in every emergency; for rapid, yet lasting, social organization; for acceptance and transformation of local institutions already at hand; for that sort of hearty, honest compromise which makes the best of circumstances and continually evolves better and better conditions under which to act. Perhaps we shall thus gain a higher faith in that republic whose children have wrought out, unknown, in silence, and under enormous difficulties, laws wise and good for the sufficient protection of life and property, adding, of their own will and

choice, the majesty of government to the careless freedom of their frontier existence. On this higher level, as
a humble contribution to the practical political experience of the race, this study of the hitherto undescribed
institutions and unwritten laws of typical mining camps
must find, if anywhere, its reason and its justification.

In 1866 the chairman of the Senate Committee upon
Mines and Mining closed his report upon a bill then before Congress, in the following language:

"It is essential that this great system" (of local law) "established by the people in their primary capacities, and evi-
dencing by the highest possible testimony the peculiar genius of the American people for founding empire and order,
shall be preserved and affirmed. Popular sovereignty is here
displayed in one of its grandest aspects, and simply invites
us, not to destroy, but to put upon it the stamp of national
power and unquestioned authority."

Chapter II. ANCIENT AND MEDIEVAL MINING SYSTEMS

*The codes of the twelfth and thirteenth centuries —
Germanic mining freedom*

M AN, as Aristotle remarks, is endowed with an instinct subservient to the ends of social union, and is led thereto by the commands of Nature. Through three great forms of productive industry, this instinct has been exercised and developed: first, by the life pastoral — the keeping of cattle, the tending of sheep, the reining of wild horses; second, by the life agricultural — the wrestling with tangled forests, the breaking of the stubborn soil, the walling-in of "tun" and "burh"; third, by the life of miners — the search for metals both useful and precious, the impetus thus given to commerce and the arts, the development of inventive skill, the closer organization akin to that of cities.

The value of the precious metals was understood in the earliest ages, as appears in the literature of ancient Oriental nations, the rent-rolls of Assyrian monarchs, and even the curious public libraries of that antediluvian race, the Accadians, who had collections at Sippera, Pantabiblia ("Book-town"), and elsewhere, and whose cylinders of baked clay speak of "gold weighed out for payment." The Egyptians are known to have had rich gold mines in Nubia and Abyssinia, also in the deserts of Sinai and on the borders of Arabia, where they also mined for turquoise, copper, and silver. A papyrus of the nineteenth dynasty still exists, containing plans of the workings of the Nubian gold mines. Herodotus gives the annual product of the ancient Egyptian mines, as recorded upon the walls of one of

[11

the palaces of the kings of Thebes, as a sum equivalent to thirty millions of dollars. This was chiefly from quartz veins, which Diodorus describes as "glittering with bright metals, out of which the overseers cause the gold to be taken." Egyptian and Assyrian methods were purely despotic, crushing and destroying the earlier freedom of the miner, which had in all probability existed, and substituting the doctrine that the ownership of all minerals was vested in the crown.

The Phœnicians mined copper in Cyprus, and gold in the mountains of Thasos, where, as Herodotus tells us, they had "overturned a whole mountain," even before the thirteenth century B.C. The Book of Job contains a realistic description of the early methods of mining extant in Arabia, and doubtless stimulated by Phœnician traders. When the merchandising of the Phœnicians began to assume world-wide proportions, their caravans developed the gold-searching instincts of many a semi-civilized nation and half-savage mountaineer tribe. Throughout Asia, the "Golden Continent," are the remains of ancient and extensive gold-workings on the Smejevka in Siberia, in the Urals and the Caucasus, along the Oxus and Indus, in Arabia, Persia, Tibet, Baluchistan, Japan, and at many other widely separated places.

The probabilities in regard to most of the prehistoric placer mines in northern Asia are that they were worked by wandering Scythian tribes, who were, perhaps, on much the same intellectual level as the turquoise-miners of New Mexico, the mica-miners of North Carolina, and the ancient copper-miners of the Lake Superior region; carrying on their mining operations with rude appliances, and without other than a tribal organization. In the same region Gmelin, during the last century, found upwards of a thousand small smelting-furnaces of brick,

evidently used for gold ores many centuries ago by miners of whom we have no further record. It is, however,
an interesting reflection that some portion of a modern
coin, ornament, or vessel of gold may consist of Siberian
metal bartered for by Phœnician merchants, sold to
Persia, conquered by Alexander, offered as a part of the
annual tribute of one hundred million dollars which
Gibbon estimates that the provinces sent to Rome, paid
by the degenerate Greeks to Harold Hardrada when he
stood among their Varingians, won at Stamford Bridge,
and lost at Senlac. Such is the permanence of gold that
in the worn wedding-ring a starving woman offers today
at a pawnbroker's counter in New York, there may be
particles that once shone in the crown of Sestu Ra, the
Grecian Sesostris, or helped to cover the Ark of the
Covenant.

Change and decay have ever been the fate of the most
famous of mining regions. Mountainous Midian furnished a hundred and thirty-five thousand fierce Bedouin
warriors in the days when her "captains and mighty men
of valor" for seven years overran Palestine (thirteenth
century B.C.) , driving the people for refuge to the mountain caves and fastnesses, until the greatest of the judges
of Israel arose, sifted his followers by the "Spring of
Trembling," and defeated the invaders in the Valley of
Jezreel. But this Midian, anciently so populous, has
now become a desert land, inhabited by only a few no-
mads. On the sea-coast, and far inland along the channels of perished rivers, are the ruins of large cities which
were chiefly supported by mining industries. The placers and rich gravel-mines, whose exhaustion caused the
decay of once wealthy and commercial Midian, are
fairly reticulated with old water-ditches; on the barren
hills are vast reservoirs and ruined walls; the country
was long ago denuded of its forests for mining-purposes;

and so waste and desolate does the region appear that its ancient prosperity is hard to understand, although the unimpeachable evidence is before the eyes of every traveler in the "land of Midian."

The historical and geographical link between Asia and Europe is Lydia. The broad, fertile, and easily tilled plains of the classic Kayster were encircled by mountains rich in mineral wealth. Among the Phrygo-Thracians were mining tribes whose chief occupation was in gathering gold and silver, learning to smelt the latter with great skill, and finally inventing a coinage. Strangely enough, the Lydian standard, the silver *mina,* afterwards used with slight changes by the Greeks, was truly the *mana* of the Accadians, given by them to the Babylonians, and so transferred, by way of Persia, to the mountaineers of Lydia. In this, as in so many greater things, Europe drew the sources of her knowledge from the remote, despotic, and mysterious Orient. But, as regards methods of mining, all the Oriental monarchies were alike in the use of the most cruel forms of slave labor and in the greatest conceivable waste. From an institutional standpoint they afford little that is worth study. The mere figures of gold yields are astounding. Solomon, it is estimated, had a yearly income of twenty-three and a half million dollars in gold alone; and Calmet thinks that he spent on Jerusalem and the temple the sum of four thousand million dollars. Diodorus tells us that out of the ashes of Susa and Persepolis seven million dollars in gold was extracted. But treasure-houses such as these were filled by forced labor and royal monopolies. In the case of the early Oriental powers, the tribes upon their borders who were developing local systems for the ownership and working of mineral deposits were crushed and overwhelmed before those systems could take permanent form. We must leave "the wide Asian fen" and turn to the hills around whose heights "the first-born olive-blossom brightened," to the rocky coasts that "sheltered the Salaminian seamen," to "nodding promontories and blue isles and cloud-like mountains," to the city "violet-crowned," whose death-less memory moves like sunlight about the broad earth forever.

In the Athenian state we discover the first orderly and effective system in regard to the management of mineral resources and the government of mines. The famous silver and lead mines of Laurium in southern Attica rose to prominence about the year 600 B.C., and were worked with varying success till the second century before the beginning of our era. In 1864, after nearly two thousand years of neglect, the old shafts were re-opened by a company of French capitalists. An estimate has been made that, during the three hundred years that the Athenians worked these mines, they procured two million one hundred thousand tons of lead, and twenty-two and a half million pounds of silver. According to the law of Athens upon this subject, the mines were not freehold property. Although belonging to the state, they were not leased or farmed out to the highest bidder, as was the Roman custom: they were granted to individu-als to use as a permanent tenancy. A small sum was paid on taking possession, and only one twenty-fourth of the gross ore-yield of the mine was required as rent. The mine was then to all intents private property, unless neglected, when the state could bring suit, and recover. The statement that before the time of Themistocles the mines were the absolute freehold property of certain families rests upon slight authority and seems improb-able. Any and all members of the community were em-powered to institute public suits against the mine-pos-sessors in case of their violation of any statute, and suits of this sort were frequently brought. There is evidence of the existence of a "director of the mines," elected by those interested. The income which the state derived from the rents was annually distributed among the citizens, in much the same way as was the "Theoricon" in later times, every one whose name was in the book of the Lexiarchs receiving his portion. Themistocles, it will be remembered, persuaded the Athenians to devote this income to the building of ships.

From Xenophon's *Treatise upon the Revenues* and Demosthenes' speech against Pantænetus we gather much about the Grecian system of managing the Laurium mines. Companies were organized to work one or more shafts, and many of the wealthier Athenians owned shares in several such enterprises. The size of each "claim" was strictly defined, and private enterprise was greatly encouraged to send out "prospectors." Secure though the tenure of mining property was, it could be transferred only to a citizen, or to aliens capable of holding agricultural lands. Any person was allowed to dig for new mines in unexplored places; but, although richly rewarded, successful prospectors had no prior right: what they found belonged to Athens, and might be rented to any other person. The labor used in the mines was that of private slaves. Each shaft was registered by the mine-inspector of the state, who examined the supports of the various drifts and galleries and saw that the bounds were not exceeded. Lessening the supports of a drift, and trespass, were punishable by fines, infamy, banishment, or death. Demosthenes addresses the tribunal as the "mining court," set to try "mining cases." Some of the island mines paid one tenth of the ore to the shrine of Apollo at Delphos.

Spain, the Peru of Europe, and in minerals the richest country of the ancient world, developed slowly, and under enormous pressure, a system of mining laws which once ruled the greater portion of the American continents, and still prevails in variously modified forms throughout Mexico, Central and South America. In that law, deeply embedded as fossils in a slab of limestone, there yet remain principles of widely differing origin — Carthaginian, Roman, Gothic, Moorish, Castilian. But the traces of mining institutions are few indeed under the dominion of either Carthage or Rome. Instead of many mine-owners, bound together, as in Athens, by a common law, having the same duties towards the state, and equal protection from it, we have in Spain, under Carthage, the almost uncontrolled authority of the proud family of Barca. Hannibal procured about three hundred pounds of silver each day from his Spanish mines. Pliny describes the method of obtaining gold from streams of Spain by using a pan, also a method of "ground-sluicing"; and he mentions the use of timber supports in drifts and tunnels, some of which extended fifteen hundred paces into the hill.

Even in Carthaginian days the almost inevitable destruction attending great mining operations was going on with unusual rapidity in Spain; subsequent Roman methods wonderfully accelerated this ruin. Their mines, farmed out to the highest bidders, were wastefully worked and recklessly destroyed. For a time the Romans employed twenty-five thousand slaves at Carthagena alone, and the silvery yield was equal to ten thousand dollars daily. The Spanish placers yielded large sums; and they also were farmed out, after the manner of the silver mines. Inventive skill of a high order characterized the early miners of Spain, who greatly improved the Egyptian methods of grinding or smelting ores and extracting the precious metals. All this implies close organization, division of labor, and severity of discipline.

The later Roman emperors made reforms in the close military system, gave more sway to private enterprise, allowed some mines to be worked by associations, granted the "prospectors" permission to search for mineral, and introduced a sort of feudal service. The Romans also knew of placer mines in northern Italy, discovered by the Etruscans, who even brought iron from Elba; but, curiously enough, the Roman senate would not allow them to be worked. The Salassians opened placers in Lombardy; and, as Polybius relates, the Taurisci found such rich placers near Aquila that the price of gold fell one third throughout Italy in the space of two months.

Thus far in our investigation we have seen that, although the gold-hunger has ever furnished a stimulating element to early society, the ancient world afforded narrow opportunities for the development of valuable institutional forms among the classes engaged in mining. We read of rich placer mines by the score, but not of their local legislation and self-government, such features being absent until the advent of miners of the race whose "political instinct" has become a familiar phrase. Golden sands of the rivers of Tibet and India set long caravans in motion past Babylon, past Palmyra, to imperious, luxurious Tyre; golden nuggets from the Chinese frontiers poured into stately Balkh, "mother of cities," cradle of ancient kings, and greatest satrapy of Persia; Grecian placers of Pactolus yielded their treasures to Crœsus, and were still worked in the days of Xenophon. But waste and barren of constructive energies were all the mining regions of ancient Europe and Asia. As the mining history of the medieval world shows, the Germanic races, and they alone, have organized true mining camps which developed into higher forms of society. Whatever elements other races have contributed, the informing spirit of such camps has been thoroughly Germanic. The organization of a Spanish mining law began with the Visigothic kings, in the days of Pelayo; the laws of the California camps of 1849 were linked in spirit to the "mining freedom" and the mining cities of the Middle Ages.

It is impossible to determine what influences from the Roman mining world, which even in its decadence embraced all the rich mineral regions of southern Europe, could have survived the chaos and wreck of barbarian conquest.

After the fall of Rome the Arabs, Franks, and Goths in Spain, Gaul, and northern Italy worked to some extent the abandoned and nearly exhausted Roman mines. To northern Spain the Visigoths brought a new force; and the *Fuero Juzgo,* or code of laws of the Gothic predecessors of Alonzo the Wise, shows greater freedom of the individual, greater respect for local institutions and for self-government, than Spain had previously known. Hints of local mining organizations in Thrace and along the Danube in the fifth and sixth centuries make it evident, though definite records are lacking, that wandering miners existed in that region and were slowly "prospecting" the mountain ranges to the north and west. Hungarian mining can be traced back to the year 750, begun by prospectors from Gaul, says Reitemeier.

But German mining history clusters about the Harz Mountains; and it is a significant fact that mining began there, at the great Andreasberg ledges, in the midst of a political and national renaissance which profoundly stirred and influenced the whole of central Europe. It began there towards the close of the tenth century, in the reign of Otho the Great, second Emperor of the Saxon line, who wore the iron crown of Lombardy and the imperial crown of Rome, reviving the glories of that holy empire, obscured since the mightiest of medieval monarchs had sunk to rest with his paladins and his sword — in the reign of that Otho whose father, Henry, had driven back the heathen in many a fierce battle, had quelled the wild Magyars at Merseburg, had taken the Mark of Brandenburg from the Slavonians to become in after-time heart of Prussia and appanage of the Hohenzollerns, had built frontier fortresses, and posted his warrior *Markgrafs* to protect the borders against Dane and Finn, Slav and Hun. With a firmer government, a stronger national life, material enterprises developed wonderfully; the forest-ways began to be trodden by peaceful merchants and explored by seekers for precious metals. In Saxony, in the tenth century, mines of vast richness were discovered by Bohemian salt-carriers, who found silver ore in the ruts worn on a steep hillside by the wheels of their rude cart. The early German miners soon began to make enactments to govern themselves. A law of mining claims, and rules of mining life, prevailed among these first Thuringian miners who struck pick into rocks of Black Forest and Harz and unveiled the treasures of Freiberg, no less certainly than similar laws and usages prevail today among the organizers of the newest camps on the Rio Grande and Yukon. The *Mark* method of dividing lands was no more certainly a product of the thought of the Germanic race than are the customs which today govern freemen in distributing with fairness the auriferous soil of Western placers. The spirit of the tribes of whose social and political organization Tacitus gave so vivid an account lives at this hour in free "miners' courts" of Idaho and Alaska.

To Germanic sources we must trace the most important principles of mining law. The local customs of the earliest Harz miners have never since ceased to exert an influence upon civilization. The *Mark* system of common lands, annually redistributed, was most likely the foundation of early German mining regulations; but it took so long to make a mine productive that the redistribution plan could not be permanently adopted. The plan of making ownership depend upon actual use, and limiting it to small, well-defined tracts, was the obvious substitute. All the early German codes express the idea of mining freedom, of a possible ownership of the minerals apart from the soil, of the right of the individual to search for and possess the precious metals, provided he infringed on no previous rights. This "mining freedom" (*Bergbaufreiheit*) contains the essence of all frontier mining customs ever since. The right to "prospect," "locate" a given claim, and hold it against all comers until abandoned is the right guaranteed, in one form or another, by the newest mining camps of Montana. This is the same right once possessed by the men of the "seven mining cities of the Harz," and by those of Freiberg, of Truro, of Penzance, and of other cities of the Middle Ages where mining guilds and organizations existed.

The first written document which embodies these rights is the mining treaty of 1185, between the Bishop of Trent and certain immigrants from Germany. Other codes appear later; in 1250 one in Moravia, in 1307 one in Styria. All these, and others of the period, were founded on the unwritten custom, on those usages "which have lasted from time immemorial." The Moravian or Iglau code provides for the appointment of officials to fix mine-bounds and defines conditions of ownership. The full size of a claim is set at four hundred and seventy-nine feet long and one hundred and ninety-six feet wide; a portion is set aside for the king, and a part for the town if on common lands, for the owner if on private property. Mining courts are granted with special rights and jurisdictions (*Bergbehörde*). In later years the miners gave effective aid to burghers and artisans in their struggles against the robber barons. The precious "mining freedom" asserted by the working miners underwent severe assaults from small landowners, from petty princes, and from the Emperor himself; but its broader principles were, as a rule, maintained intact. During the sixteenth and seventeenth centuries German mining jurisprudence grew exceedingly complicated, and covered a great range of topics. Associated mining enterprises were frequent. Miners from the most famous districts of Germany had long been in demand in other mineral regions of Europe, and often offered their services to foreign kings. Everywhere they carried with them the customs, laws, experience, and superstitions of the craft. They worked mines in northern Italy, in France, in Scotland and England, developing a strong professional pride and secrecy. They filled the place in the medieval world that Cornish miners occupy in modern times. Theirs was the reputation for dealing with the most stubborn ores and the most difficult engineering problems.

Speaking in the broadest sense, the true relationship which exists among the laws of all "mining camps" worth the name is not so much in the form of the laws themselves as in the organizing capabilities of that race which works out similar results under similar circumstances, with surprising fitness of method and fullness of harmony, and with supreme and all-conquering self-confidence. No one is able to show that there has ever been any uniform theory of law for mining camps, scarcely more than for caravans in the desert; but it has nevertheless happened, owing to this inherent political instinct, that whenever and wherever men of our Germanic race found minerals, they developed a satisfactory system of local government, based on a series of compromises, and differing in essential particulars from the sort of local government developed no less naturally by agricultural communities; their judgments grew swifter, and their justice surer, as was needed to counteract the volcanic passions and disrupting tendencies of their fascinating and hazardous pursuit. In the hands of the Germanic race alone, this fierce gold-hunger has been controlled, utilized, and made a force of primary importance in the shaping of civilized society. Communities created and built up by mining industries have thus been transformed, without danger and without loss, into communities based on agriculture, commerce, and manufactures. With men of other races, the possession of wealth-laden placers has too often meant their rapid, reckless exhaustion, the washing-away of every particle of soil, the destruction of every forest tree, the inevitable decay and desertion of towns, the absolute ruin and complete desolation of the entire region; with men of our race, the exhaustion of placer mines has only hastened the development of more potent and permanent resources, has given us the wools of later Australia, the wheat and wines of later California.

The institutional history of modern mining camps thus finds its proper place in the ever broadening story of local self-government among men of our race — the story which runs back to the days when rude, brave men lifted a chosen leader on their ringing shields and swore allegiance; when the three judges, each with his twelve doomsmen, met in yearly tribunal; when "brothers of the sword-oath" (in Icelandic, *ver svorjum Bruderskaft*) bound their rune-cut, bleeding arms together, swearing eternal *Freundschaft* over their naked war-weapons. You may find today, if you are able to recognize old types in new attire, the true descendants of the Germanic "sword-brothers" in the devoted "pards" of a raw mining camp on the outposts of civilization; and closer resemblances than this lie thickly scattered along the course of our investigation. To those who have ears to hear, the free and unconventional, yet sufficiently systematized life of mining camps is able to tell a story of the beginnings of things, of forest meetings in Saxony, of freemen in isolated villages assembling to allot the common lands, of English folk-moots in England before the waves of conquest rolled over the wild heights of Exmoor, before the hill-fortress of Exeter passed from Keltic ownership, before Lindum Colonia became English Lincoln. Since Germanic mining began, certain vital principles have been asserted by the men of camp, district, and mining town. The local mining law whose sources are as old as the capitularies of Charlemagne, and probably far older, is a living force in the world today. Professor R. W. Raymond says of early Germanic mining law:

"In the form of a local custom, obtaining with remarkable uniformity in all the original centres of German mining, the principle of mining-freedom established itself, permitting all persons to search for useful minerals, and granting to the discoverer of such a deposit the rights of property within certain limits. This principle of free mining emigrated with the German miners to all places whither their enterprise extended itself, and the original local custom became the general law. In this existence of an estate in minerals, entirely independent of the estate in soil, lies the distinctive character of German mining-law. It is eminently a special law, not subordinate to civil law but co-ordinate with it." [2]

---

[2] *Relations of Governments to Mining.* United States Mining Report, 1869.

Chapter III. CUSTOMS OF CORNWALL

Stannary courts, barmotes, and tin-bounds

THE development of local legislation among some of the miners of England furnishes most useful parallels to the development of such legislation among American gold-miners. Valuable gold mines have existed in England, Scotland, Wales, and Ireland; and mining excitements have several times occurred over the "auriferous gossan" of Cornwall and Merionethshire. A Briton tribe, the Trinobantes, coined gold, it is said, from the "placers" of Essex. Edward III issued a writ asserting royal rights over a gold mine in Salop County, and Henry IV did the same in several instances. During the reign of James V of Scotland some three hundred placer-miners worked for months at "Gold-scaur," near Wanlochhead, and collected more than a million dollars. The largest nugget found weighed thirty ounces ($480). Many instances of alluvial washings for gold in the British Isles might be given from the old chronicles, the latest being those of Wicklow, Ireland, worked in 1796. But no trace of "local law" seems to have remained, and we are forced to turn to the lead-, tin-, and copper-miners for examples of successful organization.

Local customs of the utmost importance have long existed in Cornwall, Devonshire, and Derbyshire, chiefly in Cornwall, that land of folk-lore tales and strange survivals. When, as legends declare, "St. Michael's wooded mount was six miles from the sea"; when the early Britons, or as modern Cornishmen call them "the old men," were simple placer-miners digging up "stream tin" from alluvial channels, and leaving traces of their toil from Land's End to Dartmoor; when Beltane-fires

[25

were lit, and. St. Piran became the miners' merry saint
— there was rude organization among the miners of
Cornwall. They held great public assemblies under the
open sky, upon chosen spots on the wild moor, surrounded by earthen walls, traces of which yet remain;
and these meetings were called *Guirimears* or speech-
days. Old smelting-furnaces of this Keltic period still exist, and the modern miners call them "Jews' houses." A
curious old song, apostrophizing early Cornwall, says:

"Come old Phœnicians, come tin-dealers,
    From Marazion come, ye Jews;
Come smugglers, wreckers, and sheep-stealers,
    Come tell the ancient county news."

Into this prehistoric drift — to borrow a term from
geology — an adventurous element was brought from
widely diverse sources. There was a wild freedom in the
air of Cornwall; and outlaws sought its forests, sea-
rovers the shelter of its cliffs. Literature, with its divine
instinct, loves the stormy land where Tristram slew giants, and Hereward wrought deeds of prowess; and
some of the greatest of living poets have made its shadowy legends as immortal as the tales of the Volsungs.
Long ago the miners of "wild, bright Cornwall" chose
their standard, a white cross on a black ground; until
within this century they kept "Old Christmas," the 5th
of January, and for twelve days suffered no fire to be
taken from their hearths. So tenaciously does the past
survive in the present that even now a verdant branch
is fastened on midsummer day to the highest woodwork
of the steam-engines, to mark the beginning of the Baal-
year.

Early in the Middle Ages miners from the heart of
the Black Forest found their way to Cornwall.[1] They

---

[1] There was also some migration of Cornish miners to Germany.
Camden's *Britannia* says: "After the comming in of the Normans the

left numbers of mining terms embedded in the language, and greatly modified the local laws and customs. The use of the divining or "dowzing" rod in England is not older than the advent of German miners, brought over by Queen Elizabeth to teach the Cornishmen how to work certain refractory ores. One of these, named Schutz, became warden of the stannaries. At this point, then, we discover the institutional link between English and German mining law; we also understand how it has come to pass that the Cornish miners of Nevada and Montana still use a vocabulary some of whose terms are derived from phrases in use among the miners of Freiburg six centuries ago.

The former rights of the "free prospector" or "tin-bounder" of Cornwall have only recently fallen into disuse. The ancient stannary courts, which we are now to describe, have only of late years received any serious modification; and though shorn of many of their ancient dignities, they still remain as, historically speaking, the last representatives of older and far more powerful forms.

The local mining courts, and the force of local custom, were authoritatively recognized by the organization of the chief stannary court, which long proved a most valuable right and defense of the miners. It has been modified into a court of records; but it originally existed as an original court of equity, of the vice-warden of all the stannaries of Cornwall.[2] At the present time it

---

Earles of Cornwal gathered great riches out of these mines . . . sith that in those daies Europe had tinne from no other place." He goes on to state that in the year 1240 "was tinne mettall found in Germania by a certain Cornishman driven out of his native soil to the great losse and hindrance of Richard, Earle of Cornwal."

2 Camden's account, in his *Britannia*, is as follows: "The whole commonwealth of those tinners and workmen as it were one body hee [King Edward III] divided into four quarters . . . Foymore, Blackmore, Trewarnaile, and Penwith. Over them all hee ordained a War-

has jurisdiction in certain matters over all companies engaged in tin-mining; but its local, representative, and legislative character no longer exists. The stannary court is treated of at length in various Chancery and King's Bench reports, and in papers published in the British Geological Reports; and it was established, recognized, and enforced by numbers of ancient charters.

King John granted a charter to the tin-miners, giving them the right to mine on waste and unoccupied lands. By a charter of 33d Edward I, all the working tin-miners were given privilege of being sued only in the vice-warden's court. According to this and subsequent grants, the "ancient charters, local customs, and records of lower courts" were always to be received as evidence. Henry VII increased the powers of the legal convocation, or "parliament of tin-miners," which had settled disputes and made laws respecting tin claims since the days of Edward III. This stannary parliament consisted of twenty-four influential miners or stannators, six chosen in each district. The last parliament was held at Truro in 1752. Here the men of Penzance and Carclaza, of Botallock, Carn Brea, and dozens of other mining villages and towns met and formulated Cornish mining laws. They came from quarry-like mines on the barren moor, open to the sky; from shafts sunk deep in the earth; and from drifts extended half a mile under sea, where hammer-blows sounded beneath the keels of ships, with but ten feet of crumbling rock between. To-day the descendants of these men are among the boldest and most successful miners in America. At Eureka, on

---

den called 'Lord Warden of the Stannaries and Stannum,' that is, tinne, who giveth judgment as well according to equitie and conscience as law, and appointeth to every quarter their stewards, who, once every three weeks . . . minister justice in causes personall between Tinner and Tinner and between Tinner and Forrainer. . . . In matters of moment there are general parliaments summonned whereunto jurats are sent out of every Stannarie."

the Comstock, in the Black Hills, wherever one goes, in fact, the hereditary mining lore of the Cornishmen is in demand. The miners of the Mendip district, Cornwall, as late as the seventeenth century, punished those who stole ore from the drifts with banishment, and with burning of the offender's domicile; theft being considered, as in the Western camps of today, a crime of peculiar turpitude. These Mendip miners manifested a mingling of superstitious dread and of faithful loyalty to each other in their strict rule that the body of a miner who had been killed in a drift must be dug out at any cost and given Christian burial before a stroke of work would be done elsewhere by a single miner. They also had local laws respecting the explorations of waste ground, and rights of discoverers, which were always respected.

Indeed, local mining customs have existed in Cornwall "from time immemorial," as the King's Bench Law Reports tell us. Miners' rights and privileges were definitely settled centuries ago and have been tenaciously held ever since by the descendants of those whom the varied mineral wealth of the Cornish land first attracted to its sea-girt cliffs and granitic moors. The custom prevailed, even within the past twenty years, that any person might enter upon the waste land of another, mark out a plot of ground, send a description to the stannaries' court, and lay claim to it, provided that he proposed to work it himself "in good faith." In the early part of this century a written description was required, just as in Western camps a written claim-notice is necessary; but in still earlier times a verbal statement was considered sufficient. The written notice was read in the stannaries' court at three successive meetings; when, if no valid objection was raised by any person, the court accepted it, and proceeded to deliver possession to the "bounder," who then had exclusive right to mine for tin and other minerals within the limits of his "bounds." The first act of the owner was to define the corners of his property by rearing piles of turf and stones, or by sinking small square pits. It has always been the "custom" to mark claims thus in Cornwall. When the earliest miners of the region recognized "mining claims" as property and began to ordain and enforce a general system of obtaining them, they had taken a most significant step towards organization.

The possession of this "tin-bound," thus acquired by "taking it up" — to use the American expression — involved the payment of a tax known as "toll-tin" to the owner of the land. This percentage varied according to the yield of the district, but not according to the yield of that particular shaft. In other words, the owner of the soil and the "bounder" of the mine were both subject to the usual rule in this regard, and no one need make a separate bargain unless he chose. In Cornwall, and also among the miners of the "King's Field" in Derbyshire, and in the "Forest of Dean," the lord of the soil was usually considered as entitled to one fifteenth of the gross ore yield of each shaft sunk by a "bounder," said ore being "delivered at the mouth of the pit." As high as one tenth of the ore, and as low as one twentieth, have been given in the tin-mining districts.

The right to a "bound" was inheritable property, and might be transferred by sale; but neglect to work it caused forfeiture to the owner of the soil, or, by denouncement, to another miner. The landmarks of the "bound" must be renewed annually, and kept distinct and in good condition. This reverence and care for landmarks is a characteristic of all law-abiding and mighty races; and the varied customs by which the boundaries of districts and kingdoms, and changes in the ownership of tracts of land, were fixed in the memories of men are highly curious and deeply interesting. In ancient times the "thoths" or tribal landmarks were often burial-mounds of wise chieftains and puissant warriors, who still guarded the frontiers. On the borderland, national games, annual fairs, and public assemblies were held. And of land transfers we read in the Book of Ruth: "Now this was the manner in former time in Israel concerning redeeming and concerning changing, for to confirm all things: a man plucked off his shoe, and gave it to his neighbor; and this was a testimony in Israel." In the village communes of our Germanic ancestors, "field and homestead passed from man to man by the delivery of a turf cut from its soil." The annals of Salem, Massachusetts, state that in 1695 a homestead there was transferred by "turffe and twigg," [3] an unconscious survival of the customs of those forest villages whose freemen dwelt around their moot-hills or gathered for council beneath the sacred oaks of the Odenwald. Other races, too, have transferred land with similar formalities: when, in 1670, the Raritan Indians made their final sale of Staten Island to Governor Lovelace, they "brought a branch of every sort of tree and shrub that grew on the island, for a sign; reserving only two species used in their basket-work."

Transfers of mineral lands, since the dawn of history, have been accompanied with quite as much formality as that attending the transfer of agricultural property, or of holdings in tribal community lands. The miners of the California camps showed as much anxiety to have distinct landmarks and bounds as did the Cornish and the Thuringian miners of centuries ago; and at least

---

[3] See Dr. H. B. Adams: "Germanic Origin of New-England Towns." Johns Hopkins University Studies, 1st series, *Local Institutions.*

once, as late as 1856, a transfer of mining property in California was completed by the gift, before witnesses, of a handful of gold-bearing gravel from the claim. The man who did this was a miner, whom the writer met as prospector many years after. "Why did you do it?" we asked; "was not verbal possession sufficient?"

"Mebbe so; but my father, and his father before him, always gave a bit o' land away to wind up a bargain; an' the rule's good for a minin' claim, I'll allow."

Leaving, however, for subsequent chapters, an analysis of the land laws and customs of modern mining camps, we return to the customs of the tin-miners of Cornwall, in many particulars so similar to those adopted centuries later by the free miners of the Pacific coast. The size of their "tin-bounds," so carefully marked out and set apart, varied greatly according to the old Cornish rule. It must be "reasonable," but uniformity does not seem to have been thought essential, the point being to include sufficient surface to give space for proper workings. The entire system of "taking up claims" and securing them, in the Cornwall districts during the sixteenth, seventeenth, and eighteenth centuries, was precise and effective, and "probably," as one of the English law reports says, "was the law of an extinct kingdom of Cornwall."

The Cumberland silver-miners in the time of Elizabeth had special legal privileges, and the justices of assize went there in their circuit. This was one of the "royal mines," owing to its proportion of silver.[4] They

4 The well-known definitions of Blackstone and Plowden need not be quoted here. But that quaint and rare book, *A Just and True Remonstrance of His Majestie's Mines-Royall to His Majestie*, published in 1641, contains a "declaration of learned lawyers what a Mine-Royall is, according to presedents," signed by the King's sergeant-at-law, and thirty other jurists. They say: "Although the gold or silver contained in the base mettall of a mine in the lands of a subject bee of lesse valew than the baser mettall; yet, if the gold or silver doe countervaile

do not seem to have had a court of their own for mining cases; but the "smelters, refiners, and miners held public meetings," as recorded by Bushell in 1641. Their local customs were much the same as in Cornwall. Their "tolls" were paid, however, directly to the sovereign. In Cornwall such dues were paid to the duke, whenever such a nobleman existed.

The Duchy of Cornwall was created in the fifteenth year of Henry III. Edward III made his son the first Duke of Cornwall and gave him "all profits of the court of stannary and of the mines." Slowly, and with great difficulty, the ancient tenures and privileges of many of the tin- and copper-miners were lessened and abridged; and so it soon came to pass that different degrees of tenancy were recognized. In the most important and numerous class, the bounds came to be fixed, or at least re-examined, each seven years, and reallotted by an assession court. In the "Caption of Seizin" of the manor of Tewington, in the time of Edward III, there is a list of free tenants who hold "in socage" tracts of from five to twelve acres apiece, and pay "toll-tin" upon the product of all shafts they sink. Besides these miners, there were, so states this caption, "free conventionaries," or miners who held and worked much smaller tracts on the seven-year basis; and the sort of land-tenure system which prevailed in these peculiar "conventionary holdings" was a highly interesting "survival" of ancient Keltic forms analogous to those of Brittany. Concanen's special report of the English law case of Rowe *vs.* Brenton describes the system in full.[5]

---

the charge of the refining, or bee of more worth than the base mettall spent in refining it, this is a Mine-Royall, and as well the base mettall as the gold and silver in it, belongs by prerogative to the crowne."

[5] Mr. Frederick Pollock, in *The Land Laws* ("English Citizen Series"; Macmillan & Co., 1883), speaks of ancient Cornish laws, and of these "conventionary" seven-year holdings (pp. 49, 204). He says that

In the lead districts the most interesting local institution was the barmote court, and its executive officer called the "bar-master." It was his duty to do justice between miner and miner, between miner and "adventurer," and between all the miners and the lord of the manor. The "adventurers" were what the Western miner calls "prospectors"; and they have played a very important part in English mining history, developing the richest of mineral districts by their skill and energy. Local law in the lead districts awarded to the finder "the largest share" of a new mine. Disputes were tried at the barmote; and over this court the deputy stewards presided, and the bar-master was present. A jury was summoned, composed of miners, and questions were tried before them. Arrears of the duties of "lot and cope" were properly presented by the officers of the manor.[6] In modern times English law reports show clearly the continued existence, and the recognition in mining jurisprudence, of most of the customs and local usages of tin-, lead-, and copper-miners, alluded to in the preceding pages. Local customs, as modified by acts of parliament, are still in force in Cornwall, Derbyshire, and other mining districts.

Throughout England the rule has held good that mining requires much knowledge, skill, and special training, creating in the past a constant tendency towards separate courts, towards denial of the jurisdiction of the lower civil courts, and towards a more direct dealing with higher courts of appeal. The Cornish stannaries court of today is one of the survivals of this long-continued struggle, and so is the barmote court of the lead districts. In the rocky and agriculturally worthless

in 1844 certain conventional tenants of the Duchy of Cornwall were enfranchised, and does not know whether or not other examples of this ancient tenure still remain.

6 Arkwright *vs.* Cantrell, 7 Ad. and E., p. 565.

regions, where for many centuries the entire community was dependent upon mining for its livelihood, the miners evidently governed themselves long before there was any duke of Cornwall or manorial claims: they recognized the liberty of the prospector and the sacredness of the claim-stake, in that remote past when "streamtin" gathered from the river-channels was the chief mineral resource of the region, and the veins of ore were only superficially worked. To such conclusions, at least, the nature and evident antiquity of the mining customs of Cornwall would certainly point. They seem to be fragments and remains of ancient laws adopted in meetings of freemen, for the purpose of securing equal rights, and imposing equal duties upon all within their jurisdiction. As a prominent California mining lawyer once said to the writer, "Those old Cornish miners, with their local freedom and self-government, deserved to have been born four centuries later, as prospectors in the Sierra placers."

CHAPTER IV. EARLY MINING IN
THE UNITED STATES

THE first English settlers in America hoped to find great mineral wealth; and the royal charters in most cases reserved "all mines," and claimed as rent one fifth of all gold or silver ore, "to be delivered free of charge at the pit's mouth." Massachusetts, Connecticut, Virginia, Maryland, Pennsylvania, and others of the early colonies, had clauses of this kind in their charters.[1] But the "gold ores" invariably proved worthless, much to the disappointment of the merchants in the Virginia and the Massachusetts companies, who had hoped for other resources besides those of fishing, trading, and farming. The "rights royal" never amounted to anything; and, in the process of time, mining jurisprudence came to be founded upon common law merely, the mineral being held to belong to the soil, and conveyed by one and the same title with agricultural lands.

There is little of value for our investigation in the scattered attempts at mining in Colonial and Revolutionary days. The first on record appears to be that mentioned in Stith's *History of Virginia* — the opening of an iron mine in 1622 at Falling Creek, near James River. The next was probably in New England, where Governor John Winthrop in 1657 obtained a license to work "mines of lead, tin, copper, or any mineral," and to "enjoy forever" said mines, and all woods, lands, and things necessary for their workings, "within two or three miles." He proceeded to prospect extensively, and in 1661 received a special grant of mineral lands near Mid-

---

[1] Bainbridge: *Law of Mines*, chapter ii.

dletown, Connecticut, where he opened and worked mines. President Stiles's Diary says, speaking of the "Governor's Ring," a mountain in East Haddam: "Governor Trumbull has often told me that this was the place to which Governor Winthrop of New London used to resort with his servant, and spend three weeks in roasting ores, and assaying metals, and casting gold rings." The mine was worked to a depth of a hundred and twenty-five feet, with extensive drifts. The abandoned shaft was discovered in 1852, and afterwards re-opened, though unprofitably. The first blast-furnace in the New England colonies was built by Lambert Despard at Mattakeeset Pond, Plymouth County, Massachusetts, in 1702. The copper-miners of Simsbury, Connecticut, received their charter in 1709. Arent Schuyler began to work the cupriferous ores near the Passaic, seven miles from Jersey City, in 1719. According to the centennial address of Mr. D. D. Field, Middletown, Connecticut, in 1853, a lead mine was worked in that town long before the Revolution; and from May 1775 till February 1778 this mine was operated for the citizens "by a committee of three, Jabez Hamlin, Mathew Talcott, and Titus Hosmer."

Such efforts, of which there were many, were merely business or war enterprises and had little or no organizing influence upon society. Somewhat more than this, however, may be said with justice of some of the famous gold camps of the South early in the present century. In Spottsylvania County there were numbers of placers, and from one claim, twenty feet square, ten thousand dollars was taken; in Louisa County, one placer-claim yielded seven thousand dollars; and near the Rapidan over forty thousand dollars was taken out by a miner from his placer property. These instances are noted in Mr. Taylor's report (1867) on *Gold-mining East of the*

Rockies. There were also some famous mines in Buckingham County, Virginia, and others in Abbeville District, South Carolina; but those of Rowan and Mecklenburg counties, North Carolina, and particularly the placer mines upon the tributaries of the Great Pedee, produced hosts of prospectors, who took up claims and worked mines according to a sort of local law, subject, however, to the jurisdiction of the county authorities. Wheeler's *History of North Carolina* gives interesting illustrations of this mining era and its excitements; its crude organization, its "big nuggets" (that of 1803 weighing twenty-eight pounds), its culmination, and its decay. West of the Blue Ridge, along the famous French Broad River, a number of placer-miners worked for half a century on small claims held by possessory rights. The Georgia and Alabama gold-miners had a wider field; and the operations begun in 1799, in valleys that De Soto visited, have continued with greater or less energy ever since. None of the mining districts of the South possessed any organization separate from that of the county, but some of them had simple local regulations in regard to the size of claims. In one case, that of the Hale mining tract, Lancaster District, South Carolina, over fifty years ago, the system had fostered individual freedom, though to the great detriment of all the mines. The owner of the land allowed any persons to come in and work where they chose, only agreeing to sell all gold found to him for sixty cents per pennyweight, when it was really worth ninety cents, thus paying a ground-rent of one third the gross yield. The alluvial deposits were, however, so rich that many prospectors accepted the terms. They used "pans and rockers," dug holes in search for "pockets," worked out the rich places, recklessly stripped the mine, and then deserted it. Nothing permanent could come from such a wasteful and destructive system. But as soon as gold was discovered on the Pacific coast, all these old camps of the South sent well-trained miners and prospectors to the new placers; and there they found that larger freedom in which local mining institutions were rapidly developed.

The attitude of the state and national governments towards mining interests affords a much more important theme than is offered by any of the Southern gold-discoveries. Long before the Revolution most of the colonies had recognized the rights of landowners over all the contents of the soil; so that when, in 1785, the Continental Congress reserved one third of the gold, silver, lead, copper, and some other minerals found within the states, the principle aroused the greatest opposition. It was only an extension of the "crown-right" idea of the civil law; but the rights so long recognized by immemorial custom and prescription in Germany, the Electorates, France, Portugal, Spain, and other dominions of Europe seemed so "un-American" that their assertion was soon abandoned.

The United States next tried the plan of attempting to hold, and lease to the highest bidders, the salt springs and lead mines. After the acquisition of Louisiana, lands containing lead ores were reserved from sale; and in 1807 the President received authority to lease them for five years, in tracts of not more than three miles square, afterwards reduced to one square mile — the return of six per cent of the ores being required. Under this system the first lease was issued in 1822; but after 1834 many of the miners and smelters in Michigan, Wisconsin, Iowa, Missouri, and Arkansas positively refused to pay rents, because there had been a vast number of fraudulent entries of mineral lands as agricultural lands, and the system appeared unjust. By 1846 this lease system became untenable, and was definitely abandoned.[2] Acts of Congress then restored to the several states the right to sell their salt springs, and also opened to pre-emption as public lands the hitherto leased tracts in the lead- and copper-mining districts.

The history of the disputes, protests of pioneers, and litigations among rival claimants which led at last to the abandonment of the lease system is long and highly interesting. It extends over nearly the first half of the century. The numerous complications which arose out of the entangled condition of Spanish and French land-titles in the provinces of upper and lower Louisiana, involved the best mining districts of Missouri and Iowa, and test cases were fought from court to court until settled by the highest authority in the land. The lead claims of upper Louisiana introduced hitherto unknown elements into our jurisprudence. Our government, acting in accordance with the law of nations, had agreed to recognize all lawful titles to lands in the ceded territory.[3]

---

[2] The *Annual Report* of the Secretary of the Treasury for 1865 says, speaking of the Pacific coast mineral lands: "A system of leasehold . . . after the lessons which have been taught of its practical results in the lead and copper districts, cannot, of course, be recommended."

The course of United States legislation up to this point can be synopsized as follows: Ordinance, May 20, 1785, reserved one third of the gold, silver, lead, and copper; act of March 3, 1807 dealt with lead mines; act of March 3, 1829 authorized their sale in Missouri; act of September 4, 1841 excluded salines and mines from pre-emption; case of U. S. *vs.* Gear, 1845, confirmed the previous act; April 18, 1846, mineral lands of Isle Royal, Lake Superior, reserved; July 16, 1846, lead mines in Illinois, Arkansas, Missouri, and Iowa offered for sale at two dollars and a half per acre; March 1, 1847, lands in Lake Superior district offered at five dollars per acre.

[3] Among the important decisions that bear upon Spanish and French claims, Indian rights, mineral lands, and United States title are the following: Sanchez *vs.* Gonzales, Louisiana Rep., 11 M., p. 207; Le Blanc *vs.* Victor, 3 L., 47; Landry *vs.* Martin, 15 L., 1; De Vall *vs.* Chop-

Owing to these causes, it happened that American lawyers who settled in New Orleans and St. Louis early in the century found that a knowledge of French and Spanish law was essential to success. As regards land-titles, the courts of Louisiana have decided that the colonial Spanish government of such rulers as Gálvez, Miró, and Carondelet, recognized verbal as well as written grants. The grants made by French officers during the ownership of Louisiana by France were never contested, but most of the Spanish grants were. Land-grants in some cases were referred for final decision to the captain-general of Cuba, within whose jurisdiction were Florida and Louisiana. The Indians were assigned one square league about their villages, including the town-site. A primitive land-title existing in any tribe was never recognized. Absolute ownership in their village lands was not allowed, severe restrictions being placed upon its sale and alienation. If all died or removed, the lands reverted to the crown. A simple order from the Governor was sufficient to establish these reservations. It thus followed that grants by Indian tribes to white men anywhere within the Louisiana Territory required acceptance and confirmation from the Spanish authorities. A noted case which reached the Supreme Court in 1853 decided the ownership of the Dubuque lead mines adversely to the claims of those who held under title from scheming Julien Dubuque, the old Indian trader and pioneer, who, in 1788, had received from the five chief villages of the Fox Indians in council assembled the gift of an illy defined tract of nearly one hundred

---

pin, 15 L., 566; Murdock *vs.* Gurley, 5 R., 457; Reband *vs.* Nero, 5 M.; Moes *vs.* Gilliard, 7 N. S., 314; Brooks *vs.* Norris, 6 R., 175; Breaux *vs.* Johns, 4 A., 147; Choteau *vs.* Molony, 16 How (U. S.), 203; Wilson *vs.* Smith, Yeager, 5, 347 (Mo. Rep.) ; Delassas *vs.* United States, 9 Peters, 117.

thousand acres of land.[4] Albert Gallatin also made a report to the President upon the Dubuque claims, saying
that the tract was undoubtedly government land. In
1832 there was trouble among the rival claimants to the
mineral soil; and in 1833 troops were called into requi-
sition, who drove off one party and burned their cabins.
The government then leased the land to the miners.

The St. Vrain concession of mineral lands was decided to have been perfected under the requirements of
Spanish law; and so to be outside of the jurisdiction of
the act of 1807 creating a board of commissioners for
the readjustment of land-claims. The "inchoate title"
of the descendants of "Pierre Charles Dehault, Knight,
Lord of Delassus Luzieres, and Knight of the great cross
of the royal order of St. Michael," covered a square
league on St. Francis River, Missouri, containing valuable lead mines, which had been worked by prehistoric
miners, and were reopened by the knight of many titles
in the days of Baron Carondelet, who purchased, in the
name of the Spanish Government, thirty thousand
pounds of lead annually for five years. This title, legal
as far as it went, but never made complete, was confirmed by the United States.

But while the courts and the lawyers were determining the status of hundreds of varying claims under Spanish and French titles, the region was being settled by
hardy and energetic pioneers, long before the United
States Government had arranged to sell lands. The immediate result was the formation of "squatter associations," to take up, place on record, and hold land-claims.
Professor Macy of Iowa College, in a paper upon "Institutional Beginnings in a Western State," read before

---

[4] Le Sueur, the French explorer, discovered mineral on this Dubuque tract in 1700 or 1701. The earliest notice of mines in the Northwest, however, is contained in the report of Jesuit missionaries, who in
1660 found copper ore in the Lake Superior region.

the Historical and Political Science Association of Johns
Hopkins University, November 2, 1883, and since then
published as No. 7 of the second series of the "University Studies in Historical and Political Science," has
well described the claim-laws of these agricultural settlers, whose guiding principle was to give each man his
fair and equal chance.

In the mineral region of Iowa we find early organization. Professor Macy tells us that June 17, 1830 the
Dubuque lead-miners assembled, and appointed a committee of five to draught regulations, which were unanimously adopted. They agreed to live under "the code
of Illinois," with the following additions:

"ARTICLE I. That each and every man shall hold two hundred yards square of ground, working said ground one day
in six.

"ARTICLE II. We further agree, that there shall be chosen,
by a majority of the miners present, a person who shall
hold this article, and grant letters of arbitration, on application having been made; and that said letters of arbitration shall be obligatory on the parties concerned so applying."

These simple laws, thus adopted by the lead-miners
in public meeting, form the earliest, and for thirteen
years the only, local code of Americans on the soil of
Iowa. In 1833 the Indian title to these mineral lands
was extinguished, and within a year Dubuque contained two thousand inhabitants. May 20, 1834, the
miners tried and condemned a man for murder, and a
month later policed the town, and executed him, after
the Governor of Missouri and the President of the
United States had been applied to for pardon by the
prisoner's friends and had replied that "the pardoning
power rested with those who passed the sentence."

The early local history of this interesting mineral region shows most clearly the working of forces which reached their fuller development only in the comparative isolation of later camps. Lead-miners of Iowa, tin-bounders of Cornwall, early silver-miners of Germany, all recognized the claim-stake, dwelt under equal laws of their own creation, and tried and punished their criminals.

Furthermore, as we have observed in the course of this chapter, the lead- and copper-miners west of the Mississippi came into contact, in many cases, with old Spanish grants and concessions. Here, in the heart of the continent, midway between Lakes and Gulf, the American miner first met the Spanish influence that he was to find once more, in far stronger forms, on the shores of the Pacific. Americans had no sooner controlled the lead regions of Dubuque and St. Joseph than they pushed westward, in the years preceding the great gold-discoveries of California; there to meet a current of institutional development that had come from Spain by way of Mexico, not by way of lower Louisiana, and so had retained far more of its original characteristics. It is to this Spanish-American realm that we must now turn our attention, in order to understand the elements underlying California life, and the conditions that favored peculiar local organizations in the mining camps of the Sierra and the Rockies.

CHAPTER V. THE SPANISH-AMERICAN
SYSTEM OF GOVERNMENT — MINING
LAWS OF MEXICO

SPANISH rule, and the first attempts of Spaniards to mine in the New World, are of especial significance by reason of sharp institutional contrasts to the forms of Germanic development; also because of the influence subsequently exerted upon the Southwest and the Pacific coast of the United States. The growth of the Spanish system of government, and the complete separation of mining courts from civil courts that for a time existed in Mexico, form an essential part of our investigation.

The first Spanish colonists were lazy and lustful, reckless and turbulent. They desolated the fairest isles of the West Indies, they rebelled against their governors, and they drove to suicide the unhappy race they had enslaved. Everywhere under their system, with its strange contrasts of stately indifference and volcanic energy, the Spaniards forgot their own Castilian proverb of awful significance: *"Dios consiente pero no para siempre"* ("God may consent, but not forever").

The only judicial officer of these early colonists was the alcalde, a district judge, who possessed a great variety of powers, as will be shown in a subsequent chapter. The first mention we find of this officer is at Cuba, early in the sixteenth century. The first military rule of Mexico brooked no interference from local officers of any sort; but Cortez soon developed great administrative skill and energy and rapidly introduced the local institutions known to Old Spain.

It is, however, to a colony and a mining camp that we

must look for the best Spanish example of elected officers and local organization. Early in the sixteenth century about a hundred Spaniards, led by Enciso, founded
the town of "Santa María de la Antigua del Darien."
The afterwards famous Vasco Núñez de Balboa, roused
by some acts of petty tyranny, persuaded the colonists
to depose Enciso and elect himself chief alcalde, with an
assistant and a *regidor*. A little later, in 1514 in fact,
some rich gold-placers were discovered three leagues
from "Santa María del Darien"; and a rush to the new
mines was the immediate result. Almost at once the
miners organized. They elected a mining superintendent and a surveyor of claims, under whose supervision
and authority plats of ground twelve paces square were
measured off for each able-bodied miner; no one being
allowed to hold or to work more than one claim at a
time. They paid the royal demands; but, while the
mines lasted, they managed their own local affairs with
more skill and energy than miners of their race have
elsewhere displayed. Here, in this little camp of Spaniards, a seed of local self-government had been planted;
but it could find no firm root in national characteristics,
and no abiding support from national institutions. Instead of springing up, bearing fruit, and extending itself to camp after camp northward along the Isthmus
through Central America to the placers of Yucatán and
Mexico, its blossom fell to the earth unfructified, its
stem withered and perished in a single summer.

Permanent social order, and organized self-government, could not develop from the early Spanish placer
mining, any more than from the gold-lust of Spanish
leaders like Cortez and Pizarro. Hither and thither
through the New World the freebooters of Spain had
hastened, searching for traces of gold as wolves follow
the scent of smoking blood. Impelled by this passion,

they hewed paths through tropic forests, crossed deserts, explored unknown seas, illustrated the utmost valor, cruelty, endurance, and fanaticism, and unfurled the intertwining standards of Rome and Spain at almost the same time in Amazonian and Floridian forests, in Patagonian and Oregonian wildernesses, and over hills of Arkansas, deserts of Arizona, and isles of the California pearl-coast. This breathless search was, happily, futile: the continents held no more semi-civilized kingdoms rich in treasures of gold. By the help of slaves, the baffled *conquistadores* then began to develop the mineral resources of New Spain. They still sent out expeditions by land to follow such mirages as the Golden Temple of Dabaiba, and fleets to search the North Pacific for the fabled Straits of Annian; but the fever of exploration had nearly run its course. Silver- and gold-bearing rock soon began to be worked with system and success. Humboldt says that the annual gold yield of America from 1492 to 1521 was $250,000; from 1521 to 1546, it was $3,150,000. In 1545 Potosí began to pour forth its treasures, and the annual yield of gold and silver combined was $10,300,000 for the sixty years after that discovery. The ransom of Atahualpa had been $20,000,000. Jacob, in his *History of the Precious Metals,* says that the mining industry of Europe was greatly stimulated by the mining done in America; that in fourteen years after 1516 there were twenty-five rich veins found in Bohemia; and that between 1538 and 1562 over a thousand leases and grants of new mining-ground were made by the Bishopric of Salzburg.

The Mexican system of civil law, as transplanted from the overlordships of Castile and Aragon, lasted, with few changes, until well into the present century; and its more abiding local forms of administration still rule the land that Cortez conquered. The principles upon which the colonial possessions of Spain were governed, and even the details of that government, present remarkable parallels to the complex system of authority extended by Rome over her subject provinces. Under Spain, all titles, power, and dignity flowed from the royal throne, as, under the later Roman system, they all flowed from the emperor. The viceroyalties of Spain in Peru, Granada, Mexico, corresponded with singular fidelity to the proconsulates and propraetorships of Syria, of Gaul, and of Spain herself under Rome. As in the Roman world hardly any two cities bore the same yoke or occupied exactly identical relations to the central government, whether that of senate or of emperor; so in the Spanish empire hardly two viceroys had equal rank or exercised identical powers. The most casual observer cannot but seize upon striking similarities and instructive contrasts between these vast and ultimately unsuccessful colonial empires.

The Spanish system had a feudal element, in that the land, and the Indians as attached thereto, were divided among the colonists. This royal gift of soil and people was called an *encomienda,* and first occurred in Hispaniola, extending thence to all the Spanish dominions. Cortez made a provisional *repartimiento,* or division of the natives; and this was readjusted by a royal *audiencia,* or council. Cruelty, disease, and hard work slew them so rapidly that the greater part had perished before they were set free and given land to cultivate in common, as in some of the modern pueblos.

The system of Spanish civil government extended upward from the alcalde of the village to the viceroy of the whole territory, all appointed or elected with such severe restrictions that matters were in practice kept under royal control. The detailed minuteness of the administrative affairs in even the most obscure provinces

of Peru or the Indies that passed under the eyes of the
King himself and were decided according to his wishes
is something that almost surpasses belief. Some choice in
village and district affairs was all that was left in the
hands of the people, until the mining laws differenti-
ated the powers of the system, and the local alcaldeship
was thus enabled to gain a greater dignity and influence. Spiritually, Mexico was divided into provinces,
sees, and parishes. The *visidados*, or special emissaries
of the King, and the "legates of the Pope," formed am-
bassadorial links between the Old World and the New.

Government of the towns (*pueblos*) was, in Spanish
days, entrusted to a town council, or *ayuntamiento*,
whose head was either a *mayores* or an alcalde, assisted
by several *regidors* (directors) and *síndicos* (clerks).
The villages had only an alcalde. In the large towns of
each district, the municipality chose two *alcaldes de
mesta*, to preside over semi-annual councils of the livestock-owners. This pastoral custom was carried where-
ever Mexican colonists journeyed; in a modified form it
survived in California until a few years ago, and still exists in New Mexico and the Southwest.

Studying as a whole the civil government instituted
by Spain, we can safely affirm that no nation has ever
possessed a nicer sense of the theoretical proportions of
aristocratic rule, or brought to the difficult labors of colonial government a more dignified and stately administrative genius; but the fatal facility with which department was added to department, and wheel to wheel,
made the whole cumbrous machinery break down at
last beneath its own weight. It was an ingenious mechanical contrivance, not a vital organism. Pulleys, le-
vers, and speaking-tubes, not arteries, nerves, and mus-
cles, set the mandates of the central government in
operation throughout the system. Hence its weight and

increasing weakness, its decay and final failure, its giant wrecks rusting in solitude on the hills of every Spanish-American province, its mournful problems, as of misgoverned Cuba. This overloaded mechanism of government reaches its climax in the mining laws of New Spain, more particularly of Mexico, which constitute the most unique, laborious, and complicated system of special jurisprudence ever developed on this continent.

In February 1774 the miners of Mexico petitioned the King of Spain, by whose orders a perpetual corporation was established, embracing all the mine-owners, and ruled by a great tribunal consisting of an appointed president, an appointed director, and three elected deputies. Acting under this central organization were local tribunals, one in each province. The system proposed was to have jurisdiction in all cases which concerned the mines or the miners, and it was at first received with universal enthusiasm. One of the first things done was to found a college of mines on an immense scale in the city of Mexico. Alexander von Humboldt, in his *Political Essay on New Spain*, describes this *Real Seminario de Minería* as it existed in the city of Mexico in 1803. The director of the college had then been collecting statistics from the thirty-seven *Deputaciones de Minas,* and from these reports he had perfected a mineral-map for the use of the supreme college or head tribunal. A great banking-system, whose ramifications were to extend to the remotest mining town, was early organized. The tribunal, soon after its creation, had formulated a code of laws for the government and regulation of mine towns, mine-owners, and mine laborers. In 1783 this code received the full approval of the King and the Grand Council of the Indies.[1] Thus the mining inter-

---

[1] This great Council of the Indies was created by Ferdinand in 1511, but was not fully organized till thirteen years later under

ests of Mexico were separated from direct control of the civil authorities; and the powerful corporation created in accordance with the petition of the miners received rights of separate courts, and privileges and immunities almost royal in scope and nature.

No "mine town" had a right to vote at any election for a tribunal deputy unless it contained "an inhabiting population, a church, and a curate or deputy, a judge and deputy of mines, six mines in actual working, and four reducing-establishments."

Paternal government over the mines and the miners was developed to such an amusing and exasperating degree that some of its manifestations seem almost beyond belief. Supervision was never reduced to a more exact science. This royal ordinance of 1783 declares that all cases must be decided "without any of the usual delays, written declarations, or petitions of lawyers." It sets apart the refuse ore-heaps and "tailings" as "support for the widows and orphans, old and helpless." It forbids reduction of wages, fixes rations, commands registration of laborers with a view to prevent their leaving a mine, and orders that the price of articles used in the mines shall be fixed by law so that "no undue profit" shall be taken by anyone. It also prohibits all persons from making demands of the workmen for alms, this being aimed at the beggars and the mendicant friars of the time. One of the most interesting provisions is to the effect that "persons going about to search for mines shall be allowed to have one beast to ride on, and one to carry

---

Charles V. It was a plan much favored by that wise statesman Cardinal Ximenes, whom Sir Arthur Helps has compared to the English Earl of Chatham. The *Recopilación de las Leyes de las Indias* declared that this council should consist of twenty-two councillors, presided over by the King himself as perpetual president, and of four secretaries. It was given supreme jurisdiction throughout Spanish America and the Philippines. As a rule, the councillors were men who had seen service as viceroys or captains-general in the New World.

their bedding and provisions, and shall not have to pay for their pasture, on either public or private property, whether it be customary or not to pay for the same." The reason for this provision is evidently to be found in the royal rights over mineral ground. Whoever discovered a new mine was an unofficial "king's messenger"; he was increasing the revenues of the crown. The prospector was, therefore, a more privileged character in Mexico during the days of Washington, and under the rule of pleasure-loving Charles III of Spain, than he is at the present time in any spot on the American continent.

The code ordained by the miners' tribunal further provided for certain local officers, called *disputaciones,* to reside in mining towns as arbitrators in difficulties respecting mining property, and also to discharge the very peculiar duty of "admonishing extravagant, wasteful, or gambling miners." If this warning was not heeded, the tribunal had power, which it often exercised, of "appointing a guardian for said miner, and of limiting his expenditures." In ways like this the mining code of Mexico descended to the most minute particulars and trivial details of daily life, regulating the laborer's food, attire, and hours of labor; forbidding "dice, cards, and cock-fighting," still besetting sins of the Mexican miners; punishing idlers and vagabonds; and seemingly making some provision for every possible emergency.

The use of a *disputaciones,* or arbitrator, was a favorite idea of Mexican jurisprudence. The powers of this office were, at its abolishment, transferred to the alcaldeships. The *disputaciones,* under this later form, was long in use in California. The same idea sprang up in the early "mining courts" of the American mines, as we shall hereafter see; but the "arbitrators" of the miners had little historical connection with the Spanish *disputaciones,* except that this particular function of the early alcalde courts might have aided to suggest the plan in some few of the mining camps.

That section of the Spanish mining laws which orders cases to be decided "without delay" is peculiarly characteristic of all mining communities. Time is precious; everyone is in haste; the poor are about to be made rich, the rich about to become extremely wealthy. The world over, all mining codes in whose making the miners themselves have had a hand are certain to ignore technicalities, urge swift decisions, and laugh to scorn each fine-spun argument.

The laws of Mexico, as of Spain, recognized two distinct interests in land — surface and mineral; interests not only legally distinct, but even transferred by separate and differently worded titles. One was *la propiedad del suelo,* the other was *la propiedad de la mina.* The first, the right of pasturage and of agricultural use, was transferred or conveyed from the authorities of the province, by sale, by absolute gift, or by gift conditioned on settlement; the second, the right to dig for minerals, was obtained by special gift of the king himself, by registration of discovery, by denouncement of another mine for "non-working" and its consequent forfeiture, or by purchase subject to special royal taxes and restrictions. An agricultural grant left the entire right to minerals in the hands of the Spanish Government, which right passed thence to Mexico at the Revolution. The right of miners to enter on private domains was absolute, nor was it conditioned upon payment of damages. The ideas involved in the system were, so far as regarded mineral lands, somewhat as follows: legal title complete in the crown; absolute right of the public to search for mineral. and work ungranted mines; right of eminent domain over mining lands and mining interests of every sort, such as in wood and water, vested in the government; rights of the crown to confer private ownership; ordinary mining rights, valid only during the life of the reigning king, and a renewal necessary at his death.

Many of the agricultural grants made by Mexico to citizens of Alta California were found, after the conquest, to contain mineral wealth; and in some cases such lands were entered upon by prospectors and claimed as being public lands, in the sense of the Mexican mining law, and so having passed by conquest to the United States. A knowledge of the Spanish laws thus became necessary to every American lawyer in California, as once before to the lawyers of Louisiana and Missouri, and as now in Arizona and New Mexico. They were obliged to have some acquaintance with the codes and commentaries of the famous Spanish jurist Gamboa, with the ordinance of 1783, with subsequent acts of the *Tribunal de Minería,* and with various decrees of Comonfort, Juárez, and other Mexican presidents, and acts of different Congresses.

The greatest alterations which have been made in the mining laws were shortly after Mexican independence was established. The mining deputations were brought more under the control of the government; mining courts, consisting of a lawyer and two mine-owners, were established in each one of the states, to serve as a court of appellate jurisdiction; lastly, the right of foreigners to purchase mines was recognized, though with restrictions. This was in 1823. At a later period, all "contentious jurisdiction" was transferred to the civil courts, and the separate mining courts lost the greater part of their authority. Successive modifications of the laws respecting foreign miners, and the influence of

English, German, and American capital and energy, have produced many changes, of late years, in the northern Mexican states. The local customs and district laws of that region are being superseded slowly but surely by American mining-usages.[2]

The condition of Mexican mining and civil law at the present time is, however, foreign to our investigation. Our inquiries have been only for the purpose of ascertaining to some extent the spirit of Mexican institutions, so as to understand more clearly the nature of their influence upon California, and the modifications they necessarily underwent. Before American pioneers captured California, before American miners had organized a single camp, three institutions of Spanish origin, the mission, the pueblo, and the alcaldeship, existed in the coast region, and deserve our careful study. They serve as a background for the fuller activities of the American period, and they help to explain the local political difficulties that preceded the organization of state government. The pueblo and the alcaldeship were transferred, with slight modifications, from the limits of Mexico; the "mission" was an institution that gained for a time, in the provinces of California, an influence almost as overwhelming as that it so long held in parts of South America under the Jesuits.

---

[2] "This Province [Sonora] is beginning to adopt American mining-customs" (private letter from the late Manuel M. Corella, professor at the University of California, and afterwards an eminent Arizona lawyer; written in 1880).

Chapter VI. THE MISSIONS
OF THE PACIFIC COAST

THE institution known in California as the "mission"
was, from one standpoint, missionary and ecclesiastical;
from another it was industrial and political. There was
a decided flavor of worldliness, not to say greed of gain,
mingled with the undoubted zeal and holiness of the
early priests. In all the mountainous wilderness from
Cape St. Lucas to Cape Mendocino, their missions occupied the choicest spots in the fairest valleys. They chose
for soil, water, climate, sightliness, commanding position; and subsequent years have only confirmed their
almost unerring judgment. The cash value of each convert to the gardens and pastures of the mission's broad
domains was never overlooked: Christianized Indians
meant laborers and vassals. The California natives of
whom, in 1721, Collier wrote, "Every family hath an
entire legislature, and governs at discretion," were
brought into a subjection only paralleled in Paraguay.
Students of economic subjects could not fail to find
much of interest in the internal management of these
famous missions of Alta (or Upper) California, the out-
growth of those established by the Jesuits in the peninsula of Baja (or Lower) California, where Fathers
Ugarte and Salvatierra planted Loreto, October 19,
1697. Within seventy years the priests had four flourishing missions and many minor settlements along the
shores of the Gulf, then known as the Red Sea, or the
Sea of Cortez (*el mar Cortés*). Soldiers under their command mapped out the surrounding region. Humboldt
in his *New Spain* describes early conflicts of secular and

ecclesiastical authority, terminated by the Spanish courts, which issued a *cédula real,* or writ, and put the entire detachment at Loreto under the orders of the priests. This famous shrine was soon enriched by pearls from the Gulf and silver from the mines: it possessed embroideries made by the hands of the Queen of Spain, and paintings by Murillo and Velásquez. In 1719 Father Ugarte built a missionary ship from timber dragged two hundred miles through the gray mountains and barren sand-dunes, there being no forests nearer to Loreto. At last, in 1767, the Jesuits were expelled, giving place to their successful rivals the Franciscans; and the following year they left the adobe-built missions of Lower California, the gardens, young orchards, and semi-civilized converts of their faith. The first settlement, the first church, and the first ship built in the California provinces were the result of Jesuit enterprise. The work they did was the direct means of attracting the attention of Spain to Upper California, and led to immediate efforts for its colonization. The leaders changed; but the movement which culminated at Mission Dolores on the Bay of San Francisco received its primary impulse when Fathers Ugarte and Salvatierra, with nine soldiers, set up their rude cross by the sheltered cove of sultry Loreto.

In July of 1769 — that fateful year which witnessed the birth of those mighty leaders of opposing armies, Napoleon Bonaparte and the Duke of Wellington — Father Junípero Serra, the Franciscan apostle, a man of singular zeal, piety, asceticism, and administrative ability, founded San Diego, and began the mission system in Alta California.[1] His successors completed its eccle-

---

[1] Father Serra founded six mission colonies, gathered into strict discipline over seven thousand Indians, died August 28, 1784, and was buried at San Carlos, Monterey, beneath the church altar. Father Francisco Palou, his friend, associate, and biographer, wrote Serra's life at Mission Dolores — the first book written in California.

siastical conquest and brought the coast tribes into full subjection.

The missions in their prime were little more than Indian reservations, managed, it is true, with great skill and marked industrial success, but entirely incapable of making citizens out of their Indian occupants. From the days of the good Las Casas, Spain and Mexico had honestly tried to do their best by the Indians. The laws of Mexico gave them many rights which in practice they were utterly unable to obtain. A decree of Philip II, in 1571, ordered that the property of Indians should never be sold except at public auction, before the alcalde, after thirty days' notice. Later Spanish laws created additional safeguards against the loss of their common or other lands. The *Recopilación de Indias* says explicitly that they cannot be sold nor alienated *("Por ningún caso se les pueden vender ni enagenar")*. The royal *Audencia* of Mexico, adopted in 1781, enforced with additional legislation the same idea. The object of all these regulations was purely beneficent — to interpose an insuperable barrier against all attempts of the whites to strip the newly emancipated Indians of whatever property they might receive from the government or accumulate by their own industry. Their rights in the common lands of a pueblo could not be sold or rented; and this was good law in California for some time after the American occupation.[2]

But in California, as in Mexico, the actual rights possessed by the Indians were less than their legal rights, even during the sixty years of the missions' undisputed control. For these slaves of the soil, that civil authority represented by *comandantes, ayuntamientos,* and other officials of pueblo, presidio, or province, only existed as casual apparitions, gorgeous and stately as the bandits of

---

[2] Sunol. *vs.* Hepburn, 1 Cal. Rep., p. 224.

an Italian opera. Very justly says quaint old Nicholas
Mill, in his *History of Mexico,* "In California the
monks do rule the country." In the early mission days
they discouraged settlements and colonies of whites;
and at a later period they still found means of controlling the Indian population far more absolutely than
had been the intention of the civil authorities. Mexican
laws enacted early in this century, and still in force in
California after the American conquest, provided for
Indian alcaldes, in these terms:

"Mission Indians have the right to elect their own alcaldes, who, with the advice and assistance of the mission
priests, shall make all the necessary regulations for their
own internal government."

The acts of 1833–4, secularizing the missions, pay
much attention to the welfare of the Indians. From the
point of view taken by the Mexican Government, the
only good reason for the long-continued existence of
the missions had been to train citizens. They were not
intended to be permanent establishments; but would, it
was hoped, change peacefully into prosperous parishes,
and gradually lose their peculiar industrial, political,
and communal features. But the laws relating to Indian
alcaldes were practically a dead letter. Cooke, in his
Conquest of New Mexico and California, mentions such
an alcalde at "San Phillipi" (Felipe) ; but otherwise, so
far as we are able to learn, the right was unused and
forgotten.

If the condition of vassalage in which the mission Indians were kept be considered entirely justifiable, their
treatment was, on the whole, satisfactory. Few whites
except priests and soldiers were allowed to live at the
missions, whose tile-roofed buildings of black sun-dried
bricks (adobes) surrounded a large court, cool with

flowing streams of water and shade-trees. One side of
the square was occupied by the great mission-church;
while the remaining three sides were devoted to galleries, porches, workshops, barns, stables, granaries, kitch-
ens, storehouses, cells of neophytes, and rooms of priests.
The Indians were fed and clothed, taught trades, simple
mechanical arts, and the system of agriculture practiced
in Spain; passing their uneventful lives as humble servants of the Church, which was virtually independent of
Mexico, owner of the soil, and master of the country.[3]

One might fill a volume with incidents of life in these
quaint and curious missions before their hour of doom
came. The people rose at sunrise, spent an hour at the
chapel, marched singing to the fields, returned when
the evening angelus rang, spent the evening in games
and amusements, and retired to their huts of *tules*
grouped under the mission's protecting shadow. They
planted gardens, orangeries, vineries, and olivariums —
gardens in which the choicest fruits of Granada and
Andalusia were grown; and they tended the fast-multi-
plying herds of the mission in the broad valleys and on
the fertile foothills. California became almost a sani-
tarium and refuge for army veterans and worn-out
priests; the missions where they dwelt were like highly
cultivated oases in the midst of a wilderness. Catholic
writers have strongly denounced the subsequent Mexican policy of secularization, marked as it was by the con-
fiscation of the "Pious Fund," established for missionary purposes by wealthy Catholics in Mexico and Spain.
De Courcy says that the Franciscan Fathers had seventy-
five thousand California Indians civilized and converted
before 1813. Another writer, Marshall, adds that in
eight years the secular administration of the missions

---

[3] Paper on California. Harris: Maryland Hist. Soc. Pub., 1849; now
a very rare pamphlet.

"re-plunged the whole province into barbarism," and
utterly failed in every particular; reducing at the chief
missions the 30,650 Indians to 4,450, the 424,000 head
of cattle to 28,220, the 62,000 horses to 3,800, the
331,000 sheep to 31,600, and the annual yield of 70,000
fanegas of wheat to 4,000. (A *fanega* weighed 150
pounds.) This scattering of helpless, ignorant Indians
over California has ever, and most justly, appealed to
human sympathies. Even at this day the great adobe
walls of the few mission-churches that yet stand, the
rude sculptures, gaudy frescos, and square belfries, the
neglected burial-grounds, the huge and rude crosses set
sloping on the hillsides or crowning some seaward-over-
looking peak, the mournful silver-gray olive-trees, large
as those that look down on the dark chasm of Sorrento,
all appear sacred and deeply impressive features in the
California landscape. Protestants and Catholics alike
treasure these memorials of the dreamy, romantic childhood of California, of conditions of society that have
forever departed from the American continent, and of
an ecclesiastical rule more powerful and more exclusive
than existed elsewhere in North America.

When the missions were first established, a tract of
about fifteen acres was allotted to each one; but their
lands were never surveyed, and they gradually extended
their bounds until they virtually laid claim to nearly
the entire region. The term "mission," which once had
meant only the church town, with the gardens and orchards near it, soon came to include the extensive tracts
over which the cattle, horses, and sheep owned by the
establishment were allowed to roam at will. There
were, a few years later, some separate private grants and
presidio reservations. The priests never received any
formal acknowledgment, from the Spanish Government,
of their land-claims. The Revolution of 1822 put the

subject into the hands of Mexican Liberals, who four years later freed the Indian serfs from compulsory allegiance to the priesthood. The mission lands were gradually alienated, and the decay and ruin spoken of in the previous paragraph followed as a natural consequence.

It appears evident that the missions in their best estate were triumphs of organization, and marvels of pastoral wealth. San Gabriel, for instance, once contained three thousand Indians, owned one hundred and five thousand cattle, twenty thousand horses, forty thousand sheep, and seventeen extensive ranches all well cultivated; it had fig, olive, grape, and orange plantations; and thousands of dollars were in its treasury. The twenty-one missions of Alta California in 1820 contained thirty thousand Indians, and owned a million head of livestock. By 1833, when secularization began, the number of Indians had fallen to twenty thousand, there being great mortality among them, and little recuperative energy. By 1837 the missions held only about four thousand Indians, and less than sixty-three thousand head of livestock. Seventeen years never wrought more complete ruin in a social system.

We have now to consider the legal aspects and methods of organization of the mission colonies. The Franciscan *padre* who governed each mission was at first its civil as well as religious ruler, and dealt directly with the viceroy of Mexico. He was called the *presidente,* or governor, and administered the law within his jurisdiction. Nominally it was the law of Mexico; practically it was frontier government — few and simple rules, prompt and summary enforcement, and no appeal except to the city of Mexico. Thus they governed the Indians, the soldiers, the few white settlers in the villages that grew up near the missions. The province had its *comandante,* representing the civil and military power, but never interfering with the management of the missions, nor criticizing the decisions of the priests. In Father Junípero Serra's time, there was a conflict of authority, which ended in a victory for the ecclesiastics, and the military authorities accepted the situation.

The first grant of land the priests allowed to be given in California was in 1774, to a Spanish soldier named Butron, who had married a baptized Indian girl from Carmel Mission, and received a tract in that valley.[4] By this time their claims embraced nearly the whole territory from seacoast to sierra, and from Sonoma Mountain to San Diego Bay. It was difficult, even at a later date, when secularization was evidently an inevitable fact, to secure ownership of land "against the encroachments of powerful missions which discouraged immigration, and under a weak and irregular territorial government."[5] Despite these difficulties, and the almost constant opposition of the priests, the little pueblos, or free towns, grew, and received alcaldes. In 1813 the Spanish Cortes granted right to form *ayuntamientos,* or town councils. By various enactments between 1822 and 1833 the Mexican Government took secular authority from the *presidencias* and swept away the irresponsible, undefined, and illegal power so long exercised within those jurisdictions. The *presidente,* or priest-president, became a simple prefect, and civil authority prevailed over ecclesiastical.

The mission-land claims were continued long after the American conquest. Priests in charge of missions attempted to sell or rent lands in the vicinity, and were prevented by Mason, the military governor. The noted

---

4 Tuthill's *History of California,* pp. 60–3, *passim.*
5 Cooke's *Conquest of New Mexico and California.*

case of Nobili *vs.* Redman [6] decided the legal status of
the missions, and aided greatly in settling land-titles in
California. This decision was to the effect that "the
missions established in California prior to its acquisition by the United States were political establishments,
and in no wise connected with the Church. The fact
that monks or priests governed them does not prove the
ownership of the Church. The lands the mission held
remained government lands; and the Church can only
claim mission property under the Mexican decree of
1824, and subject to all its limitations." [7] This evidently
refers to and includes the acts subsequent to 1834, carrying into effect the original announcement of 1824.

The secularization of the mission lands will be described more at length in discussing the pueblos, or free
towns, into which some of the missions were converted.
This secularization seems to have been amply justified
as a principle of public policy, though it was not wisely
conducted. It was, so far as the descendants of the first
Spanish settlers were concerned, an act of simple justice.
As early as 1763, men had removed from Mexico to California under promise of becoming landowners; and
this had hitherto been denied them. It was also an act
of patriotism; because the priests of Mexico and California had done all they could to prevent the success of
the Revolution, and whatever reduced their political
and financial influence aided the stability of the new republic. The last of the missions the priests had established was that of Sonoma, in August 1823; and between
1824 and 1834 the various decrees already alluded to

---

[6] 6 Cal. Rep., p. 325. Another interesting case is that of Santilan
vs. Moses, 1 Cal. Rep., p. 92. The position of the priest was held analogous to that of "sole corporation" in England.

[7] "*Primafacie,* that the Mexican Government of California had the
power to grant mission-lands as they chose." — *Den. vs. Den.,* 6 Cal.
Rep., p. 81.

stripped them all of their possessions. The civil officers put in charge were often dishonest; the mission-cattle were stolen, or else strayed off into the mountains; the Indians in many cases gladly returned to their savage life, or wasted their patrimony, and sank into beggary. These ten years represent a transition period from the era of missions to the era of pueblos, and in many respects the change was a trying one for the people.

The famous missions, with all their faults of theory and of practice, had been planted by men possessed of the true missionary spirit: they had done much to civilize the natives, and more to improve the country. They had often dispensed a genial and generous hospitality to strangers, and they ruled their servants with a firm and liberal hand. When the whole social fabric of the mission-system went to ruin, the suddenness of its downfall shocked all thoughtful observers. Yet it was but an artificial system, and its intrinsic worthlessness was plainly revealed the moment outside pressure and military coercion were removed. Moral suasion was futile to retain the thousands of Indian converts, who could no longer be persuaded to make soap, mold bricks, weave wool, sing Latin hymns, and repeat medieval prayers. They returned to their hillsides, their grasshoppers, their camass-roots,[8] and their idleness; while many of the priests went back to Mexico. The missions' lack of economic success was by far the least part of their failure.

The population of Alta California, exclusive of Indians, was at this time (1834) about five thousand, of whom not more than forty were English and Americans. Some of these, however, occupied very influential positions; several were alcaldes, and nearly all had married

---

8 "*Camass esculenta*," the most important food-bulbs of the Pacific coast Indians. Described by the late Hon. B. B. Redding in *American Naturalist*, and in report to Smithsonian Institute.

wealthy señoritas. But, in order to obtain any political rights, they had been compelled to become Catholics, and were objects of suspicion and hatred. Don José Castro was heard, in 1837, to declare that "a California *cavallero* cannot win a *señorita* if opposed in his suit by an American sailor. . . . These heretics must be cleared from the land." Their numbers, however, were constantly receiving accessions. The foreign element grew stronger, despite all efforts to dislodge them. They held on, with the tenacity of men in whose veins the blood of many generations of Aryan pioneers was flowing. A few swaggering trappers came wandering through the mountain passes; a few runaway sailors, such as Gilroy, who married the Spanish heiress of vast possessions, became lords of inland valleys; a few keen-witted Yankee traders settled in the towns: and the end of Spanish-American domination was close at hand. Meanwhile the light-hearted, passionate, generous native Californians established their *ranchos* in all the fertile valleys, and built their dingy, thick-walled adobe mansions on points of vantage from San Diego to Sonoma; always choosing, with some hereditary instinct of the race, the picturesque and beautiful outlooks, or nestling in the most sheltered of vales, or in the wildest of ravines. The life they lived, in its freedom from care, and its glorious physical healthfulness, was simply perfection. Dana somewhere speaks of the Californians as "a people on whom a curse had fallen, and stripped them of every thing but their pride, their manners, and their voices." But he had only seen them in their pueblos near the coast: he had not visited their wide-roofed homes, when all the descendants of the Castilian pioneer of 1763 gathered under one roof-tree in harmony and affection. Horses could be had for the asking; cattle were only of value for the hides, worth two dollars apiece, and called "California bank-notes." There were no fences anywhere, except hedges of *nopal* (or prickly-pear), walls of brush, and ditches formerly dug by the mission Indians about the adobe ranch-houses. There were no roads, except, near the towns, the occasional track of a slow, wooden-wheeled *carreta*, or ox-cart. Everyone rode on horse-back, and with an ease, grace, vigor, and fearlessness which have never been surpassed by any race. This was the people whose flocks and herds soon covered the plains and hillsides once claimed by the missions, and into whose untroubled life the American pioneers brought elements of change and confusion. This was the era of California's eventful existence, that coming artists of language will delight to portray. Its saints are such as that high-born maiden, Concepción Arguello, of whose faithfulness Bret Harte's poem tells; its shrines are mostly ruined walls of sunburned clay, the oldest architectural remains on the Pacific coast of the United States; its heroes are dark and haughty *vaqueros*, storm-ing across broad *mesa*, wild canyon, and steep *barranca*. An old Spaniard dying in a rude hut near San Luis Obispo, in the winter of 1874, sprang to his feet in the delirium of fever, and cried out, "I hear the ringing of their spurs on the mountain, the trample of their horses!" and so, repeating the names of his companions of fifty years before, he sank back in an unconsciousness from which death soon released him.

Chapter VII. SPANISH TOWN GOVERN-
MENT — THE PUEBLO IN CALIFORNIA

THE pueblos of Mexico are simply towns, as the *pueblicitos* are simply villages. In Alta California, the first pueblos were so distinct from the presidios, or nominally fortified towns under military rule, and from the missions under ecclesiastical rule, that they well deserve the title of free towns. They alone had an alcalde chosen by the people; and they alone had common lands, and gifts of town lots to all residents.

But there is an application of the word "pueblos" to the relics of an ancient, fast-fading, native civilization, which has perhaps become more familiar to most readers than is the Mexican or Californian usage. The pueblo of the southwest region of the United States is far different from those we have just described. Adventurous students such as Mr. Frank Cushing, explorers such as Major Powell, and archæologists such as Mr. L. H. Morgan, have made us acquainted with the rock-fortresses and the immense communal buildings of the race that reared Cicuyé, Quivira, Cibola, and the city of Mexico.[1] Even today the Moquis shape their black and red pottery as they did before Martin Behaim began to dream of a new world; the Zuñi priests still guard their sacred fires, and pray in their secret language for the fast-fading "children of Montezuma." It is curious

---

[1] The first of these was discovered by Coronado; the second was the city that Peñalosa saw; the third was the mystic and seven-citied realm that the Franciscan friar, Marcos de Niza, reported in his "Relations" (Hakluyt Soc., Vol. iii, p. 438) . For these pueblos, see Morgan's *Homes of the Aborigines*, Government Reports of Major Powell, Short's *North Americas of Antiquity*, Putnam's *Archæology of the Pueblos;* also, "A Pueblo Fête Day," in *Overland Monthly* for April 1884.

enough that this Spanish word "pueblo" should have come to be applied to the "joint-tenements" of the proud and brave people that drove Otermín out of New Mexico, and for fifteen years governed themselves. At the present time the pueblo Indians of the Southwest choose their own chief ruler, war-captain, and fiscal, as they have done for years. The pueblos of California had no essential relation to the Indians, and were only modifications of the Mexican town-system.

In Alta California the need of pueblos began to be felt soon after missions were first established. The presidios, where the soldiers and commandantes were, required grain, vegetables, and supplies of various sorts. Spanish vessels from the East Indies occasionally wanted provisions. The viceroy of Mexico therefore wrote to the commandante of San Diego and Monterey, under date of August 17, 1773, declaring that he "grants him the power to designate common lands, and also allows him to distribute lands in private to such Indians as may most dedicate themselves to agriculture and the breeding of cattle; but they must continue to live in the town or mission, not dispersed on their *ranchos*." The commandante is also empowered to grant lands to any new and desirable settlers, and he "must give legal titles without cost." Then follows the statement, clearly opposed to the claims of the ecclesiastics, that he "may, if he deems it expedient, change a mission into a pueblo, and subject it to the same civil and economic laws as govern the other pueblos of the kingdom." Nothing, however, seems to have come of this permission, except a few isolated grants, all under permission from, and with the full approval of, the priests.

Four years later, in June 1777, explicit directions from the viceroy ordered the establishment of two pueblos, one at San José, the other at Los Angeles, on the

Rio Guadalupe and the Rio Porcincula respectively. In 1795 the Marquis of Branciforte founded a colony, and the pueblo of Branciforte, near Santa Cruz. All the other pueblos of California were outgrowths of missions or of presidios. The regulations outlined in the letter of the viceroy, written in 1773, were adopted for the first two pueblos.

In June 1779, additional regulations respecting the pueblos were issued, and were approved and emphasized by royal orders of October 24, 1781. By these orders, each *publador,* or village colonist, was to be paid $116.44 yearly for the first two years, and $60 yearly during the next three: he was also to have the free use of horses, mules, cattle, sheep, utensils, and to be furnished with seed-wheat and other necessaries, of which a long list is given.

The officials are to lay out the streets and public squares, with which all Spanish towns are well provided; and are to choose and mark out the common lands (*egidos*), the lands for municipal purposes (*propios*), the house-lots (*solares*), and the separate sowing-lands of the colonists (*suertes*). We have here a four-fold and extremely interesting division of lands among villagers — a division of very ancient usage among the Spaniards. All the details of the system point to its origin in a community where some of the land had to be irrigated on account of the uncertainty of the seasons, and where much of the wealth of the people was in cattle. The common lands of the pueblo were to furnish water, pasturage, timber, and firewood; and these privileges were free to all dwellers in the town. Those who received grants of building-lots were obliged to fence them, make certain improvements, and plant trees thereon, within a stated time; and this they promised in their petition to the alcalde, or to the town council. The "sowing-lands" were granted in two parcels to each individual; one half being "capable of irrigation" the other half "dry ground," or upland (*de tierras*).

The object of establishing the California pueblos was set forth in a long preamble in the royal order of 1781. It was "to forward the reduction of and as far as possible make this vast country useful to the State"; and the union of white men, or "people of reason" (*gente de razón*), in close communities; also, the "better education of the Indians."

Each pueblo was furnished with alcaldes and other municipal officers (members of council, and *syndicos*), in proportion to the number of inhabitants. For two years these officers were appointed; the third year, and thereafter, they were elected. The titles to houses, lots, and water-rights for irrigation were recorded in the "Book of Colonization," and kept in the pueblo archives. The council had many duties similar to those of the ordinary town councils known to Americans: they ordered the laying-out of streets, the planting of shade-trees, the repair of roads.

In some cases the pueblo council established schools. February 11, 1797, Felipe Goycochea, of the presidio of Santa Barbara, wrote to Governor Borica, saying: "I transmit to you a statement in relation to the schools, together with six copy-books of the children who are learning to write"; and these Spanish copy-books of this pueblo school are still in the archives of California, and likely to long remain, the only thing for which history takes note of these last-century officials. The missions had their schools, also, where some of the brightest Indians were taught to read and write, to keep accounts, and superintend laborers in the field. The hero of Mrs. Helen Hunt Jackson's pathetic and beautiful novel *Ramona* is in no wise an impossible creation: a few such men grew up under the training of mission and pueblo. *Ramona* gives information about the organization of the more progressive Indian settlements of southern California, after the secularization of the missions, before their common lands were wrested away by fraud and force, and shameful neglect on the part of the United States Government.

In March 1791 the viceroy wrote from Chihuahua, Mexico, to Governor Romeu of California — the order reaching him in October — ordaining that the extent of four common leagues measured from the center of the square was sufficient for the new pueblos, into which the old presidios were transformed. The captains of the presidios were to grant and distribute house-lots and lands to citizens and former soldiers within these limits. The decree closed with the customary phrase used by the courtly hidalgos of Spain, "God preserve you many years."

President Iturbide in 1823 established new laws for the pueblos, but they were never put into practical operation in Alta California. The decrees of 1824 and 1828 of the Mexican Congress, however, set forth minute regulations regarding the colonization of the vacant lands, and the granting of town-sites to individuals who bound themselves to establish colonies. No person was allowed to receive more than one square league of irrigated land, four leagues of land dependent on the seasons, and six leagues of pasture. The lands granted must be "vacant," as the exact status of the mission lands was declared "to be as yet undetermined," and "must not be within ten leagues of the coast." This last was evidently an attempt, which proved of little avail, to populate the interior valleys. Less than twelve families were not considered as forming a colony. The government, policy, and town laws of Mexican towns were copied as nearly as practicable.

The spirit of the laws governing the granting of lands to the pueblos was manifestly liberal, as is shown in an act of the Governor and territorial deputation of California, August 6, 1834. It is there provided that when a settlement is made, and the people establish a council, that body may apply for assignments of land. This evidently contemplates the growth of free towns, not begun by formal colonies, or under large grants, but by a few settlers in the ordinary Anglo-Saxon fashion of planting communities. The municipal land so granted was rented, or given out by lot, subject to an annual tax imposed by the council — "the opinion of three intelligent men of honor being first taken." Each house-lot of one hundred varas square [2] cost the grantee six dollars and twenty-five cents for fees paid to the alcalde. Land required for warehouses and other edifices was reserved by the authorities.

August 9, 1834, the long series of efforts to secularize the missions and convert them into pueblos, of which we have previously spoken, and which had extended over so many years, culminated in the "provisional regulations" of Governor Figueroa, providing for the secularization of ten of the missions.[3] The new pueblos were given alcaldes and councils. Appointed commissioners

---

[2] The vara is the Mexican yard of thirty-two inches and four tenths. It is still in use in real-estate transactions in San Francisco.

[3] The Cortes of Spain first mentioned secularization in a decree of January 4, 1813, in reference to Buenos Aires; saying: "Steps will soon be taken to reduce vacant and other lands to private ownership." September 13, they ordered the Buenos Aires Indians to choose representatives to meet the Governor's agents, and distribute the mission lands. In January 1831 the Governor of California issued a decree based on these acts of 1813; but clearly illegal, and so at once recalled. Agitation continued till 1833, when appeared the general act under which the regulations of 1834 were passed.

took charge of the mission property and made classified inventories. They explained to the Indians, "with suavity and patience," that the missions had been converted into pueblos; that they were only subordinate to the priest in matters spiritual; and that each one must work, maintain, and govern himself, "without dependence on anyone." A few large Indian *rancherías,* distant from the missions, were allowed to form separate pueblos; but these were failures.

Thus, as we have seen, the system that prevailed during the early part of this century underwent many changes. Once the territory had been divided into four provinces — San Diego, Santa Barbara, Monterey, and San Francisco — each with a commandante,[4] and the seat of government of each being named a presidio. About it were tracts of land reserved for the use of the king's soldiers, and called *rancherías.*[5] The missions held all they chose of the remaining territory. By 1835 there were secularized missions, ruled spiritually by priests, temporally by government administrators called major-domos in the act of 1840; free towns or pueblos, ruled by officers of their own election; and private estates, controlled with almost manorial powers by lordly Spanish dons owning *ranchos* or *haciendas.* When Americans began to acquire property in the pueblos, a knowledge of their laws was essential; and many land-

---

[4] We have before alluded to the commandante. He is a classic figure in early California life. Cases from alcalde courts and from missions were often referred to him. He held his appellate court with great dignity — a naked sword on one side of his chair, and a silver-headed cane on the other. The sword awed the simple Indians and Mexicans; the cane was a perpetual writ of summons, sent to a man's door to call him as witness, or carried through the village to bring young and old to the court-room.

[5] The word has fallen from its high estate. A *rancheria* is now only a collection of Indian huts.

titles long depended on the pueblo records and procedure.[6]

Historically, the most important of the pueblos was that of Yerba Buena, at first a mere *embarcadero,* or landing-place, for boats of fishermen and hide-drogers; which grew up near the Mission of Dolores and the presidio of San Francisco, absorbed both, took the name of the latter, and has since grown into the largest city on the eastern shores of the Pacific. San José and Los Angeles have also had great prosperity, and prove, in American hands, that "the ancient and honorable pueblos" from which they sprung were admirably located.

The early courts of the State of California recognized and confirmed titles received from the pueblos, and sustained their rights to common and municipal lands.[7] In the case of the pueblo of San Francisco, the center of the old presidio square was made the initial point for a survey of the four square leagues to which the town was entitled as successor to the rights of the pueblo of Yerba Buena.[8] It was decided, under American law, that the lands of a pueblo were not subject to seizure or sale under execution.[9] The power of granting pueblo lands was usually vested in the alcalde, as before stated, but sometimes needed the approval of the *ayuntamiento,* or sometimes of the people of the pueblo. If there was no alcalde, a justice of the peace, in American days, granted lots. In all these cases, specific rules and restrictions were observed. The authorities, for instance, could only

---

[6] "Pueblos could be formed by discharged soldiers, or by a grant to a chief colonist, or to twelve or more families, or by a presidio being established, or by the secularization of a mission" (Welch *vs.* Sullivan, 8 Cal. Rep., p. 165) .

[7] Case of Welch *vs.* Sullivan, 8 Cal. Rep. Also Hart *vs.* Burnett, 15 Cal. Rep.

[8] Payne and Dewey *vs.* Treadwell, 16 Cal., 220.

[9] Fulton *vs.* Hanlon, 20 Cal. Rep., 450.

grant or lease small house-lots, or garden-lots of two hundred varas square. Certain lands could not be sold, mortgaged, or alienated, even to pay municipal expenses.[10]

'Under Mexican rule, the petition required to be sent to the alcalde must set forth that the petitioner was a citizen of Mexico, a resident of the pueblo, desired to use and possess a certain unoccupied tract, and would proceed to make certain improvements. The land was usually granted at once. The expenses of the proceeding varied at different times from five to twenty dollars.[11] The opportunities and perquisites of the office of alcalde were fully appreciated in later times by some of the American incumbents, who granted tracts outside of pueblo bounds, and seriously complicated land-titles. The American military governors of California had various difficulties on this score with the pueblos of San Francisco, Sonoma, San José, Monterey, and Santa Barbara. So far as was consonant with justice, the grants made during this period were sustained. The rights of San Francisco were continuously recognized from 1835 to 1850, except that certain grants made in 1849 by a justice of the peace were set aside as invalid.[12]

In the Mexican system as known in California after 1837, the alcalde was chief officer in all towns, and always presided over the town councils when such existed. As late as 1850 he retained the right of granting town lots.

The preceding notes upon the pueblos have thus led by natural steps to a full consideration of this chief office of the pueblo — the Mexican-Spanish alcaldeship.

---

[10] 1 Cal. Rep., 306. Also cases of Redding *vs.* White, 27 Cal. Rep., 282; Branham *vs.* San José, 24 Cal., 585.

[11] Petition of Rosalie Haro, of Yerba Buena Pueblo, to Alcalde Padilla (before American conquest), 1 Cal. Rep., 323.

[12] Cohas *vs.* Raisin, 3 Cal. Rep., 443.

Several times in the progress of this study we have found it necessary to use the term and allude to the office. Alcaldes ruled the Darien colonists and the Darien mining camp; they found a place in Mexican mine towns and Mexican pastoral communities. Transplanted to Alta California, the office still preserved its unique character, and continued its development towards higher forms. At last the American miners for a time adopted the name and the institution, transferring it from the towns of the coast to the camps of the Sierra. We must, in a separate chapter, consider the historical evolution of this office in Spain, in Mexico, and in California. How was it that a local officer of the Spanish civil system became the most important of institutional contributions from Spanish America to Germanic America? How was it that the freedom of the people to choose their own alcaldes was often greater in California than in Mexico? To answer these questions, we must consider the nature and scope of the office in its varied forms and throughout its eventful career. We must turn to the caliphate of Cordova and the three Christian kingdoms of northern Spain.

Chapter VIII. A STUDY OF ALCALDES

The heart of the Spanish local system is the alcaldeship. We must, however, turn to the fruitful Orient for the origin of the office: it is, in fact, the *kadi* of Persia and Arabia, the *alkaid* of the Saracens and Moors; it is also the village judgeship of Spain in its heroic age, when Aragon possessed the most liberal constitution in Europe.[1] Art, romance, and literature have loved to linger over the picturesque features of this office; tales of the East, and peasant songs of the Spanish peninsula, alike describe the "judge of the village," whose power for good or evil was almost unlimited.

The very forms that the word has taken in the Spanish language are evidences of the universality and importance of the thing itself. An *alcaidía* is a town warden, or governor of a town, or it is the district of his jurisdiction; his wife is the *alcaidesa;* the duty anciently levied on all cattle driven across the district or through the town was the *alcaida;* the *alcaicería* was the marketplace. These are earlier forms, and point to wider sway, and even greater powers, than the modern alcaldes ever possessed. The true alcalde was judge of the town, and *ex-officio* mayor of the council. To be given *alcalda* was to receive the protection of some powerful citizen or

---

[1] In Aragon, the citizens of the free towns, or pueblos, had provincial laws, organized guilds, and elected alcaldes. They chose deputies to the *cortes*, or legislative council; and this council elected the supreme judge, or *justicia,* levied taxes, and appointed minor officers. Aragon, Valencia, Castile, and Catalonia held *cortes* of three estates — prelates, nobles, and deputies. León in 1188 assembled the first council of elected deputies. Barcelona grew from the Spanish *Mark* established by Karl the Great, and became independent in the days of Charles le Chauve.

great nobleman; the office itself is the *alcaldia;* the judge's wife is the *alcaldesa;* lastly, as a term of contempt, anger, or sarcasm, applied to any absurd or hasty action, we have the word *alcaldada.*

Pleadings before the Spanish alcaldes were oral; and proceedings were summary, and in all ordinary cases were final. Even in very important trials, an appeal was infrequent; for to carry it farther meant to become entangled in the Spanish courts of record, a worse fate than to drift into the delays of the English chancery courts. In one of the medieval Spanish romances, a peasant says: "Yonder stone wall will rot ere thy lawsuit ends."

Under the Spanish laws, the alcaldes were the conciliators of disputes, and the head men of the village, responsible to higher authority for the behavior of those under their charge.

Wherever the descendants of Spain went, they took the main features of the alcalde system to which they were accustomed: the silver-headed official staff of the alcalde was planted beside the cross of the Jesuit missionaries and the Franciscan friars. We have previously spoken of alcaldes in the colonies of Cuba and Darien: alcaldes also accompanied the soldiers of De Soto and Narváez. When Cabeza de Vaca, afterwards pioneer explorer of New Mexico, declined to accept command of the fleet of Narváez, it was an alcalde who took the position. The alcaldes of that period were soldiers and judges by turn, leaders of expeditions, and governors of new colonies. Don Diego Peñalosa, one of the most adventurous Spanish knights of the seventeenth century, was in succession alcalde of La Paz, alcalde of Cuzco, and provincial alcalde of all the La Paz provinces.[2]

So soon as Mexico was conquered, division into dis-

---

[2] Shea's *Peñalosa Quivira Expedition.*

tricts and the planting of pueblos began, to each of which an alcalde was appointed, vacancies being afterwards filled by election. The powers and duties of the office were probably much the same as at the present time; except that, so long as the mining courts existed, no alcalde had any jurisdiction over mining cases. He could not even give a title to mineral lands; this right, as we have already seen, being vested in the "mining deputation" of the provinces. In 1812 the Spanish *cortes* extended municipality privileges to all Mexican villages of fifty or more inhabitants, and provided that several hamlets could be united politically for town government; that is, under an alcalde, for no council was considered necessary in such cases.

One of the most interesting and primary duties of the Mexican village alcalde was that of arbitration in all minor disputes. *Conciliación* was recognized as a part of the mining law: it also belonged in the civil code. No trial could take place until the alcaldes (always known in this capacity as *hombres buenos*) had tried to settle it equitably, and to the satisfaction of both parties without expense to either. "Each alcalde," the law said, "shall have a book, called the 'Book of *Conciliacións*,' in which to keep a record of all cases, and of the means taken to prevent litigation." But "ecclesiastical, military, and municipal cases, and those that affect public revenues," were not subjects for *conciliación* and compromise. The ceremony of arbitration as a necessary prelude to all lawsuits was first disregarded, in California, in February 1850.[3] The Spanish principle of *conciliación* is doubtless a gift of Roman jurisprudence. The eighth section of the fourth book of the Pandects lays down the principles almost exactly as now accepted in Mexico. Some of the old provincial laws of France

---

[3] Von Schmidt *vs.* Huntington, 1 Cal. 55.

provided for "arbiters." The principle is recognized as of great importance in international law, to settle difficulties and prevent war.

There was a form of local and special alcaldeship, first known to Mexico during the sixteenth century, that has, in modified forms, become a part of Western life in the United States. Yearly the village alcalde and the council (if one existed) chose two or more *alcaldes de mesta,* who presided over the semi-annual assemblages of the livestock-owners. This custom was carried wherever Spanish colonists went. In California these officers were known as *jueces del campo* ("judges of the plain"). They were obliged to be present at all the annual *rodeos,* or meetings on horseback in the open fields, for the purpose of collecting and branding all the livestock of the district. These *rodeos* were the most important celebrations known to the Spanish Californians. Every *ranchero* and *vaquero* was on hand with whirling *riata* and gayly caparisoned mustang. The *jueces* were often called upon to settle disputes about the ownership of cattle, the identity of brands, and similar matters; and they were very useful and dignified officials. From the first, the Californians appear to have elected their own *jueces;* and several times Americans were chosen before 1846. During the military occupation of the territory, the office of *jueces* continued; Americans serving in Los Angeles, Monterey, and San José. When the first legislature of the State of California met, it passed, on the last day of its session (April 20, 1850), a bill repealing all the old Spanish laws "except the laws of the *jueces del campo.*" For years after, and, indeed, as long as any *rodeos* were held in the pastoral regions of California, local judges to decide disputes were chosen. As late as 1870, a visitor to San Luis Obispo County saw American and Spanish cattle-raisers holding *rodeos,* and submitting peaceably to the decisions of three "judges of the plain" chosen from among their number on the first day of the *rodeo.* The great plains of California have all been fenced, and are being sown with wheat and planted with vines, so that the annual *rodeo* is now an extinct institution. But in western Texas, New Mexico, Colorado, and northward, wherever great cattle-ranges are found today, the stock-men, in their picturesque and exciting "round-ups," still follow the ancient Spanish plan; not knowing that it is a heritage from a race they despise, they choose "cattle-judges," to settle disputes, and uphold their decisions as final.

The strange vitality of that nomad institution, the *alcalde de mesta,* is explained by the fact that it was perfectly adapted to the needs of a pastoral community, as much to cattle-owners and cowboys as to *rancheros* and *vaqueros.* But the fixed and permanent office of the true town alcalde has proved hardly less enduring, and is certainly much more instructive to the student of institutions.

The Mexican alcaldeship of today is much the same office that the first Spanish colonists knew. It is a good working combination of justice of the peace, town constable, town recorder; it involves a sponsorship before the law; it possesses a sort of patriarchal authority. In each village, the power of the alcalde is supreme: his will is exercised over the in-coming and the out-going, the eating and the sleeping, the toil and the recreation, of every inhabitant. Each traveler visits him to make inquiries, to secure bargains, or to settle disputes with his servants or guides. Questions the most trivial are asked in the same breath with questions the most stupendous: to this Indian he quotes the market-price of onions, and to that blushing señorita gives advice concerning rival suitors. He has social privileges and political power. He is the chief overseer of local interests. If a traveling show wishes to visit the town, it usually bribes the alcalde to permit it to exhibit there, and the village priest to announce it from his parish pulpit. The messengers of the king used to carry letters of commendation to the alcaldes along their route. The simple and ignorant peasants have personal dealings with few other officials. Fear and reverence encircle the throne of this little autocrat, the alcalde, to whom every conceivable difficulty is brought for solution. For these reasons, the office is one of the most interesting, primeval, and romantic of yet surviving Spanish institutions upon the continent.[4]

The rule of the alcalde in California was never so firmly established or so despotic as in Mexico, but it was always of greater importance than its nominal rights and duties would seem to justify. The powers authorized by the decree of March 20, 1837 were supplemented and increased by the weight of local custom; for alcaldes had existed in California since the first pueblo was founded.

This decree of 1837 reorganized the judiciary of California, providing for courts of *conciliación,* or lower alcalde courts, for courts of first instance, courts of second instance, courts of third instance, and final appeals to the Mexican supreme court. But the revolutions and political difficulties in Alta California, then and thereafter, prevented the practical adoption of any such system: it simply remained a dead letter. The powers

---

[4] Books of travel teem with allusions. Mr. D. S. Richardson of California, the private secretary of Minister Foster, in Mexico, writes to me giving an account of the alcalde's importance in village life.

which it gave the alcalde were less than that officer really exercised. An enumeration of these powers, though suggestive and useful, must therefore be accompanied with a statement of the alcalde's unwritten duties.

"Alcaldes," it is provided in this decree, "shall secure good order"; shall execute the laws of the prefects; shall call for a military force, or upon the citizens for help, when needed; shall see that the residents of the town live by useful occupation; shall reprimand idle, vicious, and vagabond persons; shall preside over council meetings, and vote there; and may impose fines of not more than twenty-five dollars.

Jurisdiction over mining claims was expressly withheld from the California alcaldes, and was left to the mining deputation of the nearest province, Sonora.

The large towns were given three alcaldes, six *regidors,* and two *syndicos;* the nine forming the *ayuntamiento,* and the senior alcalde presiding. These officers were to be elected yearly; but the office-holding power was not limited, and it was declared that "no one must refuse to serve without having the Governor's permission to retire." Certain officers of the government were prohibited from being members of the *ayuntamiento.*

The same act of 1837 defines the duties of this council. It was to have charge of the streets and the cemeteries, of sanitary affairs, of prisons and hospitals, of the inspection of drugs, liquors, and provisions. It was to act as a committee of charity in case of pestilence; was to keep a record of births, marriages, and deaths; was to provide for market-places, straight paved streets, bridges, parks, and public fountains. One of its duties was that of "making contracts for all sorts of diversions," such as public games and shows. It was empowered to establish schools, and pay the teachers out of the municipal funds. Lastly, it was required "to be impartial to all citizens, rich or poor," to protect the weights and measures, to expend public moneys honestly, and to report annually to the Governor. Each member of the *ayuntamiento* was responsible for maladministration or malfeasance. When elected, they were sworn in by the prefect, or by a former alcalde.

In some of the Mexican towns the councils were doubtless burdened with most of the duties described in the previous paragraph. In California towns the council seldom met, since the office was not salaried; and the alcalde performed most of its functions, perhaps ordering a "horn-burning" in the pueblo square as a sufficient sanitary measure when unusual sickness prevailed.

A subsequent act of 1837 restored certain powers to the alcalde. In the departments of California, New Mexico, and Tabasco, he was empowered to perform the functions of judge of first instance in all districts where there were no such judges; and this was afterwards sustained by the American courts.[5]

But in most instances the alcaldes were even more than "judges of first instance." The disordered condition of California gave the office greater power, but at the same time rendered its tenure more precarious, than the Mexican Government had contemplated. We have before alluded to these disasters in speaking of the sudden wreck of the missions, and the scattering of the Indians. Bands of wandering trappers descended into the valleys; the Russians had settled at Bodega and Fort Ross; and the Americans in the country aided General Solis in his unsuccessful rebellion of 1830. Minor disturbances followed, and the Indians raided outlying *ranchos*. American rifles decided the success of Alvara-

---

[5] Mena *vs.* Le Roy, 1 Cal. Rep., 216; also Panaud *vs.* Jones, 1 Cal. Rep., 448. See 1 Cal. Rep., 559, appendix, on general alcalde system.

do's revolution of 1836–8; and from that time the American party began to organize, much as it did in Texas, aided in the downfall of Alvarado, and the success of Micheltorena in 1842. By 1845 the corruption of his government caused a new rebellion, headed by Castro, Pio Pico, and others; and Micheltorena was deposed. The American settlers in the Sacramento Valley, and near Sonoma, soon had reason to believe that movements were on foot to drive them out; and they organized the noted "Bear Flag" battalion, commanded by Captains Ide and Grigsby, which thrust Castro from the Sonoma and Sacramento valleys, and was on the eve of proclaiming a republic when Frémont and Stockton came to their aid.

While such political changes were in progress, the alcalde's tenure of office became precarious, because any district or town that wanted an alcalde preferred to choose him for an indefinite period. Since the alcalde made his own laws, and saw them enforced according to his own methods, an unpopular law or a disagreeable decision speedily caused discontent, and sometimes ended in an appeal to the Governor, or even in a *pronunciamiento* and a public assembly, taking the alcaldeship away, and ordering a new election. This was done, in some instances, before the American conquest.

In practice, the only judge above the California alcalde was the governor of the province, who could grant tracts of agricultural or pastoral lands in much the same way as the alcalde could grant town lots, except that the papers and applications had to be forwarded to Mexico for final approval. Castro, Alvarado, and Pio Pico granted so many "concessions" that, in some cases, a single tract was given several owners, each showing equal title to the whole. Nominally there was a veto-power vested in the governor's council, called by courtesy a "departmental legislature"; but, under the governors we have mentioned, large tracts were given away, unchecked even by Mexico. American courts sifted and tested these grants, refusing to confirm a large number on the grounds of illegality according to Mexican law.[6] After 1837 the governor held the only true appellate court in California.

We have spoken of the "Book of *Conciliacións*" that was kept by each alcalde. Besides this, he kept a "Book of Verbal Processes," recording his judgments therein; also, and of more importance, he was compelled, according to the "Plan of Pitic," a Spanish law of 1789, to record all the grants of lands made by him within the pueblo bounds, to have them signed and attested (though without seals), and a copy delivered to the petitioner. These books of record kept by alcaldes during the Spanish era, and previous to the organization of the state, were received as evidence of land-titles on proof that the signatures of the alcalde and clerk (*syndicos*) were genuine.[7] An alcalde deed to land was not void because no consideration was expressed, nor were transfers of property which he made compelled to have a price mentioned.[8]

The old Spanish forms of wills were extremely simple; and an alcalde, though appointed as executor, could authenticate the document in his judicial capacity, if only he was not named in the will as heir or legatee, nor derived any compensation for administering it. The will of Anastasio Alviso of the pueblo of San José, dated September 19, 1846, contains a list of "passive

---

[6] Cases of Ferris *vs*. Coover, 10 Cal. Rep.; Berryessa *vs*. Schultz, 21 Cal. Rep.; Waterman *vs*. Smith, 13 Cal. Rep.; and others.

[7] Cases of Touchard *vs*. Keyes, 21 Cal. Rep.; and Downer *vs*. Smith, 24 Cal. Rep. Halleck says that Governor Pio Pico made antedated land-grants, and inserted them in the blank leaves of record-books.

[8] Merle *vs*. Mathews, 26 Cal., 455.

debts" such as: "I declare that I owe Señora Romero seven hides"; also a list of "active debts" such as: "I declare that Vicente Monez shall pay for the kitchen utensils whatever he in his conscience shall think proper to deliver over." [9] Primitive habits of life are manifest in every line of such quaint documents, in spirit centuries removed from the California of today, though written less than forty years ago.

During the military rule of the American officers, who governed California before it was yielded by treaty to the United States, the powers of the alcaldes were much limited in the coast towns, though almost as extensive as ever in places where no military were stationed. In 1847, before the close of the war, while General Kearny was military governor, he appointed alcaldes whenever vacancies occurred, exercised close supervision over their acts, and removed them whenever he saw fit. He directed the alcalde of San José, John Barton, to dismiss a suit that the Mexican courts had already decided; he advised John Nash, alcalde of Sonoma, that a writ of restitution he had issued in an ecclesiastical case was illegal; he sent word to H. D. Fitch, alcalde of San Diego, empowering him to fine, imprison, or both, certain unruly persons.

When Colonel Mason succeeded General Kearny as military governor of California, he announced that "the alcaldes are not authorities of the United States, nor are they Mexican authorities. They are the civil magistrates of California, and therefore the authorities of California within their respective jurisdictions, subject to removal from office by order of the governor." He authorized them "to continue in the practice and custom of the country," and to grant lots within the town limits, but construed the word "grant" to mean "sell for the

---

[9] Panaud *vs.* Jones, 1 Cal. Rep.

benefit of the municipality." The alcaldes were not to perform the marriage ceremony in cases where either of the contracting parties was a Roman Catholic.

About this time the spirit of change and uncertainty prevailed in many places, and there were numerous instances of violation of property-rights. Squatters were taking possession of lands near the missions San José and Santa Clara, where, the previous winter, they had been permitted to occupy some old buildings. The San José alcalde was ordered to remove them. Troops were sent to the disputed lands; but a compromise was effected, and the settlers agreed to pay a small rent until the true limits of the mission property should be ascertained.

The authority of the alcalde, in all cases between citizen and citizen, was decided to be the same as under the Mexican law, and to include minor cases in which citizens and soldiers were involved. An officer was reprimanded in 1848 for interfering in such a case, and for "sending a file of soldiers to rescue a disputed saddle from the alcalde's *juzgado.*"

Indian troubles occurring in September 1847, regulations were issued that all peaceable Indians should procure protection papers from the alcaldes of their respective districts. In December a letter from Colonel Mason urges the Indian agent to have them appoint alcaldes among themselves for their own better government. A later proclamation imposed a fine of one hundred dollars on persons convicted before an alcalde of selling liquor to Indians.

During October 1847 a sailor who had stabbed the mate of the ship *Vesper* was turned over to the alcalde of San Francisco for trial. "In the old alcalde courts of California," Colonel Mason writes, "the alcalde tried such cases; and when the sentence was death, the governor either ordered the execution, or sent the case to Mexico for further advice." Some time in November, one Anastacio Ruiz of San Vicente, San Diego County, charged with murder, was tried before a jury of twelve presided over by the alcalde, Colonel Mason authorizing them to inflict capital punishment. He was probably acquitted, as the case is not again mentioned in the California Documents.

Although the acting governor had appointed alcaldes to fill all vacancies, yet in most cases he asked the people of the district to signify by petition their preferences. In 1847 native California alcaldes were in charge in only four or five towns on the coast. Everywhere else Americans ruled. At Sonoma a town council was elected, and the alcalde issued certificates of election. At San José the town council of six was twice voted for, and considerable difficulty followed; but the matter was settled by the appointment of a committee of three to examine the returns.

December 20, 1847, an American alcalde who applied for information was told by Colonel Mason that, "in cases of horse-stealing, a fine, and hard labor on public works, and in aggravated cases fifty lashes in addition, is in accordance with the old California practice." A month or so later, a commercial case, tried in San José before an alcalde and a jury of six men, was appealed to Colonel Mason, who denied it on the ground that there was no higher court.

San José pueblo at this time had two alcaldes, the first being an American, the other a Spaniard. These two officers appointed a town treasurer, who gave bonds, and at once entered upon the discharge of his duties.

The alcalde of San Luis Obispo, early in 1848, organized a party of thirty settlers to check the depredations of Indians who had been stealing cattle, and acted as their leader. Colonel Mason offered to furnish them ammunition if called upon to do so.

In March 1848 there was but one alcalde, Elam Brown, in all the "Contra Costa and San Joaquin region," a territory some hundreds of miles in extent. Stephen Cooper had just been appointed alcalde at Benicia, the new town north of Carquinez Straits.

The various alcaldes in California were notified by Colonel Mason that "notes and accounts contracted in the United States cannot be legally enforced and collected in California until the United States shall organize a territorial government in this country, and extend her laws over the same." No debts made elsewhere could be collected in California until the state constitution was in full operation.

By the close of October 1848, the evil effect of the immigration caused by the gold excitement began to be shown in some places. Several murders were committed. Three men were tried by an alcalde and jury at San José pueblo, for robbery and attempted murder of two returned miners, found guilty, and promptly executed. Colonel Mason wrote: "I shall not disapprove of this course, and shall only endeavor to secure to every man charged with a capital crime a fair trial by a jury of his countrymen." A Mr. Reed and his entire family, ten persons in all, were murdered at Mission San Miguel; and the perpetrators were captured, tried before an alcalde jury, and hung. Other murders occurred; and some of the accused were given jury-trial, some were tried before an alcalde without a jury, some were lynched.

The most important alcaldeship in California, and that which probably contains the most complete and valuable records, was that of San Francisco. Its history from the days of the marine pueblo or *embarcadero* of

Yerba Buena, established in 1833, to the days when the last alcalde under the military governors resigned his position, and was re-elected as the first mayor under the state laws and legislative Act of Incorporation, will sufficiently show the continuity of the office, and the importance of its archives.[10] No order actually announcing the establishment of the pueblo was ever issued; but its existence was assumed through all the changes, revolutions, and confusion of the last years of Mexican rule, as amply shown in Hon. J. W. Dwinelle's argument for the pueblo land-titles.

November 27, 1835, the people of Dolores Mission held their first election, and chose J. J. Estudillo as alcalde. There was then but one dwelling, the tent of an English trader named Richardson, on the Yerba Buena cove. An adventurous American, Jacob P. Leese, procured, after much difficulty, permission to lay out a new town, and by July 4, 1836 had built a shanty of rough boards as a trading-house for the *rancheros* about the bay. The only other building in the vicinity was an Indian *temiscal,* or sweat-house. The presidio contained no garrison, and only one resident, a superannuated soldier named Pina. The rule of Alcalde Estudillo extended over the entire peninsula; but he lived upon an extensive ranch on the southern shore of the bay, in what is now Alameda County, and spent little time at mission or pueblo. Extreme simplicity of life and manners prevailed among the inhabitants.

---

[10] The Spanish archives kept in San Francisco are the basis of many valuable real-estate rights. They embrace the *expediente* or record of proceedings; the petitions, maps, decree, and *titulo* or title-deed of numerous grants; the formal books *Tamas del razón* of 1828; the Jimeno Index, or list of grants, and its continuation, the Hartnell Index; and the evidences of the approval of the departmental legislation. There are five hundred and seventy-nine complete Spanish grants, and three hundred and fourteen incomplete or inchoate ones, recorded in these archives.

Several changes in the alcaldeship took place; and in 1839 the franchises, books, and papers of presidio, mission, and pueblo appear to have come into the possession of J. P. Guerrero, the alcalde, who assumed jurisdiction over all except the immediate possessions of the Mission Dolores. All the grants made by this alcalde before the war have been held by American courts to have been made in the course of his ordinary duties. After the American ships took possession, General Kearny appointed Washington Bartlett as magistrate and justice, and gave him the right to give away town lots; also, a little later, ordered the sale of certain water-lots. These orders constitute the earliest American titles to real estate in San Francisco. The title of the United States to the public domain was held to relate back to the time of the occupancy of the country,[11] when Mexican laws ceased, except as re-established by military authorities, as they were in most cases.

Alcalde Bartlett, and his successors Hyde and Leavenworth, exercised control over San Francisco affairs at a turbulent period. As soon as the war closed, Colonel Mason, and his successor, General Peter Riley, attempted to unite the civil and military functions of government; and an anomalous condition of affairs followed. There was, for a time, nothing to set things in motion; and neither law nor administration of justice existed except so far as exemplified in the alcalde courts, which had known no checks and had taken no vacations. San Francisco was growing rapidly; and the local customs and simple code of a rude Mexican population, known in written forms to but few, chiefly dependent on verbal processes and instantaneous decisions, were suddenly required to fulfill the complex and varying

---

[11] See Woodworth *vs.* Fulton, 1 Cal. Rep., 295; Reynolds *vs.* West, 1 Cal. Rep., 333.

needs of an active and enterprising people, carrying on immense business transactions, and sincerely anxious to base them on the laws of the United States. Governor Mason by proclamation enforced the Mexican civil law in its main features, and set Messrs. Halleck and Hartnell at work to make a translation and digest of such parts of the laws of 1837 as were judged applicable and still in force.[12] The people, accepting all this as a sad but inevitable necessity, began to struggle towards local organizations and a state government.

During this unsettled period the "judge of first instance," or alcalde, sat each day in the little schoolroom on the plaza of San Francisco, trying cases, and rendering that speedy justice that was then more desirable than exact justice, since men's time, in those early days of 1849, was worth from sixteen dollars to one hundred dollars per day. The judge listened to brief arguments, announced his decision, took his fees, and called up another case: hardly once in a hundred times was there any thought of an appeal to the Governor at Monterey. Criminal jurisprudence, however, was in decidedly a bad way: neither jails, district funds, nor city organization existed; so that sheriffs, guards, and other officers had to serve without pay, and seldom, until the community was fully roused, could a trial be had in cases demanding capital punishment. For lesser crimes, lashes or hard labor on the streets could always be imposed.

The powers of the alcalde increased apace, and various difficulties between that officer and two rival town councils early in 1849 culminated in the formation of an independent organization called "The Provisional

---

[12] Ready for publication in July 1849, pp. 40. Printed in the appendix to *Debates in the Convention of California.* J. Ross Browne, 1850. Washington.

Government of San Francisco." [13] Its chief feature was
a legislature of fifteen members. They met March 5,
1849, and swore "to support the Constitution of the
United States and the government of this district." They
organized for business, began to make laws, and took
the records of the town from Alcalde Leavenworth, with
whom there was great dissatisfaction, and who had refused to resign as requested. It was a government *de facto*.

March 10 they addressed a letter to Major-General
Persifor F. Smith, in which they pointed out the fact
that the civil institutions of California were "neither
Mexican nor American," but nondescript; that many
ministerial and judicial offices of the pure Mexican system had been allowed to sink into disuse; and that the
only office retained was that of alcalde, which office
"had been permitted to obtain and exercise a most extensive and unlimited jurisdiction, wholly incompati-
ble with the dictates of reason and justice. The right of
appeal to the military governor has been denied or
evaded." "Undoubtedly," the committee added, "this
office of alcalde was continued" (through the interregnum) "by the presumed consent of the people, and
without any alteration, except that the right of appeal
became inoperative. The jurisdiction, power, and duty
of the office, partially limited by martial law, became,
without it, unlimited and irresponsible. The tenure,
duty, and property of the office, as existing under martial law, without any definite or prescribed rules, was
continued so, and the people left without any law in
the adjudication of every civil and criminal issue, except the mere will of this single officer," who is "elected

---

[13] Early in 1849 the citizens of Sonoma and of Sacramento had
elected similar district assemblies. In San Francisco, February 12, the
people to the number of five hundred assembled, organized, adopted a
plan of government, appointed an election-day, and asked the council
and alcalde to resign.

by the people," and "has all public records in his hands," and "owns no superior tribunal," not even to "compel him to discharge his obligations with his fellow-citizens as a private individual. . . . All the civil and criminal issues that come before him are determined according to his own notions of right and wrong, directed and enforced by his mere will"; and, as this emphatic document reiterates in closing, "without the right of appeal." But Provisional Governor Riley, to whom a similar statement had been made, proclaimed the entire proceeding illegal, and the legislature without authority, forbade the payment of taxes to its subordinates, upheld the alcalde, and ignored the complaints formulated in the above letter to Major-General Smith. The alcalde afterwards resigned; and a new election was ordered, resulting in the choice of Mr. J. W. Geary. It was a noteworthy struggle throughout, and the temper of the citizens was admirable.

When a city government under the state constitution was established, the alcaldeship, with its varied powers, came to an end and yielded up its ancient authority. Alcalde Geary, the last of the San Francisco alcaldes, was re-elected January 1, 1850, and in April was chosen city mayor under its first charter. Thus the institutional link was established: thus the office of mayor of San Francisco derived its historical descent, not from American and English sources, but from the semi-despotic rulers of Spanish pueblos, and the tribute-levying governors of medieval towns of Castilian frontiers. The term survives; and San Francisco, metropolis of the Pacific coast, still cherishes the title of "ancient and honorable pueblo."

The story of the alcaldeship in San Francisco was repeated on a lesser scale in many other towns and villages of California. Everywhere it was of fundamental importance during the transition era, and everywhere it presented remarkable minglings of Mexican and American features. The alcaldes, whether elected or appointed, were usually honest and intelligent, anxious to deal out justice with an impartial hand, well sustained by the American settlers, and obeyed by the Mexicans. But the confusion of authorities was vexatious and amusing. Some offices contained only a few worn and smoky Spanish manuscripts, heirlooms of the last century; in some the codes of Iowa, Illinois, Missouri, South Carolina, and other states were in constant use; in some were a few volumes of French, Spanish, German, or English law that the new alcaldes had somehow obtained to add an air of impressiveness to the scantily furnished room.

Before leaving this subject and passing to the broader field of the mining camp, we must sum up and define the duties and powers of the typical alcalde. We have seen that he always wielded great power, and sometimes wielded sole authority throughout his district, in both civil and criminal cases; that he was the guardian of the common and town lands; that he summoned courts, and appointed minor municipal officers; that he exercised an almost parental supervision over the inhabitants of his pueblo. Studying his multifarious functions, we discover with admiration, not unmixed with awe, that one and the same person was often supreme judge, clerk of court, town constable, sheriff, recorder, treasurer, justice of the peace, land-officer, government agent in land deliveries,[14] superintendent of roads, town board of health, board of school-trustees, arbitrator in petty dis-

---

[14] A petition for a land-grant was often, in Spanish times, referred by the governor to an alcalde to report on. The last of the steps in judicial procedure in land-grants was the formal delivery of the tract, along with a map, by the alcalde of the district in which it lay, after examining the bounds. This ceremony was akin to the "livery of seizin" of English common law. See also United States *vs.* Pico, 6 Wall. 536.

putes, general advisory board for young and old, and even, near the coast, judge in admiralty to pronounce upon all marine cases. One and the same room was often the police court, probate court, civil court, criminal court, court of equity, court of appeal, land-office, council-hall, and *conciliación* court; it was also bedroom, dining-room, kitchen, library, and drawing-room of the busy, potent, and ubiquitous alcalde. Strangest fact of all in this unique combination, the lordly alcalde palace which sheltered such an army of officials was probably, in the mines at least, an edifice of canvas, with an empty nail-keg for a chimney-top. In the pueblos of the coast, the alcalde assembled himself in some old Mexican house, under yellow roofing-tiles molded years before by serfs of the mission, and beside priest-planted gardens of olive and orange. One American alcalde of the transition period lived and held court in a house of zinc, whose outside measurements were less than twelve feet in length and breadth. The law in which these men dealt was as concentrated, and free from waste and surplus, as were the houses in which they dwelt. The various functions of government were performed without clashing, by this happily invented alcalde system; judicial jealousies, and browbeating of lesser officers, were absolutely unknown. In the nature of the case, nothing could be less permanent than such an all-containing office as that of the alcalde in its prime; but nothing could well be more influential and arbitrary while it lasted. Its widest freedom and its fullest development were not in the quiet pastoral and agricultural districts of the coast, but in the midst of the whirling excitements of the famous mining camps of '48 and '49. The alcalde of the Sierra is the perfected American type; but so rich was the period that this forms but a small part of its institutional harvest.

Chapter IX. CALIFORNIA CAMPS — THE DAYS OF '48

The four preceding chapters have been devoted to a study of Spanish-American institutions and their influences on early California. The remaining chapters of this work deal with the organization and government, by citizens of the United States, of large and isolated mining camps; returning in some cases to primitive forms, sometimes using and modifying the Mexican alcaldeship, sometimes adopting methods suggested by New England town meetings, but always aiming to quell disorder and protect property and life. They attempt to describe what manner of men these miners were, and with what customs, laws, and usages camp and district were ruled. They discuss the influence these miners exerted, directly and indirectly, upon the political organization of California; and the acceptance, in American jurisprudence, of principles originated by gold-diggers in the folk-moots of the Sierra.

One of the most entrancing chapters of this nineteenth century's eventful history is that which narrates the gold-discovery of 1848, the rush of anxious wealth-seekers to California, and the rapid growth of new institutional life among people thus assembled from all parts of the world. When American pioneers conquered the Mississippi Valley, they made it the stepping-stone to more difficult victories. The sons of the men who settled Kentucky and Ohio crossed the mighty river and took possession of Iowa and Missouri: their sons, in turn, have made the term "West" no longer applicable to the great valley; they have even shattered the phrase into fragments, and so have given us the Southwest of New Mexico and Arizona, the Northwest of Idaho, Oregon, and the Puget Sound basin, the Central West of Colorado, Utah, Nevada, and California. The all-compelling magnet which drew peaceful armies to these wastes and mountains of the western third of the continent, there to build great cities, there to organize prosperous communities and powerful states, was a flake of virgin gold found on a California hillside thirty-six years ago.

That was the year of revolutions in Europe; of barricades in Paris, Berlin, Vienna, Milan; of Louis Blanc's "ministry of progress," and Louis Napoleon's deceitful presidency; of students in arms, and petty princes abdicating in haste their pasteboard thrones; of liberal constitutions, national assemblies, and a Slavonic congress; of Lombardy, Schleswig-Holstein, and Hungary in arms, the last, under the leadership of Kossuth, to make her death-struggle for freedom. On the Bourse, and in Lombard Street, the kings of the financial world were noting the signs of coming storm, even as the year began; but the event of most importance to the money-markets of Europe occurred unheralded before the "Revolution of February." Let us note the place and the manner of the occurrence. It was one hundred and seventy miles east of the Pacific Ocean; it was in the grizzly-haunted mountains of an obscure and neglected province only a few months before owned by Mexico, thinly populated by tribes of degraded Indians, idle Spanish Americans, musical-tongued Kanakas, wandering trappers, and a few Anglo-Saxon farmers and speculators; it was January 19, 1848, and about a fortnight before the actual signing of the Treaty of Guadalupe Hidalgo, which gave the United States 522,955 square miles of territory, including this obscure El Dorado, for the trifling sum of fifteen million dollars. Some laborers, on this California hillside, were digging a water-ditch to supply a flour-mill that was being built by the feudal-like lord of a vast tract over which wild oats waved, wild flowers bloomed, and herds of antelope roamed, mingling undisturbed with bands of cattle and horses, and even venturing at times within sight of the massive oaken gates of the adobe-built fort where this active, courtly, enterprising, and generous adventurer had established his authority as lord of "New Helvetia." [1]

Captain Sutter, at that important era in early 1848, swung his malacca cane, pulled his trim military mustache, gave crisp orders to his Indian alcalde, his commander of the troops, his general superintendent, his manager of cattle, and his head farmer; paid his two hundred laborers with pieces of tin stamped with numbers representing days' work, and redeemable at his storehouses; kept open house for every traveler, explorer, or government official: he was, in a word, the most vital, sinewy, and picturesque figure in all Alta California, beside whose manliness the plotting, irascible, treacherous, dishonest governors who disgraced the closing years of Mexican rule sink into utter insignificance. His title appeared unimpeachable, his possessions secure under the American flag, his colony enterprise well managed and certain of success. But the discovery of a flake of gold, lying concealed in the red hillside soil twenty miles away, set forces in operation that blighted and destroyed all his plans.

---

[1] Captain John A. Sutter in 1841 received from Governor Alvarado a grant of eleven leagues in the Sacramento Valley, and built a fort where the city of the same name now stands. He was commissioned "representative of the government, and officer of justice on the northern frontier." The comparison to the old courts palatinate is irresistible. He purchased from the Russians their extensive claims on Bodega Bay, and thus, perhaps, saved the United States from many subsequent diplomatic difficulties.

January 19, while unconscious Sutter governed his little kingdom, the workmen at Coloma, having finished their ditch, lifted the water-gate; and the clear mountain torrent leaped gurgling and foaming along its new-cut channel, uncovering a piece of virgin gold — first recorded nugget of American California.[2] This precious lump, smaller than the first joint of a child's forefinger, gleamed in Marshall's mill-race, attracted human eyes, was tested in a locked room by roused and excited men, and caused a rush that ended Sutter's multifarious operations, bidding the hides rot in his tanneries, his wheat fall to the earth ungathered, his herds wander untended, and perish at the hands of outlaws. The fame of this discovery drew to the spot, with magic power, the population of the whole territory; so that, a few months later, but five men were left in San Francisco, ships swung sailorless at anchor, and soldiers deserted their colors. All Alta California was concentrating in the mines. Thus the memorable gold rush began.

Soon the news went abroad to all the world. Piles of California nuggets lay in the windows of banking-houses, gazed at by thousands. The fact that in the new placers unskilled, uneducated, and penniless men were able to gather from fifty to five hundred dollars in gold-dust each day they worked was calculated to produce a profound impression. Mockers were silenced, doubters were swept into the current. Before the close of the year, fifty thousand of the healthiest and most energetic young men of the nation were on their way to California. Meanwhile the five thousand men who were fairly at work in the mines in 1848 dug out over five million dollars in gold-dust. Numbers of small parties from Oregon arrived before July, but the vast body of gold-

---

2 Small placers had been found by Mexicans near the coast in 1828, 1833, and 1838. See M. Castanare's letter to President of Mexico, 1844.

seekers known afterwards as the "Argonauts" did not reach the Pacific coast until early in 1849. The organization of the smaller mining communities of 1848 must be considered before we can discuss the more complex elements of later camps.

When, early in 1848, mining began at Coloma, near Sutter's Mill, Captain Sutter himself had alcalde powers over the region. That autumn Mr. Belt was elected alcalde at Stockton. The two thousand Americans who were living in California in February 1848 were nearly all in the mines before the end of June; and most of them knew what an alcalde was, knew that they had no legal right to elect any other officer, and knew that Colonel Mason, the *de facto* Governor, was the only other authority. But there was no general acceptance of Sutter as alcalde. Some of the very first miners attempted to own, hold, control, and rent to others a large and valuable mineral-bearing tract. After paying rent for a short time, the new-comers, who were in the majority, began to equalize matters and adopt laws respecting the size of "claims." Nothing in the early history of these camps is more evident than the unpremeditated and unsystematic nature of their first proceedings. Officers were never elected until they were needed to give an immediate decision. And, as we have said, local customs in regard to the "amount of ground a man could mine" took form before officers were formally chosen. Everyone knew that most of the land on which they worked was government land: the use of it belonged to all alike until such time as the government made other regulations. Equality of ownership was the only logical conclusion. Here, then, the laws of the camp had their beginning. Long before lawlessness and trouble with foreigners arose, long before the first California gold had reached New York, "claims" of a definite size were being measured out in the mining camps for each gold-seeker. The ownership of land was the beginning of organization; its ownership in equal parts is significant of the form of society that prevailed, for an unconscious socialism it certainly was.

The mines put all men for once upon a level. Clothes, money, manners, family connections, letters of introduction, never before counted for so little. The whole community was substantially given an even start in the race. Gold was so abundant, and its sources seemed for a time so inexhaustible, that the aggrandizing power of wealth was momentarily annihilated. Social and financial inequalities between man and man were together swept out of sight. Each stranger was welcomed, told to take a pan and pick and go to work for himself. The richest miner in the camp was seldom able to hire a servant; those who had formerly been glad to serve others were digging in their own claims. The veriest greenhorn was as likely to uncover the richest mine on the gulch as was the wisest of ex-professors of geology; and, on the other hand, the best claim on the river might suddenly "give out" and never again yield a dollar. The poorest man in camp could have a handful of gold-dust for the asking from a more successful neighbor, to give him another start and help him "hunt for better luck." No one was ever allowed to suffer: the treasure-vaults of the Sierra were too near, and seemingly too exhaustless.

To a little camp of 1848 (so an old miner writes me) a lad of sixteen came one day, footsore, weary, hungry, and penniless. There were thirty robust and cheerful miners at work in the ravine; and the lad sat on the bank, watching them a while in silence, his face telling the sad story of his fortunes. At last one stalwart miner spoke to his fellows, saying:

"Boys, I'll work an hour for that chap if you will."

At the end of the hour a hundred dollars' worth of gold-dust was laid in the youth's handkerchief. The miners made out a list of tools and necessaries.

"You go," they said, "and buy these, and come back. We'll have a good claim staked out for you. Then you've got to paddle for yourself." Thus genuine and unconventional was the hospitality of the mining camp.

The early camps of California did more than merely destroy all fictitious social standards. They began at once to create new bonds of human fellowship. The most interesting of these was the social and spiritual significance given to the partnership idea. It soon became almost as sacred as the marriage-bond. The exigencies of the work of mining claims required two or three persons to labor together if they would utilize their strength to the best advantage. The legal contract of partnership, common in settled communities, became, under these circumstances, the brother-like tie of *"pard"*-nership, sacred by camp custom, protected by camp law; and its few infringements were treated as crimes against every miner. Two men who lived together, slept together, took turns cooking, and washing their clothes, worked side by side in dripping claims, and made equal division of returns were rightly felt to have entered into relationships other than commercial.

There soon were larger associations to work deep claims, or turn the channels of rivers; but each such association came into existence when it was needed, not a moment sooner. Nowhere in the mines was there any planning ahead: men were too busy, and time too precious, for that. The result was a degree and quality of unhampered, untroubled freedom to which it is hard to find a historic parallel. Society, reduced to its original atoms, began to shape itself anew.

One of the elements in early camp life consisted of "companies," or groups of associates who had come from the same place, or had traveled together for mutual comfort and protection. Many of these companies had organized, and made rules for their own government, before they left their homes. Some were from the coast region, some from Oregon; and in 1849 many such parties arrived across the plains, or by sea. Sometimes these companies formed separate camps, sometimes only a group in a larger camp, but usually the bond of unity was preserved. The Oregonians "hung together" remarkably well, and exercised the best of influence. Some of them had helped to organize local government and a legislative body among the pioneer Americans in the Willamette Valley. Peter Burnett, who became the first Governor of California, was one of the earliest to start from Oregon, where he had been a poor and hardworking farmer. He organized a large company among his neighbors, was chosen captain, and guided them to the mines.

Ryan, in his *Adventures in California,* gives the rules of a small mining company of whom he was one. Slightly abbreviated, they read as follows:

" (1) That we shall bear an equal share in all expenses.

" (2) That no man shall be allowed to leave the company without general consent till we reach the mines.

" (3) That any one leaving with our consent shall have back his original investment.

" (4) That we work together in the mines, and use our tools in common.

" (5) That each man shall retain all the gold he finds, but must contribute an equal portion of our daily expenses.

" (6) That we stand by each other.

" (7) That each man shall in turn cook, and do his share of the drudgery.

" (8) That any one guilty of stealing shall be expelled from tent and claim, with such other punishment as a majority of our company decide upon.

" (9) That no sick comrade be abandoned."

These rules, we observe, do not provide for an appeal to the general body of miners, nor do they recognize any higher court than the law of the majority of the company. It is the idea of family rule and family justice, as opposed to tribal authority or to the supremacy of the whole body of assembled freemen. But this tendency played little part in actual mining life, though a few cases occurred where men were punished by their associates, no others interfering, not through indifference so much as because of acquiescence. The rule that "each man shall cook in turn" was probably supplemented by the unwritten proviso, still dear to Western camp life, that "no man shall grumble at the cook's failures, under penalty of cooking for twice the usual period."

When we compare the rules of different companies organized to go to the mines, we find considerable variation. Quite a number provided for an equal division of all the gold found. This was certainly a spirit that many tendencies of camp-life developed, but there were opposing forces of much more powerful nature. That chiefly which in the "flush times" prevented any general acceptance of the idea of equal division of profits among all the miners of a group, or even of a camp, was the fact that men like to take risks, run chances, and have the intoxicating excitement of sudden gains. The miners of '48 believed with all their hearts that there was gold enough for all; that the turn of the poorest miner would come; but that, as they often said, "gold belongs to the finder, and to no one else."

Several of these companies formed to go to the mines

provided for disbandment at the end of six months' labor. Quite a number forbade their members to use ardent spirits, except as medicine. Some arranged for a certain percentage of each member's gains to be paid over to the captain in trust for sick or unfortunate comrades. But enough has been said to give a general idea of their organization.

As soon as the great value of the mines was known and crowds of persons began to hasten thither, the necessity for having "wholesome regulations and laws, with a view to the security of personal property and the prevention of disputes among those engaged in mining," began to present itself to the military authorities at Monterey. There were no disturbances in the mines, however: the only crimes reported were from the coast region. But it was suggested that the entire mineral belt should be laid off in lots, by a public land-agent and a surveyor, and that they should then, under proper regulations, allow miners to occupy and work these lots, requiring them to pay a fee, or ground-rent, to the government. While this was under consideration, so many soldiers deserted, that the Governor threatened to concentrate the remaining troops in the mining districts and take military possession. One company, stationed at Sonora, lost thirty-seven men out of sixty.

In July 1848 there were about two hundred men at work on the American Fork, at "Mormon Diggings," twenty-five miles from Sutter's Fort. Colonel Mason and Lieutenant (now General) W. T. Sherman were making a tour of the mines; and the first official report about that region is dated at Monterey, August 17, immediately after their return. Along the whole route, houses were vacant and farms going to waste. At the lower mines the hillsides were strewn with canvas tents

and bush arbors. Some of the miners used tin pans,
some used closely woven Indian baskets; but the greater
part had a rude machine known as the cradle. This required four men to work it properly. A party thus employed averaged one hundred dollars a day. Mining
camps were fairly established on the American Fork,
the South Fork, the Yuba, Feather, and Bear rivers, and
on various tributaries. Colonel Mason was informed
that about four thousand men were at work in the entire gold region. The labor was very hard, but all
seemed prosperous. In many camps two ounces was considered but an ordinary yield for a day's work. A small,
shallow rock channel, a hundred yards long and four
feet wide, was pointed out, where two men had obtained seventeen thousand dollars in seven days. From
another small ravine twelve thousand dollars had been
taken. The principal store at Sutter's Fort received in
payment for goods sold in nine weeks some thirty-six
thousand dollars in gold-dust. A company of seven miners hired fifty Indian helpers to carry gravel to the "cradles," worked seven weeks, and obtained two hundred
and seventy-three pounds of pure gold; they paid off the
Indians, and each of the seven partners had about
thirty-seven pounds for his share. A private soldier who
was given twenty days' furlough went to the mines,
where in one week he made fifteen hundred dollars,
with which he returned and reported for duty. The
cash value of gold in the mines was twelve dollars per
ounce; in trade, sixteen dollars.

These instances are from Colonel Mason's report to
the Adjutant-General. He also relates an occurrence to
which he was eyewitness. At Weber's brush-built store
a man picked up a box of seidlitz powders and asked its
price; he was told that it only cost fifty cents, but was
not for sale; he offered an ounce of gold, and was re-

fused; but, promptly raising his offer to an ounce and a half, he bore off the desired article in triumph.

Colonel Mason gives the most decided testimony as to the good behavior of the community. Crimes were very infrequent: peace and order prevailed. He naïvely expresses his surprise that no thefts or robberies had been committed in the gold district, although everyone lived in a tent, a bush house, or in the open air, and frequently had about his person thousands of dollars' worth of gold. He makes no allusion whatever to any elected officers in the various camps.

It was a matter of serious reflection to him how the rights of the government in the land could best be secured. Considering the character of the people engaged, he resolved not to interfere. He suggested two plans: one, to grant licenses to work tracts of ground of a hundred yards square, at rents of from a hundred dollars to a thousand dollars per year, at the discretion of an appointed superintendent; the other, to survey the district, and sell to the highest bidder, in tracts of twenty or forty acres. The latter plan he preferred, but no steps were ever taken to carry either of them into execution. In a later letter he proposed levying a percentage on the gold found.

In August, Indian troubles led to the establishment of a small military post in the Sacramento region; but it exercised no supervision or authority over the camps of the miners, though it was situated on Bear River, near some of the richest placers. The next year troops were sent to Taylor's Ferry, on the Stanislaus, partly to quell Indian difficulties, and partly to prevent an apprehended collision between the Americans and the foreigners along the Tuolumne; but "the reports of hostilities had been greatly exaggerated." Throughout the various letters, proclamations, and official actions of the *de facto* Governor of California in 1848, nothing is more evident than the complete way in which the mining communities were left to their own devices. Even General Riley in his visit, a year after Colonel Mason's, told the miners that "all questions touching the temporary right of individuals to work in particular localities of which they were in possession, should be left to the decision of the local authorities," meaning alcaldes and other officers by that time installed in many camps.

Letters from pioneers, and all printed accounts, agree in the general features of mining life in the later months of the summer of 1848. Scattered over a large territory, the men of the various camps dwelt together in peace and good-fellowship, without any representatives of the United States Government in their midst. Legal forms and judicial machinery were as nearly nonexistent as it is possible to imagine in a civilized country. The "social-contract" ideas of Rousseau and his followers seemed to have suddenly found a practical expression. The unwritten, unformulated law that ruled each camp was the instinct of healthy humanity to mete out equal justice to all. There was no theft, and no disorder; few troublesome disputes occurred about boundaries and water-rights. The miners assembled to discuss in open meeting the size of claims that should be allowed, and the will of the majority was cheerfully accepted by the entire camp. The size, however, varied materially: most of the early camps thought that ten feet square was quite enough, or, in some cases, ten feet in width on the stream, extending from the base of the ravine to the center of the channel; fifteen feet square, twenty feet square, and more were allowed in later camps. Ardent prospectors used to tell stories of new-found placers "where four by four was enough for a claim," but no camp ever adopted so small a standard.

Definite bounds for the separate camps that afterwards became mining districts did not at first exist. No
surveyors went out from the camp to mark its subject
territory. The district grew simply and naturally about
the most convenient assembly-place, gulch, or camp; so
that, when fully organized, it conformed to purely physical boundaries. A relief-map of the Sierra region, with
all the deposits of auriferous gravel accessible to the
rude appliances of the early miners marked in yellow,
would show, at a glance, how imperious the physical
reasons were. One district must, by reason of its position, include the half-dozen camps of a circular valley
girt round about with rocky peaks; another must extend
itself along a narrow ravine, and be five miles long and
hardly an eighth of a mile in width.

The miners needed no criminal code. It is simply and
literally true that there was a short time in California,
in 1848, when crime was almost absolutely unknown,
when pounds and pints of gold were left unguarded in
tents and cabins, or thrown down on the hillside, or
handed about through a crowd for inspection. An old
pioneer writes me that "in 1848 a man could go into a
miner's cabin, cut a slice of bacon, cook a meal, roll up
in a blanket, and go to sleep, certain to be welcomed
kindly when the owner returned." Men have told me
that they have known as much as a washbasinful of
gold-dust to be left on the table in an open tent while
the owners were at work in their claim a mile distant.
Of course this condition of affairs was partly due to the
ease of acquiring gold. Men, in some cases, pulled up
bunches of grass from the gulches and hillsides, shaking
them into buckets, thus obtaining many pounds of gold;
one miner gathered sixteen thousand dollars thus in five
weeks of work. Another miner "cleaned up" eighteen
thousand dollars in one day's labor with pan and pick.

Certainly it was easier to earn money than to steal it, but it was infinitely safer also. In later days, for a man to be caught sluice-robbing was to sign his own death-warrant; with the miners of '48, whipping, banishment, or hanging was likely enough to have been inflicted upon the robber of claim or tent. For the criminality of theft was brought squarely home to each man's conscience, and to the entire community. Considering all the circumstances, a man capable of stealing from his comrades in these busy, friendly camps was hopelessly hardened, was capable of all the crimes of the Decalogue.

Throughout this Arcadian era there was not only no theft, but the bonds of fellowship were strong and sincere among all the miners of the camps. In some districts where the American element kept strongly in the majority, the entire "flush period" from 1849 to 1853 was marked by such unity. But in most camps disturbances increased; human leeches and parasites lowered the healthy tone of the community; and the miners drew farther apart than in the days when their first tents were pitched beneath the lofty Sierra pines, in clumps of chapparal and manzinita.

The miners themselves noticed how rapidly disturbances increased in number a few years later. "We needed no law," writes an old pioneer, "until the lawyers came"; and this idea is repeated in a thousand forms. "There were few crimes," says one correspondent, "until the courts with their delays and technicalities took the place of miners' law." This is, in truth, the persistent prejudice against lawyers that has existed among frontiersmen (nor among them alone) in every age of the world. Poetry and fiction have always been severe upon the "cozening, cheating, subtle-tongued lawyers." Dr. Johnson, as a withering and overwhelming assault, once said of an opponent: "Although I should be sorry to calumniate any man, yet, sir, I believe the gentleman in question to be an attorney." But it is pioneers who give the most frank expression of this time-honored opinion. And, although the fact is not generally known, there was a time when one half of the world tried, but of course unsuccessfully, to live without any lawyers. When Spain established her colonies, every one of them petitioned the king, in the most earnest and anxious terms, to allow no lawyers to sail for America; because they desired to live in peace and prosperity, freed from the malice of men and the malign presence of attorneys. As loyal Catholic subjects they prayed to be protected from the whole "lean and rascally" legal fraternity. The gallant soldier of fortune Vasco Nuñez de Balboa wrote to the King, saying:

"One thing I supplicate your majesty: that you will give orders, under a great penalty, that no bachelors of law should be allowed to come here; for not only are they bad themselves, but they also make and contrive a thousand iniquities." [3]

Pioneers of New Spain and pioneers of golden California were equally in earnest in their denunciation of lawyers, and were equally at fault in the analysis by which they reached such conclusions. In views of this sort we have a curious confusion of ideas, a curious substitution of effect for cause. The conditions of society do not change because of the lawyer's arrival: he comes because the conditions of society are already changing, and there is, or is about to be, a demand for his labor. Though we grant all that the pioneers say respecting the Arcadian simplicity and total freedom from difficulties of the camps of the earlier gold period, we must not con-

---

[3] Helps's *Spanish Conquest*, p. 338; note, *Carta el Rey,* January 20, 1513.

clude that this absence of lawlessness was necessarily due
to the absence of lawyers. There were plenty of them,
working as quiet citizens in their claim-ditches, and waiting until there was a demand for attorneys and the machinery of courts. How could there be much lawlessness where so few temptations to crime, and so few
opportunities for its commission, existed? Men could
quarrel, could steal, could kill one another; but nine
out of ten of the misdemeanors and crimes that appear
in the docket of an ordinary criminal court were impossible in the mining camps, while ninety-nine hun-
dredths of the ordinary civil cases were equally out of
the question. Land-titles all similar, transfers oral, commercial transactions for cash, borrowing and lending
simply a matter between individuals — the best of lawyers would have starved in such a community. As society grew more complex, temptations and opportunities
increased; and by the time the machinery of a state was
set in operation, California presented, as regards land-
titles, mining cases, and a thousand other subjects, so
many legal complications that for a time it became the
paradise of lawyers.

By the close of 1848, mining was actually in progress
for a distance of two hundred miles along the axis of
the Sierra. Colonel Reading was at work with his Indians on Clear Creek, Shasta County; and General John
Bidwell, in like manner, on Feather River. When winter came, most of the miners returned to their homes in
the valleys, in San José, Monterey, Sonoma, or San
Francisco. Before the summer of 1849 the pioneers of
1848 had been overwhelmed and lost in the gold rush of
that eventful year. The peace and freedom of the early
camps gave way to a new order of things; and out of
chaos and confusion the organizing faculty of the race
began to bring settled government. But so marked, so

characteristic, so different from all later types of miners was the pioneer of 1848 that it has even been said that with that year "all that was staid and primitive in or about the mines of California vanished; with it ended the old civilization and the old scenes." [4] This, however, is only true from the standpoint of a general observer: from the institutional standpoint, the camp organizations of 1849–53 had their beginnings in the camp organizations of 1848.

[4] Henry de Groot: *Recollections of California Mining-life.* Pamphlet, pp. 16. San Francisco, 1884.

Chapter X. THE EARLIEST MINING COURTS AND THEIR INFLUENCE ON STATE LIFE

The general features of the organization of the "mining courts" that were in many cases found necessary towards the close of 1848 can easily be described. There were no permanent officers, except where the alcalde plan was adopted, as in instances hereafter described; neither were there any written laws, or any records of proceedings. Anyone who desired could call a meeting. A person who thought himself wronged would tell his friends, and they would tell others, till the miners of the region would assemble if they thought the cause sufficient; but if not, would ignore the call. Some important meetings grew out of informal discussions, among groups of miners, as to the best regulations for mutual benefit and protection. As soon as "mining districts," so called, began to be laid out, they assumed exceedingly definite boundaries as regarded the actual gold-bearing territory, but were very indefinite regarding size and shape. Each district included certain gulches, ran to the top of certain divides, took in certain flats and ridges, and would have presented a very irregular appearance on a map. The district might include several camps or but one, according to convenience. The term "camp" is properly used to express the nucleus of the district, the tent town to which the miners returned at night. The discovery of new mines might at any time create new camps, but not necessarily new districts, until its miners in camp assembled made new laws and separated themselves from the jurisdiction of their former laws.

At the first meeting called to organize a camp in a recently discovered mineral belt, the boundaries of a district were drawn so as to include not only the claims of all the miners present, but also all the unclaimed ground that seemed easy of access and likely to be valuable. If, however, the district proved too large for convenience as a political unit, the dissatisfied miners would post up notices in several places and call a meeting of those who wished for a division of territory and a new district. If a majority favored such action, the district was set apart and named. The old district was not consulted on the subject, but received a verbal notice of the new organization. Local conditions, making different regulations regarding claims desirable, were the chief causes of such separations. In most of these earlier cases, district and camp were one and the same: the camp was the unit. Disagreements between two camps, as camps, were never heard of. Cases of lesser camps uniting themselves for governing purposes with larger ones were of later occurrence.

There were no county lines to consider, for this was before the organization of the state. A number of districts were therefore laid out, through which county lines were discovered to pass when surveyed a few years later; but they retained their organization as separate political units. There are in northern California, at the present time, several mining districts that include within their boundaries territory under the jurisdiction of two counties. The State of Nevada, in its laws of 1866, ordained that previously created districts through which county lines passed should be allowed to retain their autonomy and continue to enact local laws. In facts like these we find evidence of the institutional nature of the early camps, or districts, which thus created a local government area long before counties were established, and were able, when they chose, to maintain it intact. The decay of placer mining was perhaps the only thing that prevented the later adoption of districts as universal divisions of the township, or rather as areas of local authority that should disregard township and county lines much as English parishes, unions, school districts, and various local government areas intersect and overlap at the present time.[1]

The "mining court" of the camp, in its earliest form, was simply the assembly of the freemen in open council. All who swung a pick, all who held a claim, boys of sixteen and men of sixty, took part in its deliberations. It was the folk-moot of our Germanic ancestors. If the citizens had been summoned to try an important case, they elected a presiding officer and a judge, impaneled a jury of six or twelve persons, summoned witnesses, and proceeded to trial forthwith. Sometimes there was no jury; and the case was submitted to the assemblage without argument, and irrevocably decided *viva voce*. Had A trespassed on B's claim? Was C's possessory right forfeited by absence, or neglect to work? and could D assume it, or was D a "claim-jumper"? Such were the questions usually brought before the "folk-moots" of the Sierra. Changes and developments in this method of procedure occurred a year or two later, but the earlier camps seized upon the "folk-moot" plan with a true race-instinct.

Two things there were, that no camp assemblage ever attempted to regulate: no mining court ever collected debts either for or against any individual, nor did it ever take cognizance of minor personal difficulties. As regards the first of these, the miners felt and said that it was disgraceful to dun a man for money. They held

---

[1] See *Local Government*, Chalmers, chapter ii, English Citizen Series, Macmillan & Co., 1883.

that honor between men, and the strength of social and business relations, are a far better protection to the lender than bond of Shylock and execution of sheriff. In one case, in one of the camps of '48, a miner, dunned for a small debt at an unseasonable hour of the night, took a lantern, went to his claim, washed out more than sufficient, tied it up in a shot-bag, and, returning to the tent, flung it in his creditor's face with all the force of a sinewy arm. Men had to settle their financial affairs and their petty quarrels among themselves: that was mining-camp doctrine. Of course friends would interfere to separate drunken men, or to prevent a fight; but the camp as an organization set out to protect life and property, not to meddle with what seemed trivialities; so it winked at pugnacious tendencies, and possessed the most liberal definition of eccentricity conceivable. How else should it secure its Sunday-afternoon amusements, and maintain its clowns and oddities?

Crimes against society found swift enough punishment. The thief, for instance, was publicly flogged, and expelled from camp; forfeiting, of course, whatever mining ground he had occupied. But the thieves were usually the hangers-on of the camp, the idle Mexicans, or South Sea Islanders, not the men who owned and worked claims. Stealing, as we have previously stated, involved a greater degree of crime than it possibly could in a more highly organized commonwealth; because the social compact was simpler, and more clearly understood by all men.

Late in 1848 the foreign element began to find its way to the mines, and compelled better organization on the part of the Americans. When Mexicans settled the noted "Sonoranian Camp," now the town of Sonora, in Tuolumne County, nineteen white men — twelve of them Americans — followed, and, a little later, held a miners' meeting, elected R. S. Ham as alcalde, and agreed to support his authority. This district, Jamestown, was known as the "American Camp." The Mexicans and Chilians were greatly in the majority in the region, and their numbers increased during the next year. Many of them were men of the worst character, and only the closest organization prevented a reign of lawlessness. The real struggle for control of the southern mines was, however, at a later period than '48. "Sonoranian Camp" obeyed the mandates of Alcalde Ham with reasonable cheerfulness, and the few miners' meetings held were devoted to making laws regarding claims. There was no official communication between Alcalde Ham and Colonel Mason, then acting governor of California: the camp was left to govern itself.

In the camps of '48, Americans learned what strength there was in organization; but systematic development of mining courts, alcalde courts, and other forms of camp government can hardly be said to have existed until the next year. The work of the better class of miners during the winter of 1848–9 was closely connected with the beginnings of that larger life — state organization. The miners returning to their homes, forced by winter storms to desert their camps in the mountain gulches, began to seek for a remedy for certain no longer endurable evils that were afflicting the body politic. American miners who had lived in peace and friendliness all summer in their camps, had formed new bonds of fellowship, had more closely cemented former bonds, and had proved their ability to protect and govern themselves were now to take the initiative in several remarkable organizing efforts.

A "memorial," at a later period presented to Congress, reviews the political history of California.[2] It says, in effect, that, "as early as 1847," many Americans in California advocated the establishment of a civil territorial form of government; that in October of that year the military-contribution tariff was established in Californian ports, and rigorously enforced, but never once resisted though extremely onerous; that the overland immigration of 1847 strengthened the desire for a more American form of government; that the military power continued taxation without representation, and afforded inadequate protection to life and property; that the gold-discovery occurred, and in April the towns were deserted, all industrial pursuits were abandoned, and "a pall seemed to settle upon the country"; that in August the news of the treaty with Mexico was received, but the existing order of things was nevertheless continued. It describes an unsettled and unstable order of things, and a dissatisfaction and even a profound discontent as existing along the California coast in the summer and fall of 1848. It then proceeds to use the following remarkable language regarding the influence of the miners:

"Upon the coming-on of winter, the great majority of the miners returned to their homes in the towns. They came rich in gold-dust; but a single glance at the desolate and unthrifty appearance of the territory convinced them that other pursuits than that of gold-digging must receive a portion of their care and labor. . . . They felt, as all Americans feel, that the most important step they could take, and that most imperatively called for by the wants of the inhabitants, was the establishment of a stable system of government, which would command the respect and obedience of the people whose property it protected, and whose rights it

---

[2] Memorial presented March 12, 1850, by Messrs. Gwin, Frémont, Wright, and Gilbert, senators and representatives elect from California. App. to *Debates in Convention*, Washington, 1850.

preserved. Congress had adjourned without providing a Territorial government; and the public had settled into the firm conviction that the *de facto* government was radically defective, and incapable of answering the public wants."

This ample recognition of the important place in state organization taken by the returned miners appears to be fully borne out by the facts. A large public meeting was held at San José, December 11, 1848, at which the people of California were asked to organize in districts, and elect delegates to a convention for the purpose of forming a "provisional Territorial government," to go into immediate operation, and remain in full force until superseded by Congressional action. The plan was heartily welcomed and endorsed at massmeetings held in San Francisco, December 21 and 23; in Sacramento, January 6 and 8; in Monterey, January 31; and in Sonoma, February 5. Returned miners were prominent men in all these meetings. The very inclement weather and impassable condition of the roads had caused nearly two months to intervene between the San José meeting and the Sonoma meeting, and had prevented proposed meetings in other districts; but the five districts mentioned comprised more than three fifths of the whole population of California, and they elected delegates to a convention to be held early in March. Part also of this movement was the election, early in the year 1849, of "district legislative assemblies" for Sacramento and Sonoma. The legislature elected in San Francisco, for local reasons, was of a somewhat different type, and was chosen at a later date. The earlier assembly of Sacramento, which aimed to govern the entire surrounding region, was more directly the result of mining organizations than were the Sonoma and San Francisco assemblies. But all three of them disbanded peaceably in obedience to Governor Bennett Riley's orders. By the time the Territorial Convention assembled, the majority saw that California was too wealthy and populous for a territorial government; and they at once issued an address to the people, recommending a Constitutional Convention, which took place in September 1849, at the old pueblo of Monterey.

In all the important political events which began with the San José meeting of December 1848 and ended with the adoption of a state constitution, the men who had toiled, struggled, suffered, and "stood by each other" in the mining camps were leading spirits. Some of them returned to the mines; some engaged in other and more profitable occupations in the valleys and coast towns, for few of the pioneers of '48 had accumulated fortunes.

The preceding pages have in no wise exaggerated the intrinsic value of the work done by the "men of '48" in settling the foundations of society. Throughout our examination into the methods of later camps and the laws made by various districts we shall be constantly finding traces of earlier institutional organization. The debt of the Pacific coast to the few thousands of miners who first explored the Sacramento and El Dorado placers is greater than historians have heretofore acknowledged. They were the pioneers of the pioneers: without their brave and loyal work as American citizens, the greater and more dazzlingly successful work of that strange and complex era which followed could never have been accomplished.

Chapter XI. THE GOLDEN PRIME OF '49

A KNOWLEDGE of the characteristic features of the mining days of 1849 is essential to a full appreciation of the good sense and political wisdom shown by the miners as a class. Merchants, mechanics, farmers, existed but to supply the miners; and the gold of the mines was the chief resource of California. Four fifths of the able-bodied male population were living in the mineral belt, or were on their way thither, when the working-season of 1849 opened. Only four years before, in the summer of 1845, there had been but five hundred Americans in California; in February 1848, but two thousand; by December 1848 this number had grown to six thousand; by July 1849, to fifteen thousand; and by December 1849, to fifty-three thousand. Chiefly owing to the gold rush of 1848–53, the center of population of the United States moved eighty-one miles farther west. Within four years after the spring of 1849 the population of the new state was three hundred thousand; and more than two hundred and sixty million dollars had been dug from the gold-fields. The gold-product of California for all the years from 1848 to 1883 inclusive has been over twelve hundred millions of dollars, or three fourths of the entire gold-product of the United States during the past century. But, great as this total is, it would have seemed little to the minds of the excited Argonauts of 1849. Only the stories of the fortunate wealth-seekers had gone abroad to the world, and men were prepared to believe anything about California.

Dr. Stillman, in his *Seeking the Golden Fleece*, says

that at the close of January 1849 "sixty vessels had sailed from Atlantic seaports, carrying eight thousand men, and seventy more vessels were up for passage." Bayard Taylor, speaking more particularly of the land-journey, said that "it more than equalled the great military expeditions of the Middle Ages, in magnitude, peril, and adventure." John S. Hittell writes: "From Maine to Texas there was one universal frenzy."

One of the "pilgrims" wrote a song, which was soon heard on every street-corner of the Atlantic cities, in which he proclaimed:

> "Oh! California, that's the land for me!
> I'm bound for the Sacramento,
> With the washbowl on my knee."

As in the excitement of '48, so again in '49 a nucleus of camp organization often began in these companies of pilgrims, by land or by sea, who became acquaintances and friends, who decided to proceed to the same district of the mining region, and who often formed associated bodies of workers. The men who crossed the plains together, or were for months in the same ship, hold annual reunions at the present time, on the Pacific coast. Each year their numbers lessen, but the survivors cling to the observance with ever-strengthening affection.

There were many interesting features about this great onset, all the world seeming to be in haste to occupy this hitherto neglected region. Armies of emigrants were attracted by the magic of its name, and toiled wearily in wavering lines across the continent. Many a mountain valley was thus settled long before it could have been reached in the natural course of agricultural progress, and the entire frontier of the West was borne forward: the immemorial race impulse of the Aryan had reawakened with all its ancient force. In vain the

elders of lonely Deseret and the dupes of the Book of
Mormon tried by falsehood and crime to roll back or
turn aside this dreaded and hated advance of American
civilization. Some of the "Latter-day Saints" joined the
current, but most of them were faithful to their shrine.[1]
But the fierce, impetuous, resistless human torrent
swept on its way to the Pacific coast: it ran in haste, it
fairly leaped over obstacles, as one sees mountain rivers
curl down into hollows, and curve over bowlders, till,
in the rush of its advance, the smallest inequality of the
channel is reproduced in its surface.

The mining camps whose white tents and rude cabins rose so rapidly beside these rivers of this new Col-
chis in early '49 have found an enduring place in literature. The Argonaut himself has become one of the
heroic figures of the past, and is likely enough to survive, as real and strong a type in the story of America as
Viking or Crusader in that of Europe. But it is the place
held by the Argonaut as an organizer of society that is
most important. He often appears in literature as a
dialect-speaking rowdy, savagely picturesque, rudely
turbulent: in reality he was a plain American citizen
cut loose from authority, freed from the restraints and
protections of law, and forced to make the defense and
organization of society a part of his daily business. In
its best estate the mining camp of California was a man-
ifestation of the inherent capacities of the race for self-
government. That political instinct, deep rooted in Lex
Saxonum, to blossom in Magna Charta and in English
unwritten constitution, has seldom in modern times afforded a finer illustration of its seemingly inexhaustible
force. Here, in a new land, under new conditions, sub-

---

[1] The Mormon leaders told their followers that gold was to pave
streets and cover houses; and if they were faithful, they should have
more than sufficient in their own territory when the proper time came.

jected to tremendous pressure and strain, but successfully resisting them, were associated bodies of freemen
bound together for a time by common interests, ruled
by equal laws, and owning allegiance to no higher authority than their own sense of right and wrong. They
held meetings, chose officers, decided disputes, meted
out a stern and swift punishment to offenders, and managed their local affairs with entire success; and the
growth of their communities was proceeding at such a
rapid rate that days and weeks were often sufficient for
vital changes which in more staid communities would
have required months or even years.

The gateway to the mines was San Francisco. In January 1849, when Rev. Dwight Hunt, who had for several months preached to the returned miners throng-
ing the streets, organized the "First Congregational
Church," the population of the city was less than fifteen
hundred. A little later the first shiploads of immigrants
began to arrive; and, though every new-comer felt
obliged to visit the mines to see for himself, yet many
persons soon returned to enter into business; and San
Francisco had fifteen thousand inhabitants before the
close of the year.

A San Francisco pioneer of '49 writes:

"Gold-dust, provisions, and tools were safe without police. We had no disturbances at first, no rows, and no murders. Men gambled, for that was an old California vice; [2]
but they did so as honestly as it can be done. We had no
poor men, and labor was at a premium everywhere."

Before very long, however, an organization called
"The Hounds" began to rob Spanish Americans, and

---

[2] Gambling in California was permitted under Mexican rule, and
under the military government of '46–'49. It was even a source of revenue to the *ayuntamiento* of San Francisco in August 1849. It was a
legalized and important pursuit, followed with zeal by Mexicans,
French, and Americans. See Hittell: *History of San Francisco*, p. 236.

committed other outrages; and, July 16, the law-abiding citizens, who had in vain complained of the inefficiency of the alcalde, met, organized a court, elected a judge and attorneys, and by fines and imprisonments put an end for some years to ruffian supremacy.

The harbor of San Francisco became populous with ships of every nation. When scholarly Richard H. Dana, Harvard graduate, adventurous sailor before the mast, had visited Yerba Buena harbor while the Mexican "eagle and *nopal* flag" yet drooped from the presidio staff, there was not a single vessel in the harbor, not a single boat on the broad bay, and but one house where San Francisco now stands. Herds of deer came down to the water's edge; and, as in Kotzebue's time, sea-otters swam within easy gun-shot.[3] Soon after, a Russian vessel entered the harbor, but in a few days sailed away, and left the solitary hide-droger to its work. Less than fifteen years later the summer of 1849 saw no less than five hundred and forty-nine seagoing vessels in the port. In the month of August four hundred large ships were idly swinging at anchor, destitute of crews; for their sailors had deserted, swum ashore, escaped to the gold-fields. Thirty-five thousand men came by sea, and forty-two thousand by land, during the year. Australia, the Asian coasts, Africa, and South America contributed to the motley host that thronged the roads to the placers.

Society was masculine, and most of the men were under forty. In the spring of 1849 there were but fifteen

---

[3] Lieutenant Kotzebue visited San Francisco Bay in 1816, when Arguello was Spanish commandante, and Kuskoff ruled in the Russian settlement at Bodega, thirty miles northward. Twenty Russians and fifty Indians captured two thousand sea-otters that season. Count Adelbert von Chamisso, that sensitive genius, author of *Peter Schlemihl*, and Eschscholtz the botanist, were members of this expedition. The latter's consonantal name is perpetuated in the most brilliant flower of the Pacific-coast flora — the rich orange-scarlet wild poppy of field and hillside.

women in San Francisco. As one writer says, "Women were queens, children were angels." Bearded and weather-bronzed miners stood for hours in the streets to get a glimpse of a child at play. At a little later period there were plenty of women who were "vile libels on their sex"; but the reverence that Californians of the gold era paid to respectable women has received a tribute of admiring praise from all observers. Men often traveled miles to welcome "the first real lady in camp." A New England youth of seventeen once rode thirty-five miles, after a week's hard work in his father's claim, to see a miner's wife who had arrived in an adjoining district. "Because," he said, "I wanted to see a home-like lady; and, father, do you know, she sewed a button on for me, and told me not to gamble and not to drink. It sounded just like mother."

New towns were laid out in the valleys to supply the camps, and those already established grew with astonishing rapidity. Stockton, for instance, increased in three months from a solitary ranch-house to a canvas city of one thousand inhabitants. Sacramento also became a canvas city, where dust-clouds whirled, and men, mules, and oxen toiled; where boxes, barrels, bales, innumerable, were piled in the open air, no shelter being needed for months. For the City Hotel, Sacramento, thirty thousand dollars per year was paid as rent, although it was only a small frame building. The Parker House, San Francisco, cost thirty thousand dollars to build, and rented for fifteen thousand dollars per month. Speculation in promising town-sites soon reached as extravagant heights as it ever did in the Mississippi Valley or in the Pennsylvania oil region. Every cross-road, river-landing, and ferry had its "corner-lot speculators," who prophesied its future greatness. The "town of Oro," near the mouth of Bear River, had but

one house, and soon lost even that. Linda, Eliza Feath-
erton, Kearney, and dozens of others, paper towns of
the lowlands, are familiar to all pioneers.

The conditions under which business had to be conducted in San Francisco and at the interior towns were
extremely trying and difficult. The only supply-markets
were so remote that the greatest fluctuations in the stock
of goods on hand were constantly occurring, against
which no human foresight could guard. New York was
nineteen thousand miles distant by the sea-route; and
about six months were required to send an order from
San Francisco and get the goods delivered. Oregon's
few thousand pioneers had little to sell. China sent
only rice and sugar; Australia and Chili supplied some
flour. Everything else came from the Atlantic seaports.
Lumber, worth four hundred dollars per thousand one
month, would not pay for the freight four months later;
tobacco, once worth two dollars a pound, was tossed in
the streets. Saleratus fluctuated between twenty-five
cents and fifteen dollars per pound. The entire community was dependent for food and clothing upon other
communities thousands of miles distant. And the rate
of interest was ten per cent per month.

By the time goods reached the mountain camps, their
cost was so enormous that most of the miner's gains
went for necessaries of life.[4] Those who were very fortunate often indulged in curious and expensive whims
and "extravaganzas," feeling sure that their claims
would continue to yield treasure. They bought the cost-
liest broadcloth, drank the finest wines, and smoked the

---

[4] Mr. George F. Parsons, for many years editor of the Sacramento
Record-Union, and author of the *Life of James W. Marshall, the Discoverer of Gold in California*, copied the following prices from the
books of the Sutter Fort store: "Two white shirts, $40; one fine-tooth
comb, $6; one barrel of mess pork, $210; one dozen sardines, $35; two
hundred pounds of flour, $150; one tin pan, $9; one candle, $3."

best brands of cigars. "A wild, heedless, wasteful, dissi-
pated set of men," is what one of the "forty-niners" calls
his old comrades. Men who had been brought up to
keep sober, and earn sixteen dollars per month, and
save half of it, went to California, found rich claims,
earned several hundred dollars a month — of which
they might have saved three fourths — but spent every
cent in riotous living. Men who had been New York
hod-carriers paid out ten dollars a day for canned fruits
and potted meats. But only a few years later, when the
surface placers were all exhausted, these same unkempt
sybarites returned to beans and pork, strapped up their
blankets, and made prospect tours to other regions, taking their reverses more placidly than one could have
thought possible.

To many cheerful, impetuous, and intelligent men,
the ups and downs of mining-life seemed full of wild
fascination. To be there was to be a part of a scene that
each thoughtful miner knew in his heart was as evanescent as it was brilliant — an episode whose intensity
corresponded accurately to its briefness. And to many
persons of this type it certainly seemed as if the way to
make the most of the era was to take a hand in everything that came along. Reports filled each camp, almost
every week, telling of new diggings where from a hundred to a thousand dollars might easily be collected in
a day. Down came the tent-ropes, the claims were abandoned; the epidemic gold-rush fever had seized each
Argonaut in the camp. They went to Gold Lake, Gold
Bluffs, and a hundred other as loudly trumpeted regions, till the habit of following with swift feet each
new excitement became as much a part of the Argonaut's nature as the habit of running after a fire is a
part of the healthy boy's organization. The Argonaut

was well enough aware that the blaze is very apt to be only a bonfire, or else to be over long before he arrives. But he could not bear to stand by and see others run and hurrah: so off he started at the best of his speed, to come back, a few months later, "dead broke" financially, but wealthy in experience.

Fortunately there were men of quite another type, whose clear brains and steady habits enabled them to lay aside a part of their gains, afterwards to push larger enterprises, to organize mining companies, to dig great water-ditches extending for miles in a magnificent system of engineering. Some of them bought farms in the valleys, or entered into business in the towns and cities, retaining to the fullest degree their affection for the wild mountain realm where they first obtained a start in life. Even in the earlier fever-heats of the gold excitement, there were numbers of men who had come to California to remain, and make homes, who recognized vast resources other than mineral, and by whose unswerving fidelity to justice the best elements of camp life were evolved. The returned miners of 1848, and the home-hungry, home-creating few of the thousands of 1849, formed the nucleus of safety-committees and camp courts of law.

A fine example of this was afforded in what were called the Southern mines, the camps of Tuolumne, whose organization late in 1848 has been described in the preceding chapter. The several hundred dwellers in and about the Mexican or "Sonoranian" camp were reinforced as early as July 1849 by fully fifteen thousand foreigners, chiefly from Sonora, Chili, and the Isthmus. Many of them came in armed bands, and made the country unsafe. Some of them were outlaws and desperadoes of the worst types. They brought degraded women

with them, had fandangos and bull-fights, and were a thoroughly alien community. Opposed to them was the little camp of Americans who had elected their alcalde the previous autumn, and several other American camps, well organized for self-protection, founded early in 1849. The foreign invasion (for it can be termed little else) was held in check, and finally turned back, only by the energy and "inborn capacity for creating order" displayed by some of the Americans. The methods taken by the Americans were not always wise or just: in many individual cases cruelty was practiced towards weak and inoffensive Mexicans, and their claims were taken from them, as has been done in innumerable cases along the southwest frontiers within the past few years. But the central fact of the necessity for organization on the part of the Americans remains undisputed. Men had been robbed, horses stolen, and the roads rendered unsafe for travelers. In some camps "good and true men" were at once elected as alcaldes; in others there was the direct intervention of "miners' courts," such as adopted by some of the miners of '48; still a third form was the election of a committee of justice. Under all these forms, supported by public opinion, the work of purification was done rapidly and well. Suspicious characters, both Mexican and American, were notified to leave; criminals were followed, captured, and punished. Although the camps southward from Placerville (then Hangtown) were undoubtedly more turbulent than the northern mines, they struggled against greater difficulties, not only in 1849, but at several subsequent periods, as we shall see in a later chapter.

The mountain land over which mining became the chief industry of men, and to which all sea-roads and trails along the Sierra passes seemed to lead, was a region fitted by nature to attract and secure the affections of a hardy and energetic race. Its physical features are most noble and inspiring, even at the present day, when the valleys and foothills are subdued to agricultural purposes and brought under a high state of cultivation. But when the miners of '49 began to pitch their tents in the wilderness, it was unfenced, unclaimed, and almost unexplored; for the work of the previous year had only mapped out the leading features of the mineral belt. The unsurpassed wealth of what is now Nevada County was as yet undiscovered. Everywhere the land had a charm that no language can describe. Flowers of new species and wonderful beauty bloomed on slope and crag, trees of unparalleled grandeur stood in the forests, the climate of the foothills was like that of Italy. From the great and sea-like valley of the Sacramento, eastward through rolling, oak-clad hills to the broad plateau of the Sierras, and through wild forests and dim gorges to the granite heights and the pointed peaks covered with eternal snow, the ardent miners searched every gulch, traced every stream to its source, and in five years of eager, reckless toil did the work that in other communities would have taken a generation. They spread out in every direction from the Sacramento and Feather River region, searching ridge and ravine southward to the desert sands and borax deposits of Mojave, northward to the barren lava-beds of Modoc. They crossed the westward valley to explore the wildest and most difficult recesses of the Coast Range; established Redding Springs, afterwards Shasta City; rifled the Trinity basin of its riches; and discovered the placers of Klamath, Siskiyou, and southern Oregon. They went waist-deep into the ocean, and brought back tales of beaches gold-spangled by

> "All the storms
> That hurled their ancient, white-topped, weary waves

On California, since the world began."

The flickering, beckoning will-o'-the-wisp that ever led them on was the hope of new diggings, of nuggets gleaming from the moss of mountain lakes, of

> "Beds of streams that evermore
> Washed down the golden grain, and in a year
> Paid to the treasury of the insatiate flood
> More than the subjects of the richest kings
> Yield to their despots in a century."

But of all the writers who have attempted to express the splendid virility, the impetuous battle with nature's forces, the healthy outdoor atmosphere of happy, hearty toil, that the "miners of '49" knew so well, none have said the right word in a better way than Fitz-James O'Brien, poet, romancist, genial Bohemian, loyal friend, knightly soldier. Listen to the song of his "Sewing-bird" lyric:

> "Up in a wild Californian hill,
> Where the torrents swept with a mighty will,
> And the grandeur of Nature filled the air,
> And the cliffs were lofty, rugged, and bare,
> Some thousands of lusty fellows she saw
> Obeying the first great natural law.
> From the mountain's side they had scooped the earth,
> Down to the veins where the gold had birth;
> And the mighty pits they had girdled about
> With ramparts massive and wide and stout;
> And they curbed the torrents, and swept them round
> Wheresoever they willed, through virgin ground.
> They rocked huge cradles the livelong day,
> And shovelled the heavy, tenacious clay,
> And grasped the nugget of gleaming ore,
> The sinews of commerce on every shore."

I have visited the mining region, the realm of the "Argonauts of '49." Titans have been at work there. The land for miles is like a battlefield where primal forces and giant passions have wrestled. Rivers have been turned aside; mountains hurled into chasms, or stripped to the bed-rock in naked disarray. I have seen wild and steep ravines where each square rod once had its miner; where stores, theaters, and banks once stood in the flat, and gold-dust ran in the streets, and every man carried his pistol, and a day of life contained more of healthy outdoor existence and passionate energy than does a year of life in a metropolis: and in those ravines — once so populous — a few old and trembling men, worn out before their time, and pitiful to look upon, creep down from their cabins to pick and moil among the crevices for the little gold left by the gallant "forty-niners"; and creep back to brood over memories, while year after year they watch with feelings of pain and almost anger the approach of gardens, vineyards, orchards, slowly resubduing, in far more durable manner, the lost conquests of the Argonauts.

Even today the smallest of these decaying camps is worth patient study. In the hollows, grown over with blossoming vines, are acres upon acres of bowlders and debris, moved, sifted, and piled up by the hands of pioneers; on the hill's sunny slope are grass-covered mounds where some of them rest after their passionate toil, their fierce and feverish wrestle with hard-hearted fortune. Once this was Red Dog Camp, or Mad Mule Gulch, or Murderer's Bar: [5] now it is only a nameless canyon, the counterpart of hundreds of others scattered over a re-

---

[5] Names of California camps, given in books of travel, are not always to be trusted: visitors expect an eccentric title for each ravine. But the real names were remarkable enough; such were the following: Loafer Hill; Slapjack Bar; Chicken-thief Flat; Git-up-and-Git; Rattrap Slide; Sweet Revenge; Shirt-tail Cañon; You Bet; Gouge Eye.

gion five hundred miles long by fifty miles wide, each one of them all once full to the brim and overflowing with noisy, beating, rushing, roaring, masculine life. Go down and talk with those ghostly inhabitants of the ancient camp, and they will set your blood tingling with tales of the past. Twenty years, thirty years, ago? Why, it is centuries!

The saddest of all possible sights in the old mining region is where there are not even half a dozen miners to keep each other company, but where, solitary and in desolation, the last miner clings to his former haunts. He cooks his lonesome meals in the wrecked and rotting hotel where a quarter of a century before, then young, gay, prosperous, and in his prime, he had tossed the reins of his livery-team to the obsequious servant, and played billiards with the "boys," and passed the hat for a collection to build the first church; he sharpens his battered pick at a little forge under the tree on which he helped hang the Mexican who had stabbed Sailor Bill (how famous Bill was for songs and hornpipes in the El Dorado saloon whose roofless posts slant in the yielding earth!) ; he looks down in the canyon where vines and trees hide all but the crumbling chimney of the house where the "Rose of the Camp" lived, sweetening their lives with a glimpse of her girlish grace and purity as she tripped over the long bridge to the little schoolhouse, and waved her pretty hand to her friends toiling waist-deep in their claims. But that was long ago: she married, and went to Europe, and is famous, he has heard; now the bridge has fallen into the torrent, and snow-storms have shattered the schoolhouse, and the end of the story is very near.

Not one of all the thousands who hurried into the new camps of '49, who developed and over-crowded the old camps of '48, ever paused to consider how these camps would look if deserted; nor, if some prospector's tale carried them on a frenzied gold-chase, did they glance back at the camp they left. The record of the gold-returns is sufficiently suggestive. In 1849 the miners took out, by official record, twenty-three million dollars; in 1850 they increased this yield to fifty million dollars; and the probabilities are that twenty-five per cent of the gold discovered was not reported at San Francisco. By the summer of 1850, there was forty million dollars in taxable real estate in San Francisco, and as much more in the way of personal property,[6] most of which had grown directly or indirectly from the mining interest. Yet, only four years before, Webster had said, in the United States Senate, that California was worthless except as a naval station.

The typical camp of the golden prime of '49 was flush, lively, reckless, flourishing, and vigorous. Saloons and gambling-houses abounded; buildings and whole streets grew up like mushrooms, almost in a night. Every man carried a buckskin bag of gold-dust, and it was received as currency at a dollar a pinch. Everyone went armed, and felt fully able to protect himself. A stormy life ebbed and flowed through the town. In the camp, gathered as of one household, under no law but that of their own making, were men from North, South, East, and West, and from nearly every country of Europe, Asia, South America. They mined, traded, gambled, fought, discussed camp affairs; they paid fifty cents a drink for their whisky, and fifty dollars a barrel for their flour, and thirty dollars apiece for butcher-knives with which to pick gold from the rock crevices.[7]

6 "Gold in California," *International Review,* October 1880.

7 This sum was paid for a time by the miners in some districts of Tuolumne.

"They talked," as one who knew them well has written, "a language half English and half Mexican. They learned to wash and mend their own clothes, and bake their own bread, and cook their own pork and beans. They were hardy, generous, careless, brave: they risked their lives for each other, and made and lost fortunes, and went on lonely prospect tours on foot among the snow-peaks, and grew old and feeble, and found that a new race that knew them not had arisen in the State they created. They died lonely deaths, or perished by violence, pioneers to the last."

As about the typical camp there were too often loss, decay, and final desertion, so about the typical pioneer there were too often loneliness and sorrow, pathos and heroism. A few camps were germs of towns and cities. A few pioneers prospered greatly, and settled down into leading positions in the state their labors had helped to create. But the vital waste and destruction of the struggle overwhelm the observer with pity. The mines were no place for weaklings; even strong, healthy, and earnest men often sank beneath the wearing excitement of that fervid life. But these rough and busy men, whose lives were so often only the saddest of tragedies, established and enforced a code of ethics governing their relations with each other and their property rights, enforced justice though without written law, and in the end created a system of jurisprudence that has won the approval and endorsement of the highest courts of the land. Sturdy, keen-witted, courageous, independent, they left the impress of sterling natures upon all their primitive institutions.

As we have seen, there were times in almost every camp when the rowdy element came near ruling, and only the powerful and hereditary organizing instincts of the Americans present ever brought order out of chaos. In nearly every such crisis there were men of the right stamp at hand, to say the brave word, or do the brave act; to appeal to Saxon love of fair play, to seize the murderer, or to defy the mob. Side by side in the same gulch, working in claims of eight paces square, were, perhaps, fishermen from Cape Ann, loggers from Penobscot, farmers from the Genesee Valley, physicians from the prairies of Iowa, lawyers from Maryland and Louisiana, college graduates from Yale, Harvard, and the University of Virginia. From so variously mingled elements came that terribly exacting mining-camp society which tested with pitiless and unerring tests each man's individual manhood, discovering his intrinsic worth or weakness with almost superhuman precision, until at last the ablest and best men became leaders. They fought their way to the surface through fierce oppositions, and with unblenching resolution suppressed crime, and built up homes in the region they had learned to love.

Chapter XII. EVIDENCE CONCERNING LAW AND ORDER IN THE CAMPS

Let us now examine the testimony of visitors, travelers, and government officials, and of miners who have since published their observations upon the condition of the camps during the flush period. Were these camps orderly and well-governed? What impression did they make upon impartial strangers?

Ryan, in his *Personal Adventures in California*, says:

"The miners dwelt together in no distrust of one another, and left thousands of dollars' worth of gold-dust in their tents while they were absent digging. . . . A determination to punish robbery seemed to have been come to, by all, as a measure essential to security."

This was written of the camps of 1850, as a result of wide observation; and he elsewhere alludes to the admirable manner in which the camps had been conducted from the first.

We have before alluded to Colonel Mason's report on the mines of '48. Governor Riley, deciding to see the mines for himself, left Monterey, July 5, 1849, with Major Canby, Captain Wescott, Captain Halleck, Lieutenant Derby, and others, proceeded to Sacramento, and thence to the principal camps. After his return he wrote to Washington as follows:

"Order and regularity were preserved throughout almost the entire extent of the mineral district. In each little settlement or tented town, the miners have elected their local alcaldes and constables, whose judicial decisions and official acts are sustained by the people, and enforced with much regularity and energy."

In another place he says:

"The alcaldes have probably, in some cases, exercised judicial powers never conferred upon them by law; but the general results have been favorable . . . to the dispensation of justice."

The alcalde system, as adopted and modified by the miners, was all that fell under Governor Riley's observation: but there were camps in the region he visited which were governed, perhaps quite as well, though in a much more primitive manner — camps ruled by a chosen committee, to whom all authority was entrusted; or governed only by the irregular assemblage of the miners, which we have before compared to a folk-moot. Governor Riley did not inquire into the minutiæ of organization. He only knew that, copying after the system of the old Spanish pueblos of the coast, the miners in the longer-established camps had chosen, and were obeying, alcaldes; and, to assist these alcaldes in the discharge of their duties, had ingrafted upon the system the town-constableship of New England villages.

Bayard Taylor was an appreciative observer of the camps. In his *Eldorado* he describes their political organization. "There was," he says, "much order and regularity. The miners had elected one of their number alcalde (this was on the Mokelumne), before whom all culprits were tried." He says that several persons had been severely punished; some had their ears cropped, and others were whipped soundly. "It was a Spartan severity of discipline," all of which Mr. Taylor fully approves. In another place he says:

"The disposition to maintain order, and secure the rights of all men, were shown throughout the mining-districts. In the absence of law, the people met, and adopted rules for mutual security. . . . There had been," he said, "previous

to 1849, twelve or fifteen executions for murder and for
large thefts. . . . Alcaldes were elected, who had power to
decide all disputes or complaints, and summon juries.
When a new placer was discovered, the first thing done was
to elect officers. In a region five hundred miles long, inhabited by a hundred thousand people, who had neither locks,
bolts, regular laws of government, military or civil protection, there was as much security to life and property as in
any State of the Union. The rights of each digger were definitely marked out and observed."

These words of Bayard Taylor's were written of the
camps of 1850 and 1851, but apply with almost equal
force to the camps of 1849. Everywhere in southern,
central, and northern camps he reports a reign of order,
under laws of their own creation; and the sight fills him
with admiration.

One of the speakers before the First State Constitutional Convention addressed that body in October 1849
upon the permanent character of the towns built up in
the mining region, of which he was a resident. He
added:

"Every glen, every ravine, every cañon, almost every hill-
top, is lined and covered with the thousands and tens of
thousands that are scattered over the whole country."

He proceeded to speak of their peaceful prosperity,
and the constant investment, in the larger towns, of capital dug from the mines. Other speakers before the convention alluded to the quiet and order preserved in the
placer region.

Governor Peter H. Burnett, in his *Recollections*, says:

"The miners were engaged in a common pursuit, and ex-
posed to common dangers. Property was almost held in
common, — a practical socialism of a very interesting type."

Burnett says further:

"We [the miners] had the right to establish a *de facto*
government which would rest on the same basis as the provincial government of Oregon. We held a meeting at Sacramento City in January, 1849, and elected Henry A. School-
craft first magistrate and recorder for Sacramento District."

Mr. Burnett had then just left the mining camps,
where he worked during the summer and autumn of
1848, and had opened a lawyer's office in Sacramento.
The leadership of ex-miners was unquestioned in politics and in society.

A vivid account of life in the early days is furnished
by Mr. Frank Marryat's *Mountains and Molehills.* He
speaks of "Murderer's Bar," with the swift river, the
black obstructing rocks, the village of sun-bleached canvas; the miners, waist-deep, toiling to turn the course of
the river, others in pits digging to bed-rock; some alone,
some in companies; all life, vigor, and determination.
He says in one place, that —

"In most mining-villages, indignation [over theft] was
confined to ordering the offender to leave, or take the con-
sequences. . . . The mining-population was allowed to construct their own laws relative to the appropriation of
claims, and the system worked well. There was no interference on the part of the Legislature."

This observation of Mr. Marryat's was made a year or
so after the organization of state government and, as we
shall hereafter see, remained true of the mining districts
for many years.

"Every digging," Mr. Marryat continues, "has its fixed
rules and by-laws. All disputes are submitted to a jury of
resident miners. In some cases, twenty men or so from one
camp are met by an equal number from another camp."

He proceeds to say that disputes sometimes arose, and
even demonstrations with fire-arms, but that good sense

always prevailed. He speaks of the by-laws of each district as recorded in the county office, and as sometimes being stringent, ill-defined, and conflicting. His own experience of their practical workings, however, was as follows:

"I have had my placer-claim of ten feet square encroached upon. I appealed to the crowd; and a committee of three, being at once chosen, measured it from my stake; and, being found correct, the jumper was ordered to confine himself to his own territory, which he always did."

Mr. Marryat's observations are particularly interesting on several accounts. He was an English university man, and adept with both pen and pencil. He entered heartily into the spirit of life at the placers, studying mining institutions with trained intellect; and the time he visited the camps was after California had been divided into twenty-seven counties, and county government nominally established. Thus his statements regarding the amount of local government which each camp retained by tacit consent, and exercised whenever necessary, are of great importance. Committees from different camps still met in consultation: informal appeals were still made to the crowd to right or prevent a wrong. In all essential particulars the camp was still the "camp of '49."

As late as 1857, *Blackwood's Magazine*, reviewing books on California, and speaking of the entire gold era, says:

"It is an agreeable and unexpected feature in the mines themselves, that order, justice, and courtesy reign there. . . ."

And again:

"Patches of a few square feet, teeming with gold, are as sacred as if secured with title-deeds."

J. D. Borthwick's *Three Years in California* is full of
choice material for studies of this era. He describes the
daily life of the gold-miners; tells us of heaps of gold-
bearing gravel piled up in some camps to lie unguarded
but safe until the rainy season, having been made personal property by the labor performed in heaping them
together; pays a hearty tribute of praise to the universal
spirit of hospitality — the careless liberality such as led
the Downieville miners to give fully five hundred dollars in gold-specimens to a lady who sang ballads for
them at one of the first concerts ever held there. Mr.
Borthwick speaks in many places of the ample security
afforded by the mining-regulations. He also seems to
have been struck by the sharply contrasted social instincts and methods of organization displayed by the
American miners and the French miners. He says, in
effect, that the Americans wandered about the mountains, often as solitary as grizzly bears, working like de-
mons, and keeping their own counsel regarding their
prospects or claims with all the stolidity of Turkish
mutes. Sometimes the American miner worked in silence and loneliness upon a single claim, going back
and forth night and morning, a truly dangerous, reso-
lute, and deliberative animal. The Frenchmen, on the
contrary, were never seen alone: their social instinct
was irrepressible; they went in groups to their work,
and clustered together like buzzing bees. But when our
solitary and reflective Americans found quartz or gravel
that they thought would pay better to work in associated bodies, they came together at once in a way for
which the sociable Frenchman showed slight aptitude.
The Frenchman's bond of union was dependence, not
mutual confidence: the American's reserve was really
the source of his power, and the secret of his supremacy
in every camp. Their loneliness meant resolution: there-

fore their organizations always meant business, and accomplished their appointed work.

One of the interesting bits of evidence upon the condition of the camps of '49 is afforded by Dr. J. B. Stillman's *Seeking the Golden Fleece.* He says there was "no government, no law"; but "more intelligence and good feeling than in any country I ever saw. . . . Men are valued for what they are. . . . One feels that he has a standing here that it takes a man until he is old and rich to enjoy at home." This ignores the camp laws as unauthorized, but tacitly acknowledges the good order and peacefulness prevalent in the mining region. On the subject of miners' generosity Mr. Bacon, now an Idaho journalist, and an old California miner, writes me as follows:

"I have never lived in any community where there was less crime, or where people were more charitable, than they were in the early mining-camps of California. No one was ever allowed to suffer for necessaries of life, and nowhere were the sick neglected. I remember many instances where a miner with a broken constitution, who had become discouraged or unable to work, and desired to return to his family, was sent home by the miners, and, in addition, was given one or two thousand dollars for a 'home-stake.' "

Theodore Winthrop, that bright, generous poet and novelist, saw the same characteristics in the hearty pioneers of the Pacific coast, and rejoiced over "the rough sincerity impressed upon people by the life they lead in new countries." [1]

Some of the darker portions of the picture are shown by Theodore J. Johnson, in his *Sights in the Gold-Region;* and his views deserve careful consideration.

---

[1] Theodore Winthrop: *Life and Letters.* See also his description of the "appalling activity" of San Francisco, then the chief outfitting point for all the mines; p. 134.

"The thirst for gold, and the labor required to procure it," he says, "overruled all else, and absorbed every faculty. Complete silence reigned among the miners. They addressed not a word to each other for hours."

He says, further, that although enduring great hardships, exposure, and often disease, the miners as a class obtained only a moderate remuneration. The average yield per miner was, he thought, only three or four dollars a day; and not more than one man in a hundred made a fortune and invested it safely away from the mines. Out of one hundred and twenty men who went around the Horn and were at the same camps, "not one had great success." These views regarding the average yield of the mines to each toiler are well sustained by the official reports. The five thousand miners of 1848 averaged one thousand dollars apiece, though many of them did not reach the mines till very late in the season; but the hundred thousand miners of 1850 dug out only half as much proportionately, working a longer season, and with far better appliances. The gold-product of the state reached its culmination in 1853, then sinking year after year to a point below the total of 1849, but varying little during the past ten years. The introduction of capital and machinery has rendered it impossible to estimate the amount that each man's labor now produces. The annual gold yield of the state has been, for a number of years, something over sixteen million dollars; in 1883 it was $16,500,000.

Another very strong statement upon the nature of life in the mines comes from Mr. George F. Parsons, in his *Life of Marshall,* to which we have previously alluded. He says:

"It was a mad, furious race for wealth, in which men lost their identity almost, and toiled and wrestled, and lived a fierce, riotous, wearing, fearfully excited life; forgetting home and kindred; abandoning old, steady habits; acquiring all the restlessness, craving for stimulant, unscrupulousness, hardihood, impulsive generosity, and lavish ways, which have puzzled the students of human nature who have undertaken to portray or to analyze that extraordinary period."

He says that a true account of those times would be "so wild, so incredible, so feverish and abnormal," as to remind one rather of a description of a Walpurgis Night than of an era in real life. In another place we have this graphic picture:

"Take a sprinkling of sober-eyed, earnest, shrewd, energetic New-England business-men: mingle with them a number of rollicking sailors, a dark band of Australian convicts and cut-throats, a dash of Mexican and frontier desperadoes, a group of hardy backwoodsmen, some professional gamblers, whiskey-dealers, general swindlers, or 'rural agriculturists' as Captain Wragge styles them; and having thrown in a promiscuous crowd of broken-down merchants, disappointed lovers, black sheep, unfledged dry-goods clerks, professional miners from all parts of the world, and Adullamites generally, stir up the mixture, season strongly with gold-fever, bad liquors, faro, monte, rouge-et-noir, quarrels, oaths, pistols, knives, dancing, and digging, and you have something approximating to California society in early days."

Statements such as these concerning the overpowering excitement of the gold-search, and its evil effects, undoubtedly reveal a deep psychical truth. Evil men became more evil, miserly men more miserly, in the Sierra camps. There must have been many to whose souls this "yellow, glittering, precious gold" was a "most operant poison," making "black, white; foul, fair; wrong, right; base, noble"; and over whose wretched lives the spirit

of the exiled, ill-starred, man-hating Athenian's terrible
mockery prevailed in ghastly earnest, until they lived
and died in the bitter faith that "this yellow slave" of
the exile's scorn could —

> "Knit and break religions; bless the accursed;
> Make the hoar leprosy adored; place thieves,
> And give them title, knee, and approbation
> With senators on the bench."

All in all, the most unfavorable and rabidly pessimis-
tic account of California and of life in the mines that
has fallen under my observation is Mr. Hinton R.
Helper's *Land of Gold*.[2] Writing as late as 1855, he says
that the country had "no redeeming features"; the land
was "a desert"; the customs of the people were atro-
cious; murders were of daily occurrence, and men were
lying sick and uncared-for in the streets of the towns; it
was the Nazareth of states, from which nothing except
evil could come. To further prick the "California bub-
ble," Mr. Helper offers such items as the following:

Loss by fires, 1849–54	$45,870,000
Loss by freshets, 1849–54	1,500,000
Shipping lost on the coast	5,060,000
Total	$52,430,000

This certainly seems to show an astonishing degree of
waste and loss. But the table is entirely unreliable. It
furnishes the separate items of the fire-losses which go
to make up that total of over forty-five million dollars,
and by these items we can test its accuracy. The San
Francisco fire of May 3, 1851 is stated to have caused a
loss of twelve million dollars: Hittell, a most cautious
writer, gives it as seven million dollars. The Sonora fire

---

[2] *Land of Gold:* Baltimore, 1855. Printed for the author. An in-
tensely interesting work, chiefly by reason of Mr. Helper's unexampled
talent for persistent pessimism.

of 1852 is stated to have destroyed property worth two million five hundred thousand dollars: the Tuolumne County official directory places the loss at seven hundred thousand dollars. From a multitude of equally reliable sources, the grand total of over fifty million dollars appears to be at least one third, and probably one half, too great.

From the fact of Mr. Helper's temperamental bias towards gloomy views of Pacific-coast life, manners, and institutions, his unexpectedly favorable evidence regarding the miners gains a peculiar importance.

"There is," he remarks, "more real honesty and fairness among the miners than among any other class of people in California. Taken as a body, they are a plain, straightforward, hard-working set of men, who attend to their own business without meddling with the affairs of others; and I have found as guileless hearts among them as ever throbbed in mortal bosom.

"Almost every bar," he continues, "is governed by a different code of laws, and the sizes of the claims vary according to locality. In one place a man may hold twice, thrice, or quadruple the number of feet that are allowed him in another. One-fourth of an acre is an average-sized claim."

Governor Richard J. Oglesby of Illinois was one of the pioneers of Nevada County, in "the days of '49 and '50." In a letter published in the history of that county he says:

"There was very little law, but a large amount of good order; no churches, but a great deal of religion; no politics, but a large number of politicians; no offices, and, strange to say for my countrymen, no office-seekers. Crime was rare, for punishment was certain. I was present one afternoon, just outside the city limits, and saw with painful satisfaction, as I now remember, Charley Williams whack three of our fellow-citizens over the bare back, twenty-one to forty strokes, for stealing a neighbor's money. The multitude of disinterested spectators had conducted the court. My recollection is that there were no attorneys' fees or court-charges. I think I never saw justice administered with so little loss of time or at less expense. There was no more stealing in Nevada City until society became more settled and better regulated."

Among the men who "prospected" in the Nevada mines during 1849 was the late Benjamin P. Avery, afterwards editor of the *Overland Monthly,* and for some time United States minister to China. Mr. Avery, and the late Samuel Williams, long literary editor of the *San Francisco Bulletin,* were two of the noblest, purest, and best-loved men ever connected with Pacific-coast journalism; and their memories are kept green throughout the state they did so much to develop. A letter from Mr. Avery printed in Bean's *Directory of Nevada County,* in 1867, recounts his adventures in the mines, and gives a graphic picture of "the childhood of California." "I started from Mormon Island," he says, "late in October, 1849; rode a little white mule, with pork, hard-bread, and blankets packed behind me." He heard of "pound diggins" (two hundred dollars per day) near Caldwell's Upper Store, and at Gold Run, in the famous basin where Nevada City and Grass Valley now stand. There were about a dozen parties working the bars with dug-out cradles and wire and rawhide hoppers. A few tents were scattered over the flat. The "store" was a square canvas shanty, where moldy biscuit sold for a dollar a pound, pork for two dollars, flour one dollar, and boots for six ounces of gold-dust per pair. He found good prospects, and returned for his comrades. Evidently there was as yet no organization by which he could secure a claim and hold it during his absence. He seems to have posted no claim, driven no stake; and when the party returned, the ravine Mr. Avery had prospected "was occupied from end to end by long-haired Missourians who were taking out their piles." They had organized, and staked out claims of thirty feet along the ravine; and found them so profitable that "many a long-tom party took a quart tin pail full of gold-dust to their camp at night." The isolation of the place is sufficiently shown by the fact that "it cost two dollars and a half to get a letter to or from Sacramento." Mr. Avery afterwards prospected "in the savage wilds of the Middle Yuba, where only the grizzly and wildcat roamed the lofty purple ridge, four thousand feet above the sea." Eight years later he was editor and proprietor of a newspaper published there, in the midst of villages, churches, schoolhouses, gardens, vineyards, and hydraulic mines.

An unvarnished account of pioneer experiences is to be found in Lawson B. Patterson's *Twelve Years in the Mines of California*. Arriving in canvas-built Sacramento, July 29, 1849, the author set out, on foot, for Mormon Camp, where the early miners had taken out over a million of dollars. He afterwards prospected far into the wilds of El Dorado. "Georgetown Camp" contained several hundred tents, but there was not a single woman in the district. "Hudson Gulch," in the same region, "is only three hundred yards long, but the first time it was worked it paid over fifteen hundred thousand dollars," and has been worked over and over perhaps a dozen times since. American miners began to find the need of business organization; and in 1850 and 1851 a "company of one hundred members tunnelled in Cement Hill." They did most of their own work, and ran four distinct tunnels far into the solid rock before they pierced the basin of auriferous gravel whose existence they suspected. Their association was reduced to

six members, then rose to twenty, before success came.
The total expenditure was one hundred and twenty-five
thousand dollars, and yet the results paid well. Associations of miners ran twenty different tunnels into "Mam-
eluke Hill," and sank many deep shafts, taking out over
thirty-five hundred thousand dollars. The organization
of the placer camps was already leading to personal association for working the deeper deposits.

We find notes from a careful observer of mining-life
in E. S. Capron's *History of California*. He tells us that
the miners are mostly "persons in the humbler walks of
life," yet there are "no inconsiderable number connected with the learned professions. Whoever attends
one of their miners' meetings will be convinced that
neither the fools nor the drones go to the mines. Let
the visitor wend his dark way into the mountain drift,
or clamber over heaps of rocks and earth, and leap wide
artificial drains, or go to some river where a deep, broad
eddy has allured the hopeful miner, or travel over miles
of upturned earth to where a solitary toiler is at work
under the exhausting sun, and he will meet the grave
divine, the skilful physician, the shrewd lawyer, the professor, the philosopher, the gentleman of leisure, and
the student, as well as the farmer, mechanic, and common laborer. . . . Their time is esteemed too precious
to hunt, fish, or cultivate the soil. . . . Vagabond Mexicans, outlawed at home, make the miners their frequent victims."

Of mining laws and customs Mr. Capron gives a tol-
erably accurate account. He says that the miners in public meetings had established courts "summary and sig-
nal in their proceedings"; and that "their jurisdiction
embraced all actions and proceedings, civil and criminal. In most cases the presiding officer was an elected
alcalde, aided by a sheriff." The spectators constituted

the only court of appeals. Annual meetings of the miners regulated all laws regarding claims. The size of claims averaged sixty by one hundred feet, and they were numbered and registered. In earlier times meetings were held much oftener than once a year, and the great body of "local mining-law" had been thus created. The "imperious necessity for these enactments" was universally recognized.

Quotations might easily be made at much greater length, and from many more writers. Everywhere we find, among observers of mining life, testimony to the success of the system of self-government adopted in the camps; and, in no less degree, testimony to the energy and simplicity of the miners themselves. Some few among these observers give instances of abuse of mining courts, of camp justice that had for the moment degenerated into mob rule. Cases are given where men's lives were saved by the prompt and cool courage of a few persons who insisted on another trial, or pointed out defects in the evidence. But we shall hear more of these things hereafter, in studying the local history of some of the notable camps. The main point to remember, so far, is the favorable impression made upon so many different writers, English, German, and American.

Chapter XIII. ILLUSTRATIONS FROM EARLY AND SUCCESSFUL CAMP ORGANIZATIONS

Reminiscences of the pioneers of California often drift into print. Many a book, justly famous, has been hammered out of the virgin gold of stories told around the camp-fire by men who were a part of that eventful period. A number of pioneers, some of them leaders, some of them of the uncounted thousands who only followed, have written me, giving, to their best ability, accounts of the organization of various mining camps. Their recollections are often hazy upon definite points; but they all agree as to the informality and celerity of early proceedings, and the high degree of good order secured in every camp, without exception.

A gentleman, once a pioneer citizen of Marysville, before the famous Briggs orchard was planted or Yuba County organized, writes, saying that he was among the first of the miners "in quite a number of migrating camps which proved evanescent, and disappeared with the swift current of events," but "were well governed while they lasted." In one case he and a companion "found pay-dirt in a cañon which sloped to the rushing Yuba," then a clear and beautiful river. Here they toiled for several days, and were doing well, when, one morning, they were suddenly visited by a delegation of miners from a neighboring camp, where the report of lucrative discoveries in the new gulch had been circulated by men who had climbed the hills in search of a stray pack-mule. The visitors, six or eight in number, proposed to organize a new camp and share the "find."

A consultation was held; and it was decided that each miner should be allowed to own and mine a strip of land ten feet wide on the river, and three hundred feet deep. Our friend and his companion were in the minority, and could not have objected had they wished; but the plan was so entirely in accordance with the usual custom — the unwritten law of older camps — that they yielded a ready and cheerful acquiescence. In view of the fact that they were the discoverers of the mineral wealth of the gulch, it was unanimously agreed that they should have first choice of ground; that is, the privilege of abandoning the location already made and of taking up any other claim on the gulch. In many districts they would have been allowed two claims apiece in acknowledgment of their rights as prospectors, but first choice was quite as often the rule. In closing his narrative, this gentleman says that "there was seldom or never any difficulty, because such a spirit of fair play actuated the miners of '49." [1]

Another gentleman, a graduate of Yale,[2] says, in the course of a highly interesting letter, that he "ought to know something about it," for he "began to work at mining when there was not even a custom, so that a man hardly objected to your digging close beside him so long as you left him room to swing a pick."

"A little later," he goes on to say, "I was present at a miners' meeting near Illinois Town, which was called together simply by sending notices through a district four or five miles square. My recollection is, that there was nothing done of any importance, as there were so many clashing interests that we could decide upon nothing which suited everybody concerned."

---

[1] This pioneer was Mr. William C. Dougherty, now (1884) deputy postmaster of San Francisco. He was once sheriff of Yolo, and was well known throughout the northern mines.

[2] Mr. C. T. Blake of San Francisco.

The Anglo-Saxon idea of compromise as the basis of all political action could not be more clearly shown than in the above statement. At a subsequent meeting they doubtless settled upon some scheme that was the best that could be done under the circumstances; that, as far as possible, suited everybody. Americans were the only class of miners who recognized this principle as essential to any harmonious organization.

Our correspondent, in speaking of the mining camps in which at various times he lived and labored, says that they "were mostly of limited size, say a small cañon and its tributary ravines, or a ridge between two cañons, or a river-bar." A mining region of great extent, like Georgetown, Placerville, Coloma, or Nevada, "might contain numerous districts with entirely different laws. The work of mining, and its environment and conditions, were so different in different places, that the laws and customs of the miners had to vary even in adjoining districts." Nor were the laws of any district permanent: they had to be changed from time to time, as the district came to be "reworked." This reworking of a district increased the size of a claim. With rich virgin soil, ten or twenty feet frontage was a large claim; but the same gulch when being worked over for perhaps the fifth time, for what predecessors had been unable to obtain, was divided up into claims of one or two hundred feet frontage. The ground worked at first by placer-miners with pick and pan was again sifted and searched by rocker and long-tom process; then, perhaps, by ground-sluicing; and lastly by various forms of the hydraulic process, the entire gulch, where dozens of small claims had once existed, passing under one ownership.

"Almost every mining-district," our correspondent writes, "kept written records from nearly the beginning, as claims had to be registered; but most of these records have been burned in the inevitable fires which have swept over almost every mining-town in California."

Some of the mining counties of California, whose county-seats are towns that have grown from little mining camps, are unable to show any historical records of earlier date than 1851. The lesser and migratory camps carried on most of their proceedings without any written records or documents of any sort whatever.

Notes sent by a California fruit-grower [3] describe his experiences in the mines. The only officer known in his camp was a recorder of claims, elected by the miners. His duties appear to have been clerical merely: the real business of the camp was transacted in open meeting by the assembled miners, who tried all criminal cases and disputes over claims, choosing a chairman, and voting *viva voce*. He never knew the miners of one camp to trespass upon the territory belonging to another camp. Difficulties of any sort were extremely rare. The camp being in a dry region, entirely dependent upon the water-ditches for working the claims, one of the district-laws was that all claims left idle a certain number of days after mining could be commenced were considered to have been abandoned. Here we have hints of what was afterwards developed into a complete and exact system of riparian regulations.

An account of the organization of Gold Hill Camp has been secured through the kindness of a California friend,[4] who interviewed an old miner named Morey and questioned him upon various features of interest. The camp occupied a gulch and the adjoining hillsides in the western part of Nevada County, and was first prospected by several miners early in 1850, the year

---

[3] B. D. T. Clough, of Alameda County, California.

[4] Rev. W. F. B. Lynch, of Centreville, Alameda County, California; former county superintendent of schools.

that witnessed such surprising growth throughout all that region. A few hours' labor convinced the discoverers that the royal metal was there in paying quantities, and they pitched their tent on the bank. Soon the news spread; and within a week there were fifteen or twenty men at work in the low, gravelly bed of the creek. At first the camp had no organization or government, and every man's conduct conformed to his own ideas of right and justice. Each miner had chosen a spot to work in, and no question of encroachment could possibly arise until in the widening circle their operations began to approach each other. About the close of the first week after the establishment of the camp, the near approach of two miners' operations caused a dispute about the size of claims. One of the miners considered his rights infringed upon; and a few days later, after a good deal of talk, his friends circulated an informal oral request through the camp, whose population had by that time increased to fifty or more, asking for a miners' meeting in the evening. They all felt that sooner or later definite laws must be adopted for the government of the camp, or disorder would prevail. The single question that had arisen could easily be settled by arbitration, but they must have some general rules regarding claims.

When the miners of the new camp assembled, one of their number called the meeting to order and nominated a permanent chairman, who was at once elected. The chairman then stated that there had been a little trouble about claims, and might easily be more. They could no longer let matters take their own course, but must make a serious effort to get the camp into shape. Its bounds were then established, making it about three miles in length and nearly two miles in width. A few regulations were made about the size of claims; some informal talk was indulged in regarding roughs and thieves; and the meeting adjourned, to reassemble whenever called together by the chairman, who was regarded as continued in office, and, in fact, as the head of the camp, until such time as a new election took place. At subsequent meetings some further difficulties about claims were settled by vote; and the punishment of several thefts was fixed in the same way.

This camp never had a recorder or a jury, either of six or of twelve. The whole meeting constituted the jury; their decisions were final, and their punishments immediate in execution. The chairman simply named such miners as he thought sufficient to "carry out the sentence of this meeting." Every man in the camp was liable to be called upon to act as an executive officer; and each law-abiding citizen of the camp was a public prosecutor, unless he had been expressly appointed to defend the prisoner. Meetings assembled whenever an offense had been committed, and disbanded as soon as it had been punished. This crude but efficient law gave general satisfaction until the civil and criminal law of the state stepped in to take its place, and Gold Hill Cañon became a small and lessening village in one of the townships of the county.[5]

One of the Nevada County pioneers writes of the beginnings of Rough and Ready Camp. The ravine was "located" in 1849 by a company of ten persons, who were followed by another similar company; and the two parties tried to maintain a monopoly of the gulch. One of the leaders went to the Atlantic states and hired men to work for his company; but during his absence the influx of miners, who paid no regard whatever to the ex-

---

[5] The township of California is not like the township of New England. It is much larger, often containing three hundred square miles. It only elects road-supervisors and constables, and these only on the county ticket, and has a proportionate vote in the county board of supervisors.

tensive claims of the first settlers, swept everything before it. In September 1850 there were five hundred miners at work in the gulch, and they had staked it out from end to end with claims of the ordinary size. Yet there was "no trouble, no shooting, or difficulty of any sort": the monopoly scheme had failed, and that was the end of it all. Some of its members secured claims for themselves, and some were compelled to buy interests in claims already taken up. All the camps of this period rose and fell in population with a surprising rapidity. At Gold Flat there were two cabins in August 1850; in July 1851 over three hundred miners were at work there; in 1852 the place was abandoned. Washington Camp, settled in 1849, contained a thousand miners within one year; and during the winter of 1850–1 over three thousand men were at work in the immediate vicinity. Moore's Flat diggings, within a year from their discovery, grew into a camp of five hundred miners; Orleans Flat, into one of six hundred. Grass Valley had fifteen cabins in October 1850, and a hundred and fifty by March 1851: four years later its population was three thousand five hundred. In each of these camps, organization kept pace with the growth of population; and there was never any serious disorder.

A pioneer of 1849 who, after many wanderings among the camps new and old, has settled down as the editor of a Boise City newspaper,[6] lays great stress, in his reminiscences, upon the law and order maintained with little difficulty in the camps of California. In his experience, all persons who attended a meeting were allowed to take part in its deliberations, whether residents of that particular district or not. If it was a criminal case that the court had assembled to consider, the accused was granted counsel, both sides were heard, and a vote

---

[6] Mr. D. Bacon, editor Boise City (Idaho) *Republican*.

was taken. In some instances the amount of punishment awarded was excessive, but it usually inclined towards mercy's side. In one case, in the little Sierra camp in which he dwelt, a meeting was held to try an Irishman and a Dutchman on a charge of stealing an old shovel and pick from a claim where they had been left by the owner to hold possession for him; the rule of the district being that all claims were forfeited so soon as the tools were removed. They were convicted on the evidence of witnesses who saw them carry the tools off. Their plea was that the tools were so old and worthless that they supposed no one else wanted them. But the claim, it was answered, by that act, through no fault of its owners, had been thrown open to the next prospector; and therein lay the guilt of the accused, since they were fully aware of the law of the camp. They were therefore sentenced to be whipped, and expelled from the diggings. One of them received a portion of his lashes, but a motion was then made and carried to remit the remainder; and the two men were escorted to the border of the camp and told to seek fresh pastures. The miners' meeting then gravely and earnestly advised the owners of the claim to be careful and leave better tools there another time, so that the object of so leaving them might be indisputable.

After giving various regulations about the size of a claim, similar in their leading features to those previously spoken of, this correspondent says that this method avoided endless litigation; and that the system of later years, adopted in the newer territories such as Idaho and Montana, which allows a man to hold twenty acres of valuable mineral ground to the exclusion of all others, has produced bitter fruit. The smaller plots of the California miners were much better for the community. All were contented, and none were hopelessly poor. A group of California prospectors, in those early days of which we are writing, seldom attempted to determine the superficial extent of the placer and then divide it up among themselves. When they did attempt it, the effort always came to grief, as in Rough and Ready Camp. They seemed rather to wish to ascertain how much surface ground would give an operator a full season's work; they chose the richest spots they could find, marked out their small claims, and left to later comers the ascertaining of the limits of the auriferous deposits of the district. Very often, indeed, when a miner had worked out his claim, there was plenty of equally good and never-occupied ground close at hand.

But the lesser differences in all these early camps were innumerable. An old miner writes me from Chili, where he owns a large *hacienda* on the borders of the Araucanian country, and states that a Yuba County camp he helped to organize in 1850 did not permit the transfer of claims, either by sale or by gift; and disputes were referred to the oldest man in camp, whose decision was final, but was in every case so in accordance with justice that it was invariably accepted. An old miner whom the writer once met illustrated a similar method in vogue in one of his early camps: "When we come back to dinner, Bill an' I, two strange fellers was at work in our claim. We sat down on the bank an' told them there was plenty of good gravel, jest as good, a mile down the river, an' that was our diggin's. They didn't stir, so one of us went an' asked Cap'n Bob Porter, the best an' quietest man in camp, to come up; an' we all had a drink outen the cap'n's flask, an' then we talked it over, he bein' spokesman. Pretty soon they said it warn't no use making a row, an' went off very friendly."

This very summer of 1884 the dwellers in a cottage

on one of the fairest islands of Casco Bay interviewed a rugged old sea-captain, a pioneer of the gold period, and a kindly, white-haired giant of a type not unlike brave John Ridd in *Lorna Doone*. He had toiled in many different camps, but chiefly in the noisy town of Spanish Bar, Placer County, where an elected alcalde ruled, and where "everyone drinked as much whisky as they wanted." The size of claims in his experience varied, but at Spanish Bar it was ten feet square in the dry diggings. Tools left on a claim held it for three days' absence, and a claim-notice protected it for seven days. Claims on the river were one hundred feet in length, as a rule; though sometimes, when a camp was crowded, and all the best claims taken up, a new company of miners would come along and, calling a public meeting of the miners, persuade them to diminish the prescribed size of claims, so as to give all an equal chance. Sometimes the first-comers exceeded their rightful bounds, but readily yielded when other miners arrived.

This sort of evidence and illustration afforded by letters from pioneers of California might easily be extended beyond the limits of a single chapter; but we must turn to a more definite discussion of the laws of the camps, and the various systems under which they were controlled. The flexibility of the government known in the Sierra camps, and the freedom with which it assumed different forms, were quite as admirable traits as were its earnestness and efficiency. Even in the quotations already given, there are hints of different methods of governing camps; and these must now receive consideration.

CHAPTER XIV. FORMS OF DISTRICT GOVERNMENT

Folk-moot, standing committee, and alcalde

As we have seen, the forms of local organization under which laws, civil or criminal, were made for the governing of mining districts, were varied and suggestive; but they are all reducible to three types — that rule of the whole body of freemen, which we have heretofore denominated the "folk-moot of the Sierra"; that rule of a select and permanent committee or council to whom supreme authority was sometimes delegated; and, lastly, that individual rule of the alcalde, or of the miners' justice of the peace, offices of nearly similar powers and duties in the eyes of the early gold-seekers. Behind the seldom-questioned supremacy of council and alcalde, preventing them from unjust, despotic, and arbitrary extremes, was the tacit acknowledgment of the right of the community to interfere in extreme cases. Society ever kept a watchful eye upon its authorized dispensers of justice. The "folk-moot" was the original and central institution.

This assemblage of the people, called together by any person or persons, after choosing a temporary officer, proceeded to discuss subjects of interest, try cases, make laws, and enforce them. It was literally government by the miners of the district. Boys of fifteen and sixteen, broad-shouldered and self-reliant, often took part in the deliberations of the meeting. It was this miners' court, that our Norse and Saxon ancestors, could they have risen from burial-mounds like Beowulf's "on the steep, seen by sea-goers from afar," reared there by the "battle-brave hearth-companions" of the dead, would undoubt-

[167

edly have recognized as akin to those folk-moots held of old in primeval German and Scandinavian forests. In both alike were the right of free speech for all freemen, the right of unhampered discussion, the visible earnestness, the solemn judgment, not only in the name of the people, but by the people themselves, assembled to right wrong, to try offenders, to smite even to death, or to justify and set free. Out of this meeting, containing such possibilities for good and for evil, other forms of government known to the miners developed, or in this meeting were of their own free will adopted. No alcalde, no council, no justice of the peace, was ever forced upon a district by an outside power. The district was the unit of political organization, in many regions, long after the creation of the state; and delegates from adjoining districts often met in consultation regarding boundaries, or matters of local government, and reported to their respective constituencies in open-air meeting, on hillside or river-bank.

In all cases of criminal trials, the miners' court assumed much of a judicial aspect. Whatever legal talent the miners possessed was brought into service. In 1849 hardly a camp existed on the great Sierra slope that did not contain miners who were graduates of colleges and law-schools or were lawyers of considerable experience. Many of these men, in after-years, became leaders in county and state affairs. Earnest, intelligent, and cultivated speakers stood ready to defend the accused. When acting as tribunals of life and death, all who appeared were entitled to a vote and to be heard; but when deciding laws concerning claims and local government, members of other camps could not vote. The accused — camp thief, sluice-robber, horse-stealer, or murderer — was guarded by men with revolvers or was tied to a tree. The miners' court was in such cases assembled at once, not by formal notices, but by a cry running from claim to claim, from height to height, proclaiming, for instance, that "they've caught the fellow that robbed John Smiley's sluice-boxes last night." Nearly everyone then came into camp, and the case was usually brought to trial within half an hour.

Short speeches were made for and against the prisoner; the presiding officer charged the jury "to do the fair thing accordin' to common sense"; and after a brief deliberation they rendered a verdict, and the presiding officer decided the penalty. If there was no jury, the case was submitted to the decision of the miners present, who also fixed the punishment. In small camps, where only thirty or forty men assembled, this was perhaps the usual system; but in larger camps the jury system prevailed. In one case a trial was had and the prisoner hung within an hour; it being a cold-blooded murder, with a dozen witnesses to the act. In another case the jury spent four days in taking testimony and listening to arguments. When it was decided to hang the prisoner, the crowd guarded the town and the building where he was confined, having reason to fear an attempted rescue; they gave him four days to prepare for death, and then, on the ninth day after his arrest, hung him to a bridge in the presence of more than two thousand men, with all the dignity and solemnity imaginable.

Capital punishment was not, in the miners' code, confined to murder: it was often inflicted upon those guilty of lesser crimes. Thus the roads were made safe, the cabins of the lonely miners secure; as in the days of good Duke Robert, "gold bracelets might hang untouched from an oak by the public highway." Horse-stealing was sometimes considered a capital offense; partly because of the great value and scarcity of horses in the mines, partly from the fact that a desperado once mounted was infinitely more dangerous than before to society. The entire absence of jails and prisons in which to confine criminals reduced available penalties to three — banishment, whipping, and death. In practice the punishment awarded for theft was whipping for the first offense; but if repeated, it was at the peril of the offender's neck. The cases in which men were hung for theft were justified by the miners under the plea of necessity; the lawless classes being sometimes strong and defiant, only checked by the stern determination of Americans to protect their property from claim-jumpers and thieves.

Cases of whipping were very numerous. A man who stole a sack of flour, just after the Nevada City fire of 1851, was given twelve lashes. In 1850, in Grass Valley, a mule-thief received thirty lashes. In Trinity County, at Hay Fork, the first thief was whipped by the entire camp, each miner giving a blow. Hardly a camp existed in the mining region where, sooner or later, the assembled court did not decree this form of punishment to some offender. In one case a man who entered the tent of a Chileno woman one night during her husband's absence, and attempted violence, was whipped so severely that he was hardly able to drag himself out of the camp he had disgraced. A storekeeper was once whipped for swindling the miners out of their gold-dust by false balances. In Calaveras County a man stole a small amount of dust, received ten lashes; returned that night and committed another theft; was given twenty lashes and sent out of camp. He went to the next camp, and there stole a mule on which to leave the country; but the miners of this camp caught him, and the court sentenced him to fifty lashes well laid on. When stripped, however, his condition from previous punishment ap-

peared so dreadful that a vote of forgiveness was passed;
and the owner of the mule took the culprit to his tent
and dressed the bleeding wounds.

The miners' court was never wittingly cruel in its
judgments, but it was liable to be swayed by prejudice
or passion. The change to a committee or council form
of government, which occurred in quite a large number
of cases, was a decided improvement. The best example of this type occurred at Rough and Ready Camp,
Nevada County, early in 1850, after the state government had been organized, but while three fourths of the
mining region still depended upon miners' courts. This
camp, established late in 1849, had a population of several hundred persons. They held a mass-meeting and
elected a committee of three persons to administer justice. The miners then went about their business and
left the management of the affairs of this thriving camp
entirely in the hands of these three citizens. There was
no higher court; and their authority was nearly absolute, and always well sustained.

Before this council a man who was accused of stealing was tried with the forms of law, was found guilty,
and was given thirty-nine lashes, after which he was
banished and warned never again to appear in that
camp. The three members of the council had equal
powers, and all voted in such cases. Presumably a majority ruled. In quite a number of cases the punishment
given to offenders was "forty stripes save one."

The council had civil jurisdiction as well as criminal.
They settled quite a number of disputes about claims;
they laid out the streets of the town, and apportioned
the town lots among its citizens; they even appointed
a constable, issued writs as occasion demanded, and accepted bail-bonds for the appearance of accused persons.
One of these bonds is still in existence, and shows that

a person charged with horse-stealing offered bail to the amount of one thousand dollars, and afterwards came forward and stood his trial.

The nearest fully established court of justice was at Nye's Landing, afterwards Marysville, over thirty miles distant, where a justice of the peace had been elected under the state laws. Nevada City had an alcalde, but he exercised no jurisdiction outside of that district. The Grass Valley miners met in November 1850, under a large oak-tree, and elected by ballot a justice of the peace, and constable. But Rough and Ready district was satisfied with its council, which accordingly decided all disputes, administered justice with an equitable hand, and in all respects made their management of camp affairs so satisfactory that it lasted until the jurisdiction of the county was fully established.[1]

This sort of government by a committee, or council, to whom all powers are entrusted, reappears in Tuolumne, Placer, and Shasta counties. The influence of the idea is, perhaps, manifest in the adoption in many camps, almost simultaneously, of the principle of arbitration, according to which permanent officers were chosen and given the duty of acting as arbitrators whenever called upon. In some camps, as late as 1854, all disputed claims were referred to a standing committee; and the laws of many districts, as will be shown hereafter, contain traces of this principle. No case of the miners' court interfering with, or revising the action of, such a committee seems known to record or to tradition.

The third and historically the most interesting form of camp government was by means of an alcalde, that

---

1 Rough and Ready was then in Yuba County's jurisdiction. H. Q. Roberts, James S. Dunleavy, and Emanuel Smith formed this Committee of Vigilance and Safety.

Spanish-American official of time-honored authority and dignity. It seems to have given satisfaction wherever adopted, as the camps which in 1848 organized under that form made no change until their incorporation as towns under a city council, or their subjections to the general county system. The duties, powers, and manysidedness of the office in its typical development have already been described.

Removal of the office from the immediate control of the military governors of California to places far in the interior, and difficult of access, had practically emancipated it from all superior authority. We have already seen what close supervision the alcaldes of the coast towns received under Kearny and Mason, and what jurisdiction General Riley claimed and exercised; but over the alcaldes of the mining region there is no evidence that the control elsewhere exercised by the *de facto* governor of California was ever felt or acknowledged.[2] The miners were not in the habit of writing letters of inquiry when difficult cases were brought before them, or of waiting for weeks till, by slow and uncertain methods of communication, advice was received from Monterey. Even when the Constitutional Convention was called, it proved impossible for more than half the miners to vote; again, when the question of adopting the constitution was submitted to the people, the same difficulty occurred. Even a tax-gatherer could not keep the run of the new camps. Each little district in the Sierra was a body politic by itself, conscious of no outside con-

---

[2] The California Documents containing the official correspondence of Kearny, Mason, and Riley, at various times during 1847, 1848, and 1849, to various officers, are crowded with letters to alcaldes in coast towns. But no letters were written to, or received from, any alcaldes east of the Sacramento and San Joaquin rivers; nor were any removals, appointments, or changes made east of those rivers. Even when Mason and Riley visited, in 1848 and 1849, the camps, there were no appeals made to them: the miners had already organized.

trol; its alcalde seldom paid any attention to the doings of his neighbor alcaldes, nor conformed his rulings to the strict letter of Mexican alcalde law, nor, indeed, to the letter of any law whatever.

The typical plan by which a single officer was elected and clothed with full alcalde powers was often modified. It sometimes happened that at the very first miners' meeting of the district a sheriff was chosen to aid the alcalde; and a recorder to register mining claims, sometimes to act as clerk of the alcalde court. A camp provided for in this lavish manner was considered to have given proof of its permanence to all the world. The chairman of the meeting administered an official oath to the newly elected officers, who were at once installed. The alcalde issued writs and summonses according to forms copied from the nearest available law-book, or evolved from his own inner consciousness and sense of fitness, and often expressed in untechnical — even ungrammatical — language; the sheriff served these writs and summonses, made arrests, preserved order, and saw that prescribed punishments were duly inflicted.

The compensation allowed to these officers varied. The alcalde usually received about sixteen dollars for trial of a cause. The sheriff had pay for serving writs, and mileage for all travel performed in the discharge of his duties. Jurors received six dollars apiece for each case tried, and witnesses were paid their actual expenses.

Funds for these and other necessary expenses were secured by the system of registering claims. The fees for this were from fifty cents to one dollar for each registry, of which the recorder received a percentage; and miners were so restless, so constantly taking up new claims and abandoning their old ones to others, that even small camps were kept in funds for all necessary judicial expenditures. There was no waste whatever. Every dollar, except the recorder's small percentage, was used for legitimate expenses. A camp that charged no fees for recording claims had two financial resources — one, and the most frequent, by means of a collection; the other, by a direct assessment upon the claims. Thus we see that the miners had solved the problem of obtaining financial support to their courts of justice, and, in full accordance with the socialistic features of their system, had made taxation equal. The amount to be raised was small: no miner felt the payment of a dollar when he registered a new claim. No tax-collectors were needed, for the fact that unregistered claims were liable to be "jumped" in short meter was a sufficient incentive. The district thus provided for was a self-governed, independent, and self-supporting state in miniature.

The jury for civil cases was usually composed of six persons, perhaps from questions of economy; in criminal cases it was always twelve. The alcalde's decision, it need hardly be said, was final.

In many cases a camp was long governed by occasional miners' courts and did not adopt the alcalde system until nearly the full organization of state and county courts. Thus, in March 1850 "the need of more authority was felt at Caldwell's Upper Store"; and a man named Stamps was by ballot elected alcalde, two hundred and fifty votes being cast. At the same miners' meeting the name of the camp was changed to "Nevada City." Only two months later the county officers at Marysville ordered an election for justice of the peace to supersede the alcalde, so his reign was a brief one.[3] The evidence of Governor Riley, as noted in a previous extract from his report of a visit in 1849 to the Tuolumne camps; also the evidence of Mr. Bayard Taylor,

---

[3] Thompson and West's *History of Nevada County;* chapters on Early Courts, and on Nevada City.

who describes alcalde rule as "nearly universal in the Butte-county region" — is sufficient to show the extent to which the system was adopted. It suited the demands of the mining community, being simple, efficient, thoroughly representative, and always responsible to the people.

Stories of curious alcalde decisions are numerous in the mining region, and some of them are extremely characteristic.

In Columbia district, Tuolumne County, the first case brought before the alcalde was an American miner's complaint against a Mexican for stealing a pair of old leather leggings. That official, himself an American, remonstrated; but, justice being demanded, he fined the Mexican three ounces (about fifty dollars) for the theft, and the miner one ounce for making a complaint over such a trifle. The second case in this court was a miner's suit against a neighbor for a pick stolen from his claim. Judgment for plaintiff, for value of pick, one ounce; and costs, three ounces.

In 1849 an El Dorado alcalde had a case of trespass on mining ground brought before him, and settled it to the satisfaction of both parties. The district treasury was nearly empty. Turning to the astonished sheriff, the alcalde ordered him to pay the costs, since the trespassing miner was poor and had infringed unwittingly upon his neighbor's rights, while the mulcted officer owned the best claim on the gulch. "If you don't do it, the boys will have to take up a collection." Protests were ineffectual, and the sheriff paid the costs.

In one of the Calaveras camps of 1849 a sailor deserter, too lazy to work, stole several thousand dollars in dust and coin from under a miner's pillow, was captured, left tied to a tree the rest of the night, and in the morning given a jury-trial, and found guilty. The alcalde sentenced him to one hundred lashes well laid on, though the crowd wanted him hung as an example and warning. All the miners favored stringent and rigidly enforced laws against theft. A law permitting capital punishment for theft remained for a few months on the state statute-book.

One more story of early alcalde methods will suffice. It was in one of the northern mines; and the alcalde had a slow, oracular delivery, and a mild, gentle, persuasive manner. To him one day a well-dressed young man who had stolen a purse, and tried to escape on horseback, was brought for punishment; the evidence being so clear that after five minutes' listening to the testimony, the alcalde said in his most seductive accents:

"Would you like to have a jury-trial, my son?"

"No, judge: it isn't worth while to do that."

"All right, my son. Now you must return the dust you stole."

"Certainly, judge."

"And the court regrets the necessity, but really, my son, you ought to pay costs — two ounces."

"Oh, I can stand that: here it is, and thank ye, judge."

"Now the court is fully satisfied, with the exception of one trifling formality. — Boys, take him out, and give him thirty-nine lashes well laid on."

We must remember that all the various forms of camp government existed in one place or another at the same time; that the older and more prosperous camps were assuming the appearance of towns, and perhaps had a town council, sheriff, and recorder, besides the alcalde; while the newer camps were in the first stages of growth. Nevada camps of 1849 were in somewhat the condition of El Dorado camps of 1848; Trinity County comps of 1851 were ruled as simply and directly as were

those of Nevada in 1849. For months after the state judicial system was adopted and established at the various county-seats, the remote camps saw only the tax-
collector, and continued to govern themselves by their
favorite local methods. Long after Sonora Camp had organized a town government and elected a council and
mayor, though without state authority, there were hundreds of small camps where no officer except the chairman of the miners' court had ever been known. The
primitive folk-moot reigned supreme in these temporary camps. A chronological study of the life of various
camps is impossible. Some were blossoming, others decaying; some began under committee-rule, others with
one-man power. But none, after electing an alcalde,
chose to abandon the system and return to primitive
methods; although in more cases than one they asserted
the right of the camp to sit in judgment on the actions
of their elected ruler.

Brief though the reign of the mining-camp alcaldes
was, it left a deep impress upon mountain society, as an
occurrence in northern California a few years ago will
perhaps illustrate. There is a school-teacher there, a
man of mighty frame and great energy, whose boyhood
was spent in the placers of Siskiyou, and his young manhood on the cattle-ranges of eastern Oregon and in adventurous wanderings along the frontiers of British Columbia. When the late war began, he went East and
joined a regiment; returning to his mountain wilderness in 1865, a crippled and battered veteran. He had
always been a close reader and hard student: so, as a
teacher, he soon won a reputation for success over three
counties. Under these circumstances he was called to
take charge of what, with undoubted justice, was called
one of the worst schools in northern California. The
mail-rider threw off the trustee's letter at the door of

this man's summer cabin, perched on a pine-clad height of the Sierra; trout-stream within a stone's throw; grouse, deer, and bear in the woods; his gun and rod in the corner, his "Marcus Aurelius" and *Noctes Ambrosianæ* on a rustic shelf. He saddled his horse the next morning, and reached the village, once a mining camp, before nine o'clock. When school was called to order, he found that efficient work demanded a reclassification; because the previous teacher had tried to gain cheap favor by advancing grades without reason, and skipping the hard places. After a few weeks he had come to grief by trying to persuade a large boy not to smoke a cigarette in school-hours; for the playful innocents had ducked him in the adjacent stream, sousing him up and down until he escaped, waded to the farther bank, and sought other fields for his pedagogic prowess. But the new teacher possessed frontier freedom of resource and military discipline of character.

"I must turn you back in your grades," he said after several hours of examination. An ominous murmur of rebellion followed. Several boys rose in their seats and announced that their parents "would see about that."

The teacher then made his first and last speech to the excited school. He took a book from the table and addressed the most noisy of the rebels.

"Do you know what this is?"

"Yes, sir — the school-law."

"And it defines the grades; and you think that last year you passed an examination, and that I cannot go behind the law?"

"Yes, sir."

"Very well, you are quite mistaken. I am the alcalde of this school. I am sheriff, and register of claims, and judge of the camp, and the whole jury. I am absolute finality here!" With this comprehensive statement, he threw the school-law out of the open window and then, in the midst of an awe-struck throng, proceeded to break up and consolidate class after class.

"Yes, an alcalde was what the district needed," was the opinion of the old pioneers of the village when the story was told; and a better school, for the rest of the year, northern California never knew.

Chapter XV. HOW AN ALCALDE WAS ONCE DEPOSED

W E have said that in the mines there always was a tacit recognition of the power vested in the people of the camp to depose an alcalde from his high office. One of the best known instances of the exercise of this power occurred in the southern Oregon mines, as late as the autumn of 1852; and its history throws more light upon the ideas of justice and law which underlie these frontier courts than could be obtained by pages of barren generalization.[1]

It is not our purpose to describe the beginnings of local government in Oregon, the famous "Wolf Meeting" of the settlers of the beautiful Willamette Valley in 1843, and those earlier local organizations in that region in 1838 and 1839, which preceded and made possible that notable assembly. The Spanish-American and gold-seeker elements were entirely foreign to the struggle that organized Oregon under a legislative committee and supreme judge while the ownership of her territory was as yet undetermined. That interesting struggle of Americans to gain control in the Northwest must be studied elsewhere.[2]

But in southwestern Oregon there were placer mines; and to these narrow gulches, clad with spruce and fir, California miners went, bearing with them the organiza-

---

[1] The points for this chapter are obtained from an article, "Pioneer Justice in Oregon," *Overland Monthly*, first series, vol. xii. p. 225, and from letters of correspondents.

[2] Barrows: *Oregon*, American Commonwealth Series, p. 265. Mrs. Victor's articles on Early Oregon, *Overland Monthly*, first series. W. H. Gray: "History of Oregon," *Overland Monthly*, November 1884, p. 555.

tion perfected through fierce struggles and dire necessity in the camps of 1848 and 1849. They governed their Oregonian camps on the plans adopted in Siskiyou and Shasta, in Amador and Fresno, in Tuolumne and Nevada. North of the Calapooia Mountains the pioneer Oregonians were, and always remained, totally unacquainted with that famous Spanish office, the alcaldeship: south of those mountains there were several alcaldes chosen by the settlers and given the extensive powers of the office as known in California camps. Before January 1852 there were no county organizations in the southwestern fourth of Oregon, and for a year later the alcaldes continued to rule supreme in that region. Returned Oregonians who had determined to prospect nearer home after one or two seasons in California were influential forces in all the earlier Oregon camps.

The miners of Jackson Creek Camp, Rogue River Valley, had an alcalde named Rogers. He was not at all popular, but was thought to be honest and capable until events showed him in an unexpected light. His election had occurred before the camp had "boomed": the few early miners on the creek had chosen him, and the crowds that came later had accepted his authority.

It happened that there were two mining partners named Sim and Sprenger, who worked a claim together, and were unnoticed and unknown in the mass of busy workers till a sudden difficulty brought them into prominence.

Sim took money from the funds of the concern and went to Portland to lay in their winter's stock of provisions. During his absence his partner, Sprenger, met with an accident, and was crippled, helpless, and sick in the cabin, nursed by a few sympathizing friends, when Sim returned. The real nature of Sim revealed itself:

without any compunctions he at once ejected Sprenger
from their cabin and their claim. Of what use was a sick
and crippled partner?

The wronged and unfortunate miner secured the
services of a young man named Kinney as his lawyer,
and took his complaint to Alcalde Rogers. But Sim, as
events proved, had forestalled him by arguments of another sort: putting little trust in his claim of an oral
sale, and his extremely doubtful witnesses, he bribed
the unworthy alcalde, who, disregarding local custom,
mining law, and the plain dictates of reason and justice,
rendered his verdict against Sprenger. The plaintiff, in
sad destitution and misery, and urged as a forlorn hope
by some of his friends, begged the alcalde for a rehear-
ing of the case, which was promptly refused: a judge
could not be expected to overrule his own decisions.
Nor would he grant a jury-trial. Restitution, and rein-
statement in his possession of one undivided half of
cabin, tools, provisions, and claim, appeared unattain-
able for poor Sprenger.

The story was told throughout the camp, and it was
openly said that there had been bribery of the witnesses,
perhaps of the alcalde; but the camp, though populous,
was a scattered settlement, and concerted action was
difficult. There was indignant talk, but the men and the
hour had not yet arrived. Sprenger found shelter in a
friendly cabin, and Sims began to look about for an
able-bodied partner who wanted to "buy in." But no
one desired the situation of partner to such a man.

Matters were in this condition when Sprenger, still
brooding over his wrongs, still urged by sympathizing
friends, heard that a miner in the camp, named Prim,
was a first-rate lawyer, a graduate of some law-school,
and an attorney of considerable experience. Hoping
against hope that some new mode of procedure might

yet be devised, Sprenger hobbled to Prim's claim and
begged for his assistance. At first this was denied; and
Prim even said he was no lawyer and could not leave
his work. But Sprenger's penniless and piteous condition became an appeal that could not be disregarded:
the miner threw down his tools, hunted up Sprenger's
former attorney, Kinney, and they held a conference.

Further appeal to the alcalde was clearly useless. But
Prim proposed to reach the territorial courts north of
the Calapooia Mountains — to go, in fact, to Portland
itself — and there obtain powers to organize a district
court with appellate powers over the entire region.
There was constant need, he argued, for a more complete scientific system. They could not continue the un-
balanced, uncontrolled, irresponsible alcalde system
without a higher court to check its abuses. The practical difficulty in the way was that all this would take
months, and their unfortunate client would probably
starve long before the close of the approaching winter.
Then, too, the value of the interest he owned in the
claim from which he had been ousted was steadily di-
minishing, as Sim worked there from daylight to dark.
And if Sim should succeed in finding a partner, a new
element of difficulty would be added.

At last Kinney is reported to have exclaimed: "Who
but the people made the damned scoundrel alcalde,
anyhow? We can organize our own court of appeals."

Prim caught eagerly at the idea. They sent a man up
and down the gulches, and over the ridges, to the extreme limits of the district within Alcalde Rogers's jurisdiction. It took a day of hard travel to summon them
all, but nearly everyone heeded the appeal to his sense
of justice. There was no attempt to prejudge the case or
to bias men's opinions. Each miner was told that numbers of persons thought a great wrong had been done,

and that it was desired to examine the entire subject with all fairness and deliberation, sustaining or reversing the former judgment as the evidence should warrant.

So the eventful morning dawned; and over a thousand miners threw down their picks and shovels, left their rockers, long-toms, and sluices, and came hastening to the main camp. Every man of them all suffered a loss, by his day's idleness, of whatever his work that day would have earned — perhaps five dollars, perhaps fifty dollars; but the miners of Jackson Creek were willing to suffer loss if justice, as between man and man, could thereby be established.

The court met in the open air and chose a presiding officer. They then elected a committee of three well-known miners to wait on Alcalde Rogers and respectfully request him, "in the name and by the authority of the citizens of Jackson-creek Camp," to reopen his court and give the case of Sim *vs.* Sprenger a new trial; they asked also that a jury be allowed. Rogers refused point-blank, and retired grimly defiant to the entrenchments of his log cabin. The committee returned and made a report in open meeting. It was then discharged, and the first act of the drama had closed.

Only one course was left for the miners' meeting — to organize their higher court and invest it with full authority to review any and all proceedings of the court below. This seems to have been done by these bold reformers on the supposition that it might have to be a permanent thing: it was not merely an expedient by which to reinstate Sprenger in his rights, if such rights a fair trial proved him to possess. It had dawned upon the minds of those earnest men assembled in that winding Oregonian ravine that the time had come for a higher judicial organization. With strong good sense and sturdy independence they grappled with the problem.

First, a miner named Hayden, one of the most respected and intelligent men in the entire community, was nominated and elected to serve as chief judge of the district. He declined the responsible position, begging them to choose someone else; but the duties of the office were urged upon him until he was forced to accept.

Judge Hayden displayed the greatest promptitude, dignity, and good sense in his proceedings. He at once asked for a sheriff and a clerk, who were immediately elected, and reported themselves ready for duty. Within an hour after Hayden's acceptance, a writ of *certiorari* commanding Alcalde Rogers to appear in the new and duly established court, before Judge Hayden, and submit the records of his proceedings, was served upon that officer by the newly installed sheriff of Jackson Creek. To the surprise of all concerned, the stubborn alcalde refused to yield, and proceeded to impugn the motives of certain leaders and deny the legal existence of the court. History has failed to keep an exact record of his language; but, beyond a doubt, it was profanely belligerent.

The crowd of miners were by this time tired and angry. It was suggested to batter down Rogers's cabin, take possession of his records, and lay them before the newly chosen superior judge. But to this Judge Hayden objected, as defeating the ends of justice. He called the sheriff and issued new writs, ordering both parties in the original controversy to appear before him at once for a trial: in other words, he ignored all former proceedings and asserted original as well as appellate jurisdiction over the camp. The impressiveness of the scene had now become indescribable. Those hundreds of brawny, bare-armed, red-shirted men, grouped in the open air, under giant oaks, were moving without noise or excitement to the full accomplishment of their appointed task.

Plaintiff and defendant came before the new court and were assured of a full and fair trial. Witnesses were summoned; a jury impaneled, sworn to do their duty; and lawyers appointed for each side. Tradition reports that Sim's lawyer was able and courageous, but that his witnesses weakened under the severe cross-questioning of his opponent. Both lawyers made appeals to the jury, and the case was submitted. No one can doubt, from the dignity and earnestness which had hitherto prevailed, that a verdict for the defendant, though contrary to the general expectation, would have been accepted by the assemblage. By the verdict of that jury those freemen who had left their claims lying idle for miles were tacitly pledged to abide; and Prim, Kinney, and Hayden would have been the first to acquiesce, the last to propose any "new deal."

The court, in his charge to the jury, said that they must strip the case of technicalities, regarding no law but right and wrong, no test but common sense. They listened with approval, and at once proceeded to disagree on a vital point: some wanted to hang Sim, who had been proved guilty of bribery; several wanted to hang Alcalde Rogers. This dangerous phase soon passed away; the jury found a verdict for the plaintiff, and left the sentence with the court, where it evidently belonged. Judge Hayden then, amid breathless silence, announced his decision: Sprenger was to be reinstated in all his former rights, as half owner of cabin, tools, provisions, and claim; Sim was also ordered to pay the costs of his partner's sickness. The court then adjourned.

But some of the evidence offered had revealed so much rascality and malfeasance on the part of Alcalde

Rogers that none of the miners were satisfied to let him longer hold the office he had so disgraced. Who could any more put confidence in so untrustworthy an official? How could a thousand men, some of them living five miles from the central camp, be expected to leave their claims and administer justice by newly organized courts each time there was need thereof? The crowd proceeded to Rogers's cabin, growing angrier and more tumultuous each moment. A cry that he should be hung swelled like a mountain torrent in time of flood; but Hayden, Prim, Kinney,. and Jacobs (who had been Sim's lawyer) made speeches, and reason again prevailed. One thing, however, was certain — Alcalde Rogers must resign; and this he did without demur. Judge Hayden's court was then reassembled, and it levied an instant execution upon some mining property which ex-Alcalde Rogers had illegally and unjustly obtained; it being part of the Sim-Sprenger claim, given to him by Sim as a retainer at the time of the first trial.

The Hayden court lasted until county organization, a few months later, but no other case of any importance was brought before it. The lesson taught by the sight of those assembled pioneers had proved sufficient.

The typical nature of this remarkable case is best shown by the facts that Sim's lawyer, Mr. Jacobs, has since become chief justice of Washington Territory; that Mr. Prim has been chief justice of Oregon; that Judge Hayden for many years has been one of the leading citizens of southern Oregon; that the full records of the case are on file in the archives of Jackson County, Oregon; and that variants of the story can be heard in mining camps hundreds of miles from Jackson Creek. Years ago, in Douglas City Camp, Trinity County, California, the writer first heard of "Judge Hayden's appellate court": today, perhaps, the story is told in the Kootenay passes and under the Uintah pines.

In points of interest and importance this case is only surpassed by the equally famous Scotch Bar case of the Siskiyou mines. But at Scotch Bar the problem was of a different nature and cannot be considered in this connection: we must first return to the California camps of the early gold era, and discuss a curious institutional link between the alcalde of full and unlimited powers, and the ordinary justice of the peace of ten years later.

Chapter XVI. THE MINERS' JUSTICE
OF THE PEACE

THE most important officer the miners had under the early state and county organization was a justice of the peace, on whom, in practice, partial alcalde powers were bestowed in a number of cases.

The state law of 1850 ordered the election of justices of the peace in every township and abolished the office of alcalde. The length of term was fixed at one year; jurisdiction to extend over the township, often as large as the average county of an Atlantic seaboard state. The justice had cognizance of action to recover damages, or specific property of not more than two hundred dollars in value.

In 1851 the powers of this office were greatly enlarged. The justice of the peace was given authority to try all civil cases when the amount involved did not exceed five hundred dollars, all cases of forcible entry and detainer, and all disputes over mining claims and cases involving mining properties, whatever their value. It was this last clause that made the miners' justice of the peace a much more powerful potentate in 1850-2 than was his brother of the valley townships. His criminal jurisdiction included all cases punishable by a fine of not more than five hundred dollars, or not more than a year's imprisonment.

Hon. A. A. Sargent, in his valuable *Sketch of the Nevada-county Bar,* says:

"The jurisdiction of justices of the peace in 1850–51, who were then the only judicial officers known in these diggings, was a little shadowy, or very substantial, as the reader pleases."

190]

Some examples are given by Mr. Sargent. In 1851, in Rough and Ready, just after the famous council retired to private life, a case which involved possession of a mining claim on Lander's Bar — a claim worth fully one hundred thousand dollars — was tried before Justice Roberts. Among the counsel was Mr. Lorenzo Sawyer, now on the supreme bench of California. The trial lasted three days, and the jury disagreed. A new trial was commenced on the following day, which lasted ten days, and was one of the most closely contested legal struggles of the period. Able and brilliant lawyers fought the ground over, inch by inch, and exhausted every resource of the profession. This trial resulted in a verdict, and the losers paid a bill of costs amounting to nineteen hundred and ninety-two dollars in gold-dust.

In September 1850 one of the "coyote-hole claims," near Nevada City, was owned by several Frenchmen, and is said to have paid as high as nine hundred and twelve dollars to the pan.[1] Several Americans coveted the mine, and so demanded to see the owners' foreign-tax receipts. The Frenchmen had none less than two months old, but were ready to pay whenever the collector appeared. The Americans drove them off, took possession, and began work. Suit to recover was brought before the justice of the peace. The case went to a jury, and the chief plea of the Americans was that "they wanted a slice." Of course the verdict was against them; a sheriff's posse at once reinstated the true owners, and the claim-jumpers were warned against repeating such exploits.

Quite a number of cases are on record where a justice of the peace issued writs of injunction to restrain par-

---

[1] "Coyote claims," small holes on the hillside to reach rich gravel, which is carried to the nearest stream and washed out.

ties from working valuable mines until their true ownership could be decided. In one case this injunction was
made perpetual.

The justices were not always fit men to hold office. A
miner near Placerville was once on trial before a justice
for assaulting a claim-jumper. The story is admirably
told in Parsons's *Life of Marshall*. The trial began at
eleven p.m.; and the justice kindly adjourned the court
every few minutes, so that prisoner, prosecutor, jury,
witnesses, officers of the court, and spectators could frat-
ernize at the bar of the neighboring saloon. When
morning came, "a drunken lawyer addressed a drunken
jury, on behalf of a drunken prosecutor, and, a drunken
judge having delivered an inebriated charge, a fuddled
verdict of acquittal was rendered."

At Nevada City, in 1852, a thief was sentenced by the
justice to receive twenty lashes: so he was tied to a pine-
tree and given his punishment before the court adjourned. Stories of equally summary judgment and execution are told of pioneer justices of the peace at "Piety
Hill" Camp in Shasta, and at camps in Klamath and
Butte.

In one very amusing case reported from Nevada
County, two alleged horse-thieves were brought before
an old justice of the peace whose fame for honest, original, and usually sensible decisions had gone abroad.
The friends of the two lawyers who conducted the case
had laid wagers as to which lawyer would make the best
speech; but of this the justice was, of course, kept in ig-
norance. The lawyer for the prosecution made out an
unusually clear case; but the defendants' attorney called
up a man from a neighboring camp and asked: "What
was the prisoners' character at the East where you knew
them?"

"It was good," replied the witness.

"Good character!" squealed the brusque and excited old justice. "Good character, when they have been proved to be damned thieves? That evidence won't do. They stand committed. — Sheriff, take them to jail." A shout went up from the assembled crowd, and all wagers were declared "off."

The early justices of the peace in Tuolumne County were endowed with the same miscellaneous assortment of judicial powers that we have noted in Nevada: in some respects the survival of alcalde powers was more complete in the southern mines, where those powers had always been more despotic.

Justice Barry of Sonora, successor of the last alcalde of that region, was a type of a large class. He had an advertisement inserted in the Sonora *Herald* of July 4, 1850 (the first issue of the first newspaper published in the mines of California) which read as follows:

"All persons are forbid firing off pistols or guns within the limits of this town under penalty; and under no plea will it be hereafter submitted to; therefore a derogation from this notice will be dealt with according to the strictest rigor of the law so applying as a misdemeanor and disturbance of the peaceful citizens of Sonora."

In the foregoing, "the judicious printer" had evidently corrected the orthography; but no printer could destroy the expressiveness of "derogation" and "strictest rigor." The following decision is given *verbatim et literatim,* and in the annals of frontier-justice documents it certainly deserves a high place. The affair which drew out this paper was a case in which the state was prosecutor, and a Mexican named Barretta was defendant. The trial lasted nearly two days, lawyers being engaged on both sides. Justice Barry, after several hours of study and reflection, returned his decision in the

form of a written document, still in existence. It reads
as follows:

Having investigated the case wherein —— Barretta has
bean charged by an old Mexican woman named Maria
Toja with having abstracted a box of money which was
buried in the ground jointly belonging to her self and
daughter, and carrying it, or the contents away from her
dwelling, and appropriating the same to his own use and
benifet, the supposssed ammount being over too hundred
dollars; but failing to prove posittively that it contained
more than twenty, and that proven by testimony of his
owne witness, and by his owne acknowledgment, the case
being so at variance with the common dictates of humanity,
and having bean done under very painful circumstaces, at
the time when the young woman was about to close her ex-
istance, the day before she died, and her aged mother the
same time lying upon a bead of sickness unable to rise or
to get a morsel of food for her self, and he at that time presenting him self as an angel of releaf to the poor and destitute sick, when twenty poor dollars might have releaved the
emediate necessitys of the poor, enfeabled, sick, and destitute old woman, far from home and friends. Calls imperi-
tively for a severe rebuke and repremand for sutch inhu-
man and almost unprecedented conduct, as also for the
necessity of binding him over to the Court of Sessions in the
sum of 500\frac{00}{000}$.

                    (Signed)   R. C. BARRY, J.P.
SONORA, NOV. 10, 1851.

Amusing as is this summing-up, this special pleading,
this honest indignation, and characteristic of the mining-camp justice as is the entire document, yet the
reader cannot but feel a sense of disappointment at the
outcome. One fully expects a sentence that shall fitly
punish the Barretta enormities. But Justice Barry recog-
nizes the rights of the newly established court of sessions — though evidently with a struggle — and he will

keep strictly within his powers as defined by state law. The court of sessions consisted of the county judge and two justices of the peace, and had original jurisdiction in all criminal cases except murder, manslaughter, and arson. Justice Barry was a member of this court. Sonora was in 1851 the county-seat of Tuolumne. In 1863 the sessions courts of California were abolished by a constitutional amendment.

From papers still in the Tuolumne County records, it appears that Justice Barry acted as town coroner, for which his fees were ten dollars in each case. Between October 20, 1850 and July 28, 1851, we have the following record of violent deaths: William Doff, Michael Burk, James Haden, and William A. Bowen, all murdered, "no clue to the perpetrators"; George Williams, suicide; William Bowen, hung at Curtis Creek, for killing A. Boggs; T. Newly, killed by an outlaw named Fuller, who made his escape; Leven Davis, "killed by a rifle-shot in a Jumping Claim Row"; two homicides decided to have been justifiable. Almost every document winds up with: "Justice fees ten dollars," or "Coroner's fees ten dollars."

One document (No. 997) in Justice Barry's court was a writ issued to the sheriff ordering him to summon parties charged with having jumped a town lot belonging to "one Donnalld," who "claims his rights as an American cittizen by claiming a writ to disposess them, and to have restitution according to law with appropiate damages for the imposission now about to be carried out against him by sutch high-handed and mercenary arrowgance on the part of aforesaid accused." [2]

---

[2] These records of Justice Barry's courts are taken from a very rare pamphlet, published at Columbia, Tuolumne County, in 1856, by Heckendorf and Wilson, and entitled a *Miner's and Business Directory*. It was lent me by the kindness of Mr. William G. Dinsmore of Oakland, California.

Many other stories of the early courts of justices of the peace might be told, but enough has been said to give some idea of their methods and powers. Calaveras, Stanislaus, Amador, El Dorado, and Tuolumne appear to have contained a large number of camps where these officers had more extensive powers than elsewhere.

The men who were chosen justices of the peace in these mining camps were often eccentric and illiterate, but as a rule their honesty and good judgment were unquestionable. They had the full confidence of the people, and were conscious of the responsibilities of their office. In many a town of the mining region the pioneers still remember their names with respect, and still smile over their eccentricities. One of them, when dying, left "all his money, after paying funeral expenses" (some five hundred dollars), to "the boys for a treat"; and it was duly spent in the saloons of the camp. Yet he is said to have dealt out justice with firmness and good sense: his official conduct was satisfactory.

The race of such "miners' justices" has disappeared; and the office has shrunk each year to lesser powers and narrower duties, until it is now only the smallest wheel in the complex judicial machinery of the commonwealth. But there is no doubt of the fact that socially the position held today by a justice of the peace in the old mining region retains something of its former prestige and dignity: the justice is often "judge" or "squire," terms that one seldom hears thus applied in the valley counties.

Chapter XVII. ORGANIZATION OF TOWN GOVERNMENTS BY THE MINERS

The nature of the town organizations adopted by the miners in a number of instances next claims our attention. As soon as a camp was thought to be "permanent" — that is, supported by rich mines, and by lesser and tributary districts — there was always talk of town government; perhaps from those used to the town councils of the Eastern states, perhaps from ambitious politicians. Sometimes the compromise that was made consisted in the election of a "committee of management," a council of three or five to attend to town affairs. Of fully organized town government, however, the best examples that the mines afford are those of Sonora and of Nevada City.

Mention has already been made of the struggle to obtain control of Sonora Camp in the days of '48, when an American alcalde was first chosen. The border-land position of the camp makes all its history interesting. Few of the mining camps offer material of equal value for our investigation. The Americans of Sonora and that vicinity were from the first outnumbered by the foreign population, and only united action saved them from being overwhelmed. There were but nineteen "white men," two of whom were Frenchmen, four Spaniards, and the rest English, Scotch, and Americans, in Sonora Camp in 1848: the rest of its population were Mexicans and Chilians. Before the close of 1849 the total population was five thousand, and the camp was ruled by Americans. The manner in which town organization then arose was entirely unforeseen and unpremeditated.

[197

As soon as the rainy season of 1849–50 set in, multitudes of miners, many of them Mexicans, were attacked with scurvy, owing to their exclusive diet of salt meat, since vegetables could be obtained only in small quantities, and at enormous prices. The resources of charitable individuals were evidently inadequate to cope with the evil, and it was proposed to organize and establish a town hospital. November 7, 1849, this idea took form in the creation of a town government, it being felt that everything had best be kept under one management. Mr. C. F. Dodge was then the alcalde of Sonora, and he was asked to act as mayor of the town. A council of seven members, five Americans and two Frenchmen, were elected to serve until further notice. They at once established a hospital, which was successfully maintained for more than six months, or until the ravages of scurvy were checked.

Expenses were enormous. Lime-juice cost five dollars a bottle, potatoes one dollar and a half a pound; canned fruits and all anti-scorbutics were twenty-fold the usual prices. Wages of servants were eight dollars a day.

The alcalde dedicated his official fees to hospital uses, and the citizens contributed largely; but the chief financial resource was soon seen to consist of the vacant town lots. The council, shortly after its organization, ordered a survey of the town, and had quite a number of new streets laid out. Up to this time, anyone who chose took possession of a vacant lot, with the understanding that no one was to occupy more than one such lot of a reasonable size. All the hillsides not claimed under the mining laws of the camp were unfenced and used as common pastures until thus taken up for building-purposes. The winding streets of the earlier portion of the town followed the base of the canyon, or the lines of old pack-mule trails on the hillside. Land had possessed no value, except as used; and no one had taken more than he needed, for that only involved the building of more brush or picket fence. But when the new council had streets laid out, and lots surveyed, it gave them a positive value. Seldom, if ever before, has an American town attained to a population of several thousand without a great deal of very lively land-speculation; but the miners of Sonora Camp had lived in blissful unconsciousness of that resource.

Just about the time the survey was completed, but before the town council had asserted any particular rights over outside lands, the first state legislature met, divided the state into twenty-seven counties — of which Tuolumne was one — and selected Sonora as its county-seat. Before the latter fact was known outside of the committee-rooms, one of the legislators wrote to a member of the Sonora town council, informing him that the county-seat question had been settled in favor of Sonora, and asked him to "take some of the boys, and secure possession of just as many town lots as possible," expecting, of course, to share in the profits.

The councilor was thoroughly indignant. He walked into town meeting that very night, with the letter in his hand, read it to the mayor and council, and offered a resolution, which was unanimously passed, that no one should be permitted to take up vacant lots, "because all such unoccupied lands do belong to this town in its corporate capacity." This action was promptly enforced. From time to time the lots were sold to the highest bidder, and the proceeds devoted to the town hospital.

When the county of Tuolumne was fully organized, it was found that the town government could have no legal existence without a special charter from the legislature. It was therefore disbanded; and, the office of alcalde having been abolished, the only officer to rule the town was the "miners' justice of the peace," the Justice Barry mentioned in the previous chapter. But a charter was procured; and under it, in 1851–2, a mayor, marshal, attorney, sheriff, treasurer, clerk, recorder, assessor, and seven aldermen were elected. This proved too expensive; and in 1855 the town government was simplified, under a new charter, to a board of five trustees, with merely municipal powers.

The early Sonora town-council experiment seems interesting chiefly because of its spontaneity of growth. Established to secure a town hospital, and relieve the alcalde of its extra duties, it at last took all the management of town affairs upon its shoulders; while the mayor, still acting as alcalde, decided disputes and criminal cases brought before him. The councilors received no salaries, and most of them could devote only their evenings to their official duties.[1]

Nevada City also had an experience of town government under the mining *régime*. The camp that in the spring of 1850 was only a collection of a few tents and brush huts, grew by August to a town of two thousand inhabitants; while within a radius of four miles a population of eight thousand men were at work, in a dozen or more lesser camps. On December 22 the *Alta California* called Nevada "a frost-work city"; for hundreds of miners had abandoned the region, and the town seemed in the last stages of ruin. In the spring of 1851 all mining interests revived, and the town soon recovered its former prosperity. Its enthusiastic citizens now pro-

---

[1] As illustrating with clearness the "political atmosphere" of the mining camps of 1850–1, the following instance deserves attention. Tuolumne County elected as one of its representatives a young man whose poverty was so great that, after he was chosen, the citizens of his district assembled, regardless of party, and voted him a gift of several hundred dollars to buy clothes, pay stage-fare to the capital, and live comfortably till he could draw his salary. He made the best of records, afterwards practiced law, and gained a competence.

cured a charter for a city government, and incorporated it on a liberal scale, providing for a mayor, marshal, clerk, recorder, and nine aldermen, including the "president of the council." They purchased a city hall, built a jail, and established a hospital; for here, also, miners were dying of scurvy.

But Nevada City had no common lots to sell, no taxes, and few license fees were collected; and the financial resources of the organization were soon at an end. By September the town government had run itself eight thousand dollars in debt, and a public meeting was called to consider the problem. The aldermen agreed to discharge all the city officials and suspend operations. Early the following spring, the state legislature repealed the charter. Some of the scrip issued by the city was never redeemed, because the very disastrous fires which occurred late in the gold era crippled its resources for some time. In 1853 the town was again incorporated, under a less expensive form of government.

Fifteen or twenty mining towns received charters and organized some sort of town government during the gold era. Weaverville, Shasta, Oroville, Grass Valley, Nevada City, Jackson, Placerville, and some places that are now but waste and almost deserted villages, organized on a liberal plan, so soon as the day of tents and rough shanties had passed. It must be remembered that a great deal of capital went into permanent investments in these thriving and energetic towns. Brick blocks, three-story hotels, stores, banks, and fine residences embowered in blossoms and surrounded by lawns were not infrequent long before 1856 in all the towns we have named. Population lessened as the mines decayed; and in many cases such investments proved unprofitable, or, indeed, nearly worthless. But the spirit of confidence that led miners to organize town governments so soon

was eminently praiseworthy. Some of the schemes of the
time were notable. A costly plank road between Grass
Valley and Marysville was discussed; plans for railroads
were made public; the toll-road system developed rapidly, and was very important; local improvements, town
halls, theaters, costly bridges, met with hearty endorsement. Unity of action, and sympathy of interests, gift of
early camp life, are peculiarly characteristic of mountain towns of the gold region, even at the present time.
The towns are but overgrown and permanently settled
camps. Nothing that is likely to happen will ever destroy this mining-camp atmosphere, that still pervades
such peaceful and orchard-surrounded towns as El Dorado, Auburn, Grass Valley, with the loyalty and earnestness, the strength and freedom, of their tent and
rocker period.

Chapter XVIII. THE DIFFICULTIES WITH FOREIGNERS IN VARIOUS CAMPS

The heterogeneous population of the mining region included a strange medley of races from the islands and shores of the Pacific, from the provinces of Mexico, and the countries of southern Asia. Outlaws, desperadoes, men who had long before flung defiance in the face of law and society, were far too abundant in this conglomerate mass. Difficulties with such foreigners were inevitable, and they only served to weld the Americans into a closer union. Sometimes, however, the Americans were unjust and overbearing, or were at least careless and indifferent to the rights of others. It is an old story, still told in the mines, that idlers and gamblers have often been known to "raise a stake" by a double collection of the foreign miners' tax from Chinese or Mexicans. The treatment of the early French miners, who, in 1849 and 1850, were forcibly driven from their claims in several camps, was simply outrageous; and the better class of miners did not always interfere to protect them against the bands of ruffians who desired their property. The filibustering expedition of Count Raousset to Sonora, with its romantic features and tragic termination, would probably never have occurred, had it not been for the attacks which drove so many Frenchmen from the mines.

As for the Chinese, there were large numbers of camps where none were allowed to work or hold claims at any time. They now find employment in many of the old and nearly exhausted gulches, working over the gravel, and often, it is thought, making quite valuable "finds." Their patience, perseverance, and industry are

[203

tireless. Even at the present time, however, there are camps within whose precincts no Chinaman is ever allowed to set foot. The local laws of Churn Creek District, Shasta County, as late as 1882, forbade any miner to sell a claim to a Chinaman or to give employment to one. The feeling is that so long as white races find it pays to work the district, they shall be allowed to do so; when they desert the camp, the Chinamen may, of course, take possession. In many of the camps of the flush period, however, Chinamen were allowed to hold and work claims, by paying their foreign-tax. It was the experience of American miners that many of the Chinamen were adept claim and sluice-box thieves; and to this fact the beginnings of the undoubted prejudice against them can be traced.

One of the cases where indignation against foreigners had much justification was during 1850 and 1851 in the southern mines. In June of the former year the collector appointed by the state to receive the "foreign miners' tax," then thirty dollars a month, arrived in Sonora. This sum had not been exorbitant in the newer camps, but in many cases men began to find it difficult to obtain so much. The foreigners, chiefly Mexicans, met, and denounced it, held public meetings, refused to pay a cent, and seemed so determined that rumors went abroad to the effect that armed resistance could be expected. The miners of the surrounding camps armed themselves and, to the number of several hundred, marched into the town, set a watch, organized patrols, and offered their services to the alcalde "for the preservation of peace and the suppression of crime." The Spanish Americans in Sonora and in several Mexican camps adjoining, or not over four miles distant, seem to have far outnumbered the tax-supporters, and there was every reason to expect a collision.

About this time many of the Mexicans left their claims and, retiring to the mountain fastnesses, became outlaws; so that, in a few weeks, robberies and murders were of almost daily occurrence. July 3 the citizens of Sonora met in public meeting to discuss "the public safety, and methods of self-protection." They resolved to organize a rifle company "of twenty-five men good and true"; they elected a captain and ordered him to raise his company at once and report to the new "court of sessions." They also chose a finance committee of three members and began to take subscriptions from different individuals and camps.

July 10, four Mexicans were discovered piling brush upon and burning the bodies of two American miners. They were arrested and hurried into Sonora. A crowd assembled; a jury was empaneled, and a judge chosen. The defense set up was, that the bodies had been lying there for several days, that the real murderers were unknown, and that it was the Mexican custom to cremate the bodies of the dead. But by this hasty and illegal trial — illegal, because the court of sessions was fully organized, and the case came within its jurisdiction — the prisoners were condemned. A *riata* was passed over the limb of an oak, and the trembling Mexicans brought forward to meet their doom. At this exciting moment Judge Tuttle, one of the bravest and best of the pioneers of that region, accompanied by Judges Marvin, Radcliffe, and other gentlemen, arrived. Judge Tuttle made a thrillingly earnest appeal, saying that now the county had law, had courts, and could not afford to disgrace its record. The prisoners were given up, and taken to jail by the town officers.

The next week district court and county court were both in session, and for the first time. Monday morning over eighty armed citizens of the town marched through the streets; and three hundred miners from "Green Flat Diggins," where the murdered Americans had been found, arrived to see the laws carried out in the punishment of the murderers. Every knife and revolver in every camp within a radius of a dozen miles was strapped to some stalwart miner's side, and either already in Sonora or on its way to that place. The assembled miners were assured that speedy and reliable justice would be afforded, and they prepared to remain till the end of the trial.

Rumors of an uprising in a Mexican camp three miles distant were so numerous that the sheriff, with a posse of thirty American miners, went thither, arrested one hundred and ten Mexicans, marched them to Sonora, and confined them in a corral until the next day, when they were cross-examined by an interpreter, and, proving their innocence, were released.

Tuesday was the beginning of the famous trial. Fully two thousand armed and excited men were in the streets of the town. There was much talk; but the resolution to support the law and abide by the decision of the court was steadily increasing in strength. Part of Tuesday and all day Wednesday the trial continued. "There did not appear a tittle of evidence against the prisoners, and the jury acquitted them." So, at least, runs the report of the newspapers of the time. And the crowd, ashamed, it may be, of their haste and eagerness for blood, signified their approval, and separated in silence.

Before the close of this eventful day, there were accounts of new outrages and murders. A public meeting was held, and Judge Tuttle was the speaker. He urged the necessity of active organization to arrest the progress of crime and secure the safety of citizens. The chairman of the meeting appointed a committee of safety, which called a mass-meeting to assemble four days later, and strengthened the town patrol.

Resolutions adopted at this mass-meeting were to the effect that —

"*Whereas,* The lives and property of Americans are in danger from lawless marauders of every clime, class, and creed under the canopy of heaven, and scarcely a day passes that we do not hear of the commission of murders and robberies:

"*Resolved,* That all foreigners in Tuolumne County, except persons of respectable character, be required to leave within fifteen days unless they obtain a permit from the authorities hereinafter named.

"*Resolved,* That the authorities referred to be a committee of three, to be chosen by the American citizens of each camp.

"*Resolved,* That all foreigners in this county (except such as have a permit) are notified to turn over their weapons to the committee, and take a receipt for the same."

The other resolutions provide for carrying this plan into effect. But the really dangerous men, the scattered Mexican outlaws, whose camps were in the mountain fastnesses, and hardly two nights in the same place, could not be reached by any such method; and it was not enforced except in a few camps where difficulties of an aggravated type had occurred.

The next year, an attempt having been made to fire the town, and an organized band of thieves having been discovered, a new vigilance committee was established, which was in session several times a day for three or four weeks; which punished petty crimes by whipping, and banished a number of suspected persons. This committee seems to have refrained from all excesses, and it turned over to the civil authorities the only man that was brought before its tribunal charged with a capital offense. When order was restored, the vigilantes disbanded, and left the regularly constituted authorities in full jurisdiction.

The "southern mines" furnish some of the worst cases of mob law, as well as some of the best examples of law-abiding, justice-seeking organization. The greatest number of difficulties with foreigners occurred there, and some of the worst quarrels over disputed claims were in those southern camps. It has been said by some observers that men were readier to resort to the arbitrament of the revolver in the southern than in the northern mines. If such were the fact, it would not be surprising; for gold-seekers from the Southwest and South predominated in those camps, as men from the Northwest and North did in the camps north of Placer County. Organization in the southern camps was under greater difficulties, but it seems to have been fully as complete and successful as in the more northern camps. Some of the most orderly of the southern camps were controlled by New England men, some by Georgians and Virginians. The steady evolution of society in these camps, out of the chaotic mixture of men of every race and characteristic, deserves our admiration; but a close study of the newspapers of the time, and the evidence of pioneers, convinces us that it is difficult for the American frontiersman to avoid treating the Mexican frontiersman with a sort of contemptuous defiance. Joaquin Murrieta, and his outlaw reign of years, were the natural result, not of deliberate injustice on the part of the American miners as a body, but of blameworthy carelessness that too often permitted the viler elements of the camp to enforce by actions their rude race-hatred of the "greasers." This tendency to despise, abuse, and override the Spanish American may well be called one of the darkest threads in the fabric of Anglo-Saxon frontier government.

Chapter XIX. THE FAMOUS SCOTCH BAR DECISION

THERE was a very remarkable example of the gold-seekers' methods of settling serious disputes which once occurred in the northern part of California. It fairly deserves to be termed one of the most important and interesting of litigations in the early history of the mines. In many respects it is even entitled to rank as the unique example of a higher type of organized effort to do the best thing possible under each and every circumstance than is shown in the history of any other mining camp of the period. The following brief account of the case rests upon the recollections of one of the most genial, generous, and intelligent of early Californians — Mr. Anton Roman, first publisher of the *Overland Monthly,* who spent sixteen months during 1850 and 1851 in several of the most successful mining camps in Klamath and Siskiyou. Upon his stories and recollections some of Mr. Francis Bret Harte's best prose work is founded; and they still afford a mine of invaluable material, literary and scientific.

Scotch Bar is rather indefinitely located by my informant as "in the Siskiyou-Klamath region." It was a highly prosperous camp, "booming," as the miners said; and the fame of its rich placers had already extended to Trinity, Shasta, and Butte, attracting traders, prospectors, and parasites of the camp. Exactly what local laws and local officers the camp had, we do not know; but probably much the same that were known to districts in the central part of the state. It is likely that they had elected a justice of the peace, allowing him to settle their disputes over boundaries and to keep a record of their claims. At least, so it appears; the camp had been peaceable, law-abiding, and contented; the miners had dwelt together in concord, much in the spirit of the Arcadian days of '48; and it was "a royally good camp to live in."

Some time early in 1851, a discovery of some very "rich gravel," or mining ground, was made, and made in such a way, also, that two equally strong parties of prospectors laid claim to it at the same time. There were about a dozen men in each party, and both groups were entirely honest in their belief of the justice of their respective claims. Each clan at once began to increase its fighting numbers by enlistments from the rest of the camp, till twenty or thirty men were sworn to each hostile assembly. The ground in dispute was so situated that it was best worked in partnership, and thirty claims of the ordinary size allowed in the district would occupy all the desirable territory of the new find. So there were two rival companies ready to begin work, and no law whatever to prevent a pitched battle.

It began to look more and more like fighting. Men were asked to join, and bring their bowies, revolvers, and shotguns. Men were even forced to refuse the honor, against their wills, because, forsooth, there were no more weapons left in camp. The two opposing parties took up their stations on the banks of the gulch; there was further and excited talk; at last there were eight or ten shots interchanged, fortunately injuring no one. But by this time the blood of the combatants was fairly roused; the interests at stake were very large; neither side proposed to yield; and the next minute there probably would have been a hand-to-hand conflict, except for an unlooked-for interference.

The camp, the commonwealth, the community at

large, had taken the field the very moment the first shot
was fired. Dozens and hundreds of men, five minutes before mere spectators of the difficulty, at once compelled
a parley, negotiated a truce, and urged a resort to legal
methods. The moment this compromise was suggested,
the combatants laid aside their weapons. They knew
there was no legal authority within twenty miles, and
not even in the camp itself any force able to keep them
from fighting; for persuasion was the only argument
used, and it is not supposable that the rest of the miners would have actually fought to prevent fighting. It
was a victory of common sense, a triumph of the moral
principles learned in boyhood in New England villages
and on Western prairies. "Men more thoroughly fear-
less never faced opposing weapons"; but the demand
for a fair and full trial in open court found an answering chord in every bosom. Both parties willingly agreed
to submit to arbitration; but not to the ordinary arbitration of the "miners' court," or of the "miners' committee," or of the "miners' alcalde," all of which we
have heretofore described. They thought out a better
plan, and adopted it after a few moments' discussion.

The rude and often biased jury of the camp was re-
pudiated by both contestants alike. None of the ordinary forms of tribunal known to the mining region
seemed to them entirely adequate to this momentous
occasion. They chose a committee, and sent it to San
Francisco. There they had three or four of the best lawyers to be found, engaged for each party; and they also
engaged a judge of much experience in mining cases. It
was a great day at Scotch Bar when all this legal talent
arrived to decide the ownership of the most valuable
group of claims on the river — claims that had been lying absolutely idle, untouched by anyone, guarded by
camp opinion and by the sacred pledges of honor, ever

since the day of the compact between the rival companies.

Well, the case was tried with all possible formality,
and as legally as if it had occurred within the civil jurisdiction of a district court. It is not reported in any of
the California law-books; but no mining case ever commanded better talent or elicited more exhaustive and
brilliant arguments. The lawyers and judge were there
to settle the case; the entire camp wanted it settled;
both parties to the dispute were anxious to find out who
the real owners were. In order to show the childlike
sense of fairness the miners had, we should mention
that before the trial began, it was arranged by mutual
consent that the winners should pay costs. To the losers,
it was sufficient to have failed to prove title to such rich
claims: they must not be made still poorer.

Now, in ordinary cases of camp rule there is often
too much compromise: one claimant gets less than he
deserves, while the other gets more. But in this justly famous Scotch Bar case there was in the end a verdict
squarely for one side and squarely against the other.
The defeated party took it placidly, without a murmur;
nor then, nor at any other time, were they ever heard
to complain. The cheerfulness of their acceptance of the
verdict was not the least gratifying episode of the famous trial.

"Ah! it was a great case," writes our informant, after an
interview with Mr. Roman. "The whole camp was excited
over it for days and weeks. At last, when the case was decided, the claim was opened by the successful party; and
when they reached bed-rock, and were ready to 'clean up,'
we all knocked off work, and came down and stood on the
banks, till the ravine on both sides was lined with men.
And I saw them take out gold with iron spoons, and fill
pans with solid gold, thousands upon thousands of dollars.

Ah! it was a famous claim, worth hundreds of thousands of dollars."

On the bank, along with these hundreds of spectators, stood the defeated contestants, cheerful and even smiling: it was not their gold, any more than if it had been in Africa. And the successful miners brought their gold out on the bank, divided it up among themselves — so many pounds apiece — and each went to his tent to thrust the treasure under his blankets till a good opportunity arrived for sending it to San Francisco.

The community capable of that Scotch Bar case was a community which could be trusted to the uttermost. Put it down on a desert island, and it would organize a government, pick out its best men, punish its criminals, protect its higher interests, develop local institutions; and soon, unless its natural surroundings forbade, there would be a healthy, compact, energetic state, with capital city, seaports, commerce, navy, and army. Put it down on a new continent, and it would eventually possess, control, and develop all its resources and energies; doing the work that Rome did for Italy, that the Puritans did for New England, and through New England for the United States. And if the evidence of travelers, of the pioneers themselves, and of the institutions they organized can be trusted, there were many such camps in California. The Siskiyou region did not monopolize that habit of self-control, of acceptance of the situation, of submitting questions to the best obtainable courts, and of abiding by their decisions. From Klamath to Colusa, from Siskiyou to Fresno, from Lake Bowman to Trinity Peak, manhood and honesty ruled the camps of the miners. Some were ruled better than others, but all were ruled well.

Chapter XX. SPORADIC ORGANIZATIONS — CASES OF MOB LAW

This portion of our subject would not be complete without some allusion to irregular and sporadic forms of miner organization, to burlesque meetings, to later forms connected closely with the earlier assemblages of "all the miners of the district," and, lastly, to cases of mob rule.

Rough and Ready Camp, in Nevada County, so interesting by reason of its simple and effective standing committee, or council, affords a valuable though eccentric example of independence. The township contains about a hundred and twenty-seven square miles, and was very prosperous in 1850, when a miner named Brundage conceived the idea of having a permanent and separate organization to be called the "State of Rough and Ready." He called a meeting evidently in dead earnest, and proposed the scheme; urging that none of them had voted for the state constitution, nor helped, through delegates, to make that instrument. About a hundred persons favored the plan, and for some time he continued to agitate its adoption; but the funny and absurd elements of the proposal so appealed to the miner's abundant sense of the ludicrous that the entire scheme disappeared at last, in a fit of irrepressible and Homeric laughter. It became a topic of conversation in every cabin, and beside every long-tom, for miles; but the State of California was good enough for the light-hearted, keen-witted miners.

A curiously burlesque assembly gathered together in Grass Valley in the winter of 1852–3, and is known in local history as "the Hungry Convention." The winter had been so severe that supplies were short: bacon and flour had once again risen to the prices of 1849. Miners could not work their claims, and were assembled in the town, spoiling for some enterprise or excitement. So a meeting was called, in dignified earnest, to consider whether the scarcity of provisions could in any manner be relieved. Everyone soon saw that, in the condition of the roads, there was nothing for it except patience: the merchants would secure supplies at the earliest moment possible. The meeting immediately degenerated into a wild burlesque. Speeches of the most desperate and communistic order were made, and hailed with shouts of laughter and applause. A duly elected committee reported, declaring war upon San Francisco, and their resolve to have supplies thence "peacably if we can, forcibly if we must."

The later history of the mining camps affords innumerable examples of the keen pleasure that the average American pioneer takes in public meetings, in resolutions, in committees, chairmen, and "big talks." He does it in sober earnest most of the time, but now and then he does it for the mere fun of the thing. The men of the mining region are even now, after all the changes of the past thirty years, a race of men peculiarly ready to assemble for free discussion, peculiarly apt to have debates in the district schoolhouse, to start arguments, and listen to stump speeches. The early training of miners' courts and of camp life has left its impress upon the people of the mining region. They differ from the people of the valleys as the mountaineers of Tennessee differ from the dwellers in the lowlands. But they have closer and better organization, a more abiding habit of seeking each other's counsel, of meeting in assemblies and of discussing their affairs, than ordinary mountaineers have. The life of the gold-seeker brings men closer together in their camps and districts, and creates links of town life, while the purely pastoral mountains still remain almost a wilderness.

Yet one must ask, in reviewing the subject of camp government: Did the machinery of justice set in operation by the miners never degenerate into the weapon and excuse of a mob? Were the innocent never punished, the guilty allowed to go free? Did not feverish excitement and unreasoning violence too often rule? What, after all, was the miners' court but an appeal to lynch law, as that term is now understood? Were not council government and alcalde government, scarcely less than the miners' court itself, based on the will of the mob, and liable to strange outbursts, fluctuations, and monstrosities?

We find, throughout the mining era, sporadic cases of true mob law; of men being hung without judge or jury, without fair trial, and perhaps without justification. Considering the population, these cases were scarcely more numerous than in the Western states today. Regularly organized miners' courts proceeded with great care, and gave the prisoner the benefit of every doubt. Those men who were killed by mobs were usually caught red-handed in the act. In one notable case a murderer was beaten to death before he was a hundred yards away, by pick-handles caught up hastily from a barrel in front of a store. In another instance the murderer was stoned to death, with more than Hebrew energy, before he could climb the steep banks of the ravine where his victim lay.

The men who had led in organizing miners' courts were the first to advocate their abandonment in criminal cases so soon as the county organization was possible, and were the first to oppose mob violence. In Ne-

vada County, in 1850, a man named Studley was falsely
accused of stealing a nugget worth three hundred and
twelve dollars from a miner; and the crowd seized him,
tied him to a tree, and proceeded to administer a flog-
ging. Judge Roberts and several friends were passing;
and they rushed into the crowd, released him, and soon
proved his entire innocence of the theft. At Rough and
Ready, in 1851, two miners, Stewart and Watson, rode
into the town one afternoon and saw a stranger being
led by a mob who purposed to hang him. They drew
their pistols, ran into the crowd, shouting: "You have
the wrong man: let go of that man!" organized a committee, secured a fair trial; and in an hour the prisoner,
who was accused of having stolen three hundred dollars,
was set free. Cases like these were not the work of camp
organization, but of the roughs and hangers-on of the
camp. And even the courts at that time awarded capital punishment for grand larceny.[1] "Law-abiding citizens from the first" is what Hon. A. A. Sargent calls the
old "forty-niners." Nearly always, when passion and
prejudice swayed the crowd, men of nerve and courage
were at hand to check the tendency to mob law. Sometimes it was the county or township officers who first in-
terfered; as at Beckman's Flat in 1852, when a miner
was accused by his partner of theft and was about to be
hung by the crowd when the county sheriff and the district attorney arrived on horseback and rescued the prisoner, who was proved innocent. Perhaps the worst case
of mob violence that ever occurred in the northern
mines was at Newtown Camp, in March 1852, where a
jury of twenty-four, a presiding judge, and a clamorous
crowd condemned on the merest suspicion of theft a

---

[1] For about a year, 1850-1, a law which permitted a jury to bring
in a verdict of death for grand larceny was on the statute-books. Under
this law, one man was hung in Nevada County, one in Marysville, one
in Sacramento, and one in Tuolumne County.

Negro and hanged him immediately. As late as September 1855 the Grass Valley community, roused to deep indignation against incendiaries, came near hanging a man who was found lighting his pipe near some unfinished buildings. In 1874 the mountain town of Truckee, infested by persons of bad character, was purified by a secret organization known as "601," which killed one person and severely wounded another, besides banishing quite a number.

Cases of lynch law occur from time to time in almost every frontier community, and too often in older communities also. But the difference between the true miner courts of the gold era, and such cases of mob law, is fundamental and generic. Lynch law, in the plain, everyday acceptance of the term, is the work of an association of men who have determined to violently expedite, or to suddenly change the course of, judicial procedure in one individual case. They announce no new laws, create no new system, add nothing whatever to the jurisprudence of the land. The moment the piece of work they were banded together to do is accomplished, they separate, and the association ceases to exist. They keep no records of their proceedings; the names of their leaders are sedulously concealed; and the regular officers of the law are often, in the discharge of their duty, brought into open collision with the lynchers. The utmost that may be said for them is that they often, though unintentionally, compel better administration of the laws; but, on the whole, lynch law is manifestly selfish, cowardly, passionate, un-American.

In every important particular the organizations of the typical mining camps which we have been considering offer sharply outlined contrasts. Camp law has never been the enemy of time-tried and age-honored judicial system, but its friend and forerunner. Axe of pioneer and pick of miner have leveled the forests, and broken down the ledges of rock, to clear a place for the stately structures of a later civilization. Rude mountain courts, rude justice of miner camps, truth reached by short cuts, decisions unclouded by the verbiage of legal lexicons, a rough-hewn, sturdy system that protected property, suppressed crime, prevented anarchy — such were the facts; and on these, frontier government rests its claims to recognition as other than mob law, and better than passionate accident.

Later illustrations of vigilantes' justice than those of California can readily be found. When, after a reign of terror almost unexampled in American frontier history, the tried and true miners and merchants of Montana organized during the winter of 1863-4 and in a few weeks hung twenty-four desperadoes and murderers, they performed a solemn duty laid upon them as American citizens. The present peace, order, and prosperity of that empire in the high Rockies, the "land of the silver bow," as its children love to call it, are the result of this acceptance of weighty responsibilities. Not until nearly a hundred persons had been waylaid, robbed, and slain in various parts of the territory by members of a fully organized band of assassins, did society accept the challenge, and supply the absence of civil authority with the military firmness of the Vigilantes. It is a matter of history that this organization, like that of San Francisco, never hung an innocent man, and that, when its work was done, it quietly disbanded.

In studying the nature of the mining camps of California we are irresistibly compelled to think of the whole race of American pioneers, from the days of Boone and Harrod to the days of Carson and Bridger; heroic forest chivalry, heroic conquerors of the prairies, heroic rulers of the mountain wilderness, ever forcing back the domains of savage and wild beast. Well did one of the most eloquent of American lecturers once exclaim:

"Woe to the felon upon whose track is the American borderer! Woe to the assassin before a self-empanneled jury of American foresters! No lie will help him, no eloquence prevail; no false plea can confuse the clear conceptions or arrest the judgment of a frontier court." [2]

When the pioneers of the newer West pushed into California, adding the leaven of such ideas to the mass of ancient Spanish civilization; when youth and energy from older communities of the Atlantic states, and adventurers from every land under the sun, joined in the famous gold rush of 1849 — the marvel of marvels is that mob law and failure of justice were so infrequent, that society was so well and so swiftly organized.

---

[2] Dr. John C. Lord, lecture on "Land of Ophir"; delivered in Buffalo, February 1849.

Chapter XXI. LOCAL LAND LAWS AND LEGISLATION FROM 1848 TO 1884

HERETOFORE we have considered only the appearance, general government, and criminal procedure of the early mining camps; but there is a broad field of special mining jurisprudence as yet comparatively untouched, and that, also, the field of most permanent value and greatest historical interest. The civil regulations of the miners were more varied and numerous than their criminal codes; and, reduced to their primary significance, they were "land laws of the frontier."

It is difficult to express the supreme importance of laws which govern the ownership of land. The social, economic, and political history of the human race has turned upon the pivot of changes in systems of land tenure; and here is a battle-ground of the future, as of the past. Nothing which serves to illustrate the workings of any land system, or of any method by which lands were actually held in any community, can ever be called irrelevant or worthless; for the entire field of study is so broad, and broken into so many angles, that each ray of light is needed. Earnest students have explained the prominent features of the land system of the ancient Germans, and have followed its history to the present time: they have told us how the primitive equality of the *Mark* system gave way in some remote past to the allodial system of village life, and how the holdings of lands in common yielded slowly to rights of separate ownership and inequality of estate, until thus the foundations of royal families and of feudal duties were laid. The ownership of land among the Saxons of the fifth century "was the outward expression, rather than the basis, of political freedom," so Mr. Stubbs tells us, "and in itself a usufruct rather than a possession." Landed property in England before the Norman conquest was of four distinct kinds — the *folk-land*, belonging to the nation; the *common-land*, held by communities, as it is still held under the Russian *mir* system, by the villagers of India, and in the pueblos of New Mexico; the *heir-land*, which had become partially alienated from the common-lands, and could pass by will, perhaps by purchase, with the consent of all the members of the community; lastly, the *book-land*, with its full and separate ownership, under a grant from king and witan. At last the hereditary freemen of the township became the tenants of the lords' manor, and the modern system of individual ownership of land was ultimately developed.

Now, the study of the mining camps of the Far West reveals the presence of primitive Germanic ideas more clearly in their land laws than in any other department of their jurisprudence. The rights of the individual over land were strictly subordinate to the rights of the camp, for use was made the proof of ownership. Then, also, the legislative enactments of the mining camp clustered with peculiar force about the central question of land tenure; and a large body of laws was thus created, setting forth with great exactness the size of a claim, the conditions under which it could be held, the circumstances which would work its forfeiture, and the methods of settling disputes in reference to its possession. Moreover, the establishing of district land laws led inevitably to meetings of the miners of many districts, who harmonized their diverse district codes into one which should be binding upon all the miners within the county — a still further step in institutional progress.

The claims of each district were numbered and recorded, and their size was according to local regulation. The miners' meeting, when sitting to decide upon questions of this sort, was in fact like a local legislature, or a committee of the whole. It decided how many claims a person could hold; how much work he had to do upon each one to retain possession; what forms of conveyance were requisite; what relative rights and duties the owners of adjoining claims had; what constituted abandonment of a claim; in what manner riparian rights could be secured and maintained; lesser regulations about water-supply; rights of, or restrictions upon, aliens in the camp; and hundreds of cognate subjects. It could levy assessments for general or particular expenses of the camp as a body corporate, and could at any time adopt such new regulations as seemed desirable for preserving and protecting private rights. And these powers of the miners' meeting, or of committees, or officers appointed by them, lasted long after the state was organized.

In each new district the framing of local mining laws became the most important legislative duty of the miners. The laws of the hundreds and thousands of camps that grew and decayed in the Pacific coast region, differing though they did in many particulars, all agree in recognizing discovery and appropriation of mineral property as the source of title; and development by use and working as the condition of continued possession. This acceptance of the law of equal ownership in the gifts of nature deserves more than a passing notice. Probably every man in the gold region had been educated in the doctrine of individual ownership of land; yet this instinctive return to first principles, this adoption of the ancient idea of "free mining lands," common to all as once the woods and fields and pastures of

England were common, will ever prove an attractive theme for students of historical and social topics.[1]

That mining claims should become a subject of speculation, of sale and purchase, of transfer from owner to owner, seems to have been foreign to the views of the earliest placer-miners of California; and in some camps a man who sold his claim could not take up another. But it was not long before claims were everywhere acknowledged as real-estate property, held by "miners' title"; and the process of perfecting minor regulations went on with great rapidity. For all this, the miners' sole and all-sufficient plea was "imperious necessity"; and so thoroughly did they accomplish the work of creating a land law that until a comparatively recent date the titles to all the mining property of the newer states and territories has rested upon these local laws and miners' enactments.

We therefore proceed to a minute analysis and comparison of the land laws and consequent regulations by which mining camps were and are governed. We have taken the laws actually enforced for a period of years in

---

[1] Mr. Henry George, in his *Progress and Poverty*, writes:

"For the first time in the history of the Anglo-Saxon race, these men were brought into contact with land from which gold could be obtained by the simple operation of washing it out. . . . The novelty of the case broke through habitual ideas, and threw men back upon first principles; and it was by common consent declared that this gold-bearing land should remain common property, of which no one might take more than he could reasonably use, or hold for a longer time than he continued to use it. This perception of natural justice was acquiesced in by the general government and the courts; and while placer-mining remained of importance, no attempt was made to overrule this reversion to primitive ideas. . . . Thus no one was allowed to forestall or to lock up natural resources. Labor was acknowledged as the creator of wealth, was given a free field, and secured in its reward. The device would not have assured complete equality of rights under the conditions that in most countries prevail; but under the conditions that there and then existed, — a sparse population, an unexplored country, and an occupation in its nature a lottery, — it secured substantial justice."

many of the leading camps of various states and territories; sometimes abbreviating their enactments, but
omitting nothing essential to a full understanding of
the subject. The laws in their complete form are usually concise, well-worded, and clear in meaning. In some
cases they were evidently drawn up by lawyers; in other
cases, by persons of good general education, but as evidently ignorant of law. The period to which they refer
ranges from the summer of 1848 to the close of 1884.

As regards the important question of the number of
mining districts which have been governed by local laws
of their own devising, the United States Reports on
Mineral Resources state that in 1866 there were over
five hundred organized districts in California, two hundred in Nevada, and one hundred each in Arizona,
Idaho, and Oregon. There were, perhaps, fifty each in
Montana, New Mexico, and Colorado. Here is a total of
more than eleven hundred camps in the Far West, as
late as 1866. Since then the number of districts has di-
minished in the older mining regions, and increased in
the newer ones; but state and national legislation has in
a great degree restricted the field for local enactments.
The number of actual placer camps in California during
its "flush period" is not recorded; but it could not have
fallen below five hundred, and probably exceeded that
figure. Mining was carried on vigorously in twelve large
counties, and to some extent in three others.

The first camp to which we shall invite the attention
of our readers was situated five miles from Sonora, the
county-seat of Tuolumne County, California, and was
in one of the richest ravines known to the early miners.
It bore the homely appellation of "Jackass Gulch" from
the days of its first organization in 1848, but its earliest
laws were not committed to writing. A square of ten
feet of ground "often yielded ten thousand dollars from

the surface dirt," and ten feet square was the maximum size of the claim allowed. After 1851 the laws, as adopted and enforced by the camp, were as follows:

"First, That each person can hold one claim by virtue of occupation, but it must not exceed one hundred feet square.

"Second, That a claim or claims, if held by purchase, must be under a bill of sale, and certified to by two disinterested persons as to the genuineness of signature and of the consideration given.

"Third, That a jury of five persons shall decide any question arising under the previous article.

"Fourth, That notices of claims must be renewed every ten days until water to work the said claims is to be had.

"Fifth, That, as soon as there is sufficiency of water for working a claim, five days' absence from said claim, except in case of sickness, accident, or reasonable excuse, shall forfeit the property.

"Sixth, That these rules shall extend over Jackass and Soldier Gulches, and their tributaries."

The greatly lessened value of the mining ground is shown by the size of the claim being increased from ten feet square to one hundred feet square. Requirement of claim-notice renewals during the idle season was common in most of the camps, unless a miner lived upon his claim. Thriving though the camp was in 1851, still crowded with miners by the hundred, it was rapidly exhausted; and in 1856, according to the Tuolumne Directory of that year, had only twenty-two voters.

Springfield District, whose leaders were men of New England, trained in town meetings and local self-government, was able to create an organic law far superior to that of the preceding camp. Its laws were adopted in written form at a mass-meeting of the miners, April 13, 1852; were revised August 11, and again December 22,

1854. After describing the boundaries with great minuteness, the preamble (of 1852) declares:

"That California, is and shall be, governed by American principles; and as Congress has made no rules and regulations for the government of the mining-districts of the same, and as the State legislature of California has provided by statute, and accorded to the miners of the United States, the right of making all laws, rules, and regulations that do not conflict with the constitution and laws of California, in all actions respecting mining-claims; therefore we, the miners of Springfield District, do ordain and establish the following rules and regulations."

There are sixteen articles. The size of the claim is fixed at one hundred feet square, no person under any circumstances to hold more than one; work must be performed upon it at least one day out of three during the season for mining. Claims must have substantial stakes at each corner, and must be "registered and described in the book of the precinct registry," to which the owner or owners shall sign their names. Several persons, each owning a single claim, may concentrate their labor upon one of those claims.

Disputes are to be referred to a standing committee of five miners, or to any member or members of this committee, as arbitrators; or a miners' jury may be summoned. Each member of the standing committee shall in each case be paid two dollars for his service. It is easy to see that a single arbitrator was in many cases entirely satisfactory for both disputants. The laws proceed to further define the process of arbitration. The head of the committee is to be sworn by a justice of the peace, provided such an officer be appointed in this mining district, and is to administer the oath to his associates and to the witnesses. In some of the early camps the al-

calde administered this oath "to honestly arbitrate" to
his deputies. The decision arrived at in either jury-trial
or arbitration must be received as conclusive and binding upon the parties thereto, and be deemed and considered final in all such cases. Either party may compel
the other to come to trial, by giving three days' notice
of time and place. Costs shall be paid in the same way
as in magistrate's courts. Disputes over water-privileges
are especially named for arbitration.

Thirty days' desertion of a claim during the working-
season results in forfeiture without remedy.

Article thirteen reads as follows:

"No person not an American citizen, or where there is a
reasonable doubt of his being entitled to the privileges of
an American citizen, shall be competent to act on any arbitration, or trial by jury."

The next article provides that "companies which go
to great expense running tunnels" are allowed "two
claims for each member of the company." The first code
of "tunnel-claim laws" adopted in this region was several years later — January 20, 1855; and it defined a legal tunnel-claim as "one hundred feet along the base,
and running from base to base through the mountain."

Article fifteen provides for the election of a district
recorder, who is to have fifty cents for recording the
title of each mining claim.

The last article provides that "all claims held by foreigners who have failed to secure their State license"
shall be forfeited. This was to aid in the enforcement of
the State Act of April 13, 1850, passed at San José. A list
of the unnaturalized foreigners was to be kept in each
county. The recorders of the different districts usually
aided in its preparation.

These laws of Springfield District show plainly how

much dependence was placed upon the arbitration —
or, as the Spanish termed it, the *conciliación* — plan.
We shall find equal care in this regard in many other
districts. Springfield is said to have been the first district
in the Sierra Nevada that built a church before it built
a gambling-house. It has remained an orderly, flourishing, and energetic community since the days of its first
organization.

Jamestown District, settled in August 1848 by Southern and Western men, was regulated by miners' meetings assembled every six months, and sometimes special
meetings held to consider particular cases. In 1853, several persons having attempted to pass unpopular laws,
the miners held a rousing assembly, repealed "all previous laws, of every sort whatever," enlarged the boundaries of the district, adopted the usual standard size for
claims — one hundred feet square — and declared that
all claims secured under former laws were publicly acknowledged as legal.

In this district, within three days from the time of location, a claim must have a ditch one foot wide and one
foot deep cut about it; notices must also be posted, and
stakes driven at the corners. Failure to work a claim
within six days after the mining-season begins causes its
forfeiture. A miner can hold other claims only upon
proof of purchase. Miners shall have the use of water
from the ditches according to the date and situation of
the location of their claims.

An important clause is to the effect that miners may
dig up any farm, or enter within any enclosure, by giving the owner security that they will pay all damages
inflicted. In no case, however, shall they dig within
twelve feet of a building, or obstruct the entrance. Payment of damages meant only compensation for growing
crops and improvements.

Shaw's Flat District required the claim to be "in one lot, and square in form." A notice would hold a claim for ten days after the season began. Part of a company could not "hold the claims of a whole company during the absence of a part of its members." Claims in "deep diggings," where pay-dirt is twenty-five feet or more below the surface, may be laid over without work from December 1 to May 1 if they are well defined by marks and notices and recorded in the district register, which shall always be open to inspection. For some years there was an annual meeting to revise the district law, besides several meetings called by the chairman when it seemed desirable.

The laws of Sawmill Flat, Brown's Flat, Mormon Gulch, and Tuttletown districts present many points of resemblance. Two of them begin by saying:

"*Whereas,* This district is deficient in mining laws and regulations, and disputes have arisen: therefore we, the miners of —— district, in convention assembled, do pledge ourselves to abide by the following laws."

In three of the districts named, the laws provide that the discoverer of new diggings shall be allowed to hold twice the usual amount of mining ground.

The laws of Sawmill Flat provided for a committee of three persons, elected by the miners, to call meetings of all the miners of the precinct, either to enforce the laws, or whenever, for any reason, they deem such meeting necessary. The arrangement for arbitration is as follows:

"Whenever any dispute shall arise respecting claims or water-privileges, each party shall choose two disinterested persons; the four thus selected shall choose a fifth; and the five thus selected shall hear evidence according to the laws of this precinct."

The law of Brown's Flat provided that "all arbitrators shall be appointed by the committee" of three which then governed the camp. They were to be five in number; and were to "examine all disputed territory, hear testimony, and decide accordingly." This governing committee of Brown's Flat was elected "to hold office until superseded." It was the court of appeals in cases where the arbitrators failed to satisfy the parties. Its members were paid "wages for summoning the arbitrators, and for other duties"; but the amount is not named.

The Tuttletown laws say: "No person shall hold more than two claims, either by purchase or otherwise." They also provide that anyone who destroys a notice or claim-stake shall be fined not less than five dollars nor more than fifty dollars. Notices of discontinuance of work on deep claims during winter are to be posted in some convenient and public place in the district. Tuttletown was so named because Mr. Tuttle, afterwards first county judge of Tuolumne, built and occupied the first cabin there. The miners of the district organized a water-ditch company in June 1851, and carried their enterprise to a successful termination. Mormon's Gulch and Brown's Flat were first mined in 1848. Sawmill Flat became a great resort of Mexicans, Chilenos, and Peruvians, in 1850–1. Joaquin Murrieta, the notorious outlaw, was a monte-dealer there in 1852.

Yorktown, Poverty Hill, and Chili camps had similar laws; and these pioneer camps were organized early in 1849. The first and last were settled by Mexicans and Chilenos, but Americans soon ruled all three. At Yorktown, within a month after its discovery, the Americans and other miners met, "and elected P. Cutrell for alcalde, and Mr. Rochette (better known as *'Frenchy'*) for sheriff," under whose administration the district was

governed well and quietly. The alcalde system was retained in its main features until superseded by county
organization. In these districts the miners assembled
to pass legislative enactments; but they only referred to
size of claims, and possession thereof, not in any case to
"arbitration," because that was one of the alcalde's most
important duties. The camp laws limited "deep diggings" to claims "of thirty feet square on unworked
ground, and to fifty feet square on previously worked
ground." A claim of sixty feet square was set apart for
the discoverer of a placer. A claim must be worked
within three days after staking it out and placing a
claim-notice upon it. Ten days' absence in the working-
season subjects it to forfeiture and throws it open to re-
location as an abandoned claim.

Chinese Camp also had an alcalde system; and its
laws, passed at a miners' meeting September 17, 1850,
were in operation for many years, without change. The
alcalde elected at this meeting had "power to decide
upon all disputed claims"; his fees were fixed at three
dollars for his decision, and a dollar a mile for traveling
expenses from the central point of the camp to the disputed claims and return. The legislative enactments of
the district confirmed all claims "as made by the present settlers"; confined all future claims to "twenty feet
square"; and required a ditch two feet wide and one
foot deep to be dug about each claim, "unless prevented
by rock or clay," in which case the removal of the surface soil and the erection of cornerstones were considered sufficient. In this district Isaac Caps was the first alcalde, and S. E. Chamberlain the first sheriff.

The laws of Gold Spring Camp presented some features differing materially from those of other districts
in the region. Claims must be worked one day in every
seven. Arbitrators were "earnestly recommended," but

not made essential. Miners were compelled to make a new road if they destroyed the old one in their operations. This is often a bone of much contention in mining districts. Gold Spring Camp had a population of about eight hundred, and was ruled in 1850 by an alcalde; in 1854 the population was five hundred. The gold of this district minted more than that of any other of the early diggings.[2]

Columbia District was always a large and important one, including several lesser camps, such as Yankee Hill, where many fine nuggets, one weighing twenty-three pounds, were found in the early days. The history of this camp was highly characteristic of the mining era. March 27, 1850, five prospectors — all New Englanders, and three, at least, from the woods of Maine — camped beside a gulch and tested the gravel. To their delight, it was found that they could make eight or ten ounces a day to the man, though water was very scarce. They named the place Kennebec Hill, and proceeded to wash gravel with their utmost energy, knowing that others would soon find the gulch. Within a week another prospector joined them, and succeeded in taking out two pounds and a half of gold-dust during his first day's work. Within thirteen days from the time the five original prospectors camped on Kennebec Hill, there were eight thousand miners in the new town. Many gamblers came with the crowd; and at one time there were not less than a hundred and forty-three monte and faro banks in operation, the funds of which were nearly half a million dollars. Men were often seen to turn a card for three or four thousand dollars, sometimes for several times as much. It was one of the most rapid devel-

---

[2] Gold-dust, which at first passed at uniform rates in the mines, and in San Francisco, at one time falling to seven dollars per ounce, was carefully tested by the express companies; and they found that it ranged in value in different localities, from $14.50 to $19.50 per ounce.

opments of a great and prosperous mining camp ever known in California.

Within a fortnight the need for some system of government was manifest. A public meeting was called to talk up the subject; but nothing in particular was done except to give the camp a name — Columbia. Two or three days later, at another and much better attended mass-meeting, Major Sullivan was chosen alcalde, and allowed fees collected from registry of mining claims. June 1 the new state tax on foreigners was enforced, and the population decreased greatly. In 1852, 1,229 votes were polled in the district.

The points in the mining law in Columbia which differed from those previously noted were as follows: Full regulations respecting "dry diggings," and gold-bearing earth thrown up in heaps to remain till winter rains, such heaps being held to be private property; full regulations to prevent persons from diverting water flowing naturally through gold-bearing ravines, from its course, without the consent of all parties interested; the presence on a claim of tools, sluice-boxes in condition for use, or other mining machines accepted as *prima-facie* evidence of occupation.

There are no regulations for arbitration, that being one of the alcalde duties in this camp. The alcalde appointed jurors in civil cases when asked for. The other officers were sheriff and recorder; and the sheriff chose his own assistant, or selected a posse whenever thought necessary. Recorder-fees were at first a dollar, but afterwards fifty cents.

But far the most important sections of the Columbia District law were as follows: "Neither Asiatics nor South-Sea Islanders shall be allowed to mine in this district, either for themselves or for others." "Any person who shall sell a claim to an Asiatic or South-Sea Is-lander shall not be allowed to hold another claim in this district for the space of six months." "None but Americans, or Europeans who intend to become citizens, shall be allowed to mine in this district, either for themselves or others." These laws were in full operation in 1856, when Columbia had more than five thousand inhabitants.[3]

Montezuma Camp, Tuolumne, allowed "three squares, of a hundred feet each," to constitute a surface claim; a hundred and fifty feet in width was a "tunneling-claim"; a hundred feet wide by three hundred feet long was a deep-sinking claim. All shaft-claims must be recorded within one week after location, and must receive three full days' labor each week. The recorder was elected "for one year, and until his successor is chosen, unless dissatisfaction occurs": then the miners of the district "may call a special meeting, and by a two-thirds vote declare said office vacant, and proceed to elect his successor." Arrangements are made for an annual meeting, called by the recorder. His fees are a dollar for recording each claim, and a dollar for each arbitration. He presides over the arbitration court, which consists of two miners chosen by each of the disputants. If either party refuses to choose arbitrators, the two others and the recorder shall decide; and their decision is final.

Jacksonville Camp allowed for a claim fifty feet in width on the river, and extending from the center of the stream to the adjacent mountain; in the small ravines three hundred feet constituted a claim, one hundred and fifty feet on the flat, and sixty feet in certain

---

[3] In 1854 the town was incorporated. In 1855 the miners were anxious to aid the progress of a water-company's ditch; and three hundred or more of them took their picks and gave several weeks' work to the enterprise. This company, in ten months, constructed forty-four miles of canal and fluming, and supplied twenty-five square miles of mining ground.

deep diggings. Fifteen days' idleness in the working-season destroyed claim-rights. In Garote District fifty yards up and down the creek were allowed, and seventy-five yards on neighboring gulches.

In 1856 the mining laws of French Camp, Stanislaus County — then called La Grange — contained the following, after providing for arbitrators: "In the event of any of the disputing parties not acknowledging the decision, then the miners of this district will assemble, and compel said party to recognize the umpire's decision."

The Sweetland mining district, Nevada County, was organized in 1850, claims then being thirty feet square. Two years later the privilege was increased, and claims of eighty by a hundred and eighty feet allowed. In 1853 the miners met, and subdivided the district into three; and different regulations were adopted in each. North San Juan, one of these districts, and long the great hydraulic-mining center of California, provided, in its earlier code, for "one claim by location, and an unlimited number by purchase. The claim-notice must be renewed every thirty days, unless obviated by the daily presence of the owners or their representatives." An expenditure of five hundred dollars in prospecting or opening up a claim secures it for two years. A recorder was to be elected annually by the miners, with the usual fees; and each sale or transfer was to be placed on record within a week.

Pilot Hill, Calaveras County, passed laws about 1855, to the effect that each "gulch-claim" should be a hundred and fifty feet long and fifty feet wide; each "surface-claim," two hundred feet by a hundred feet; and each "tunnel or shaft claim" should be a hundred feet in width, and extending through the hill. On the last class of claim, work to the value of twenty-five dollars per week is required from each company. "Occupation and use" are required of the owners of the other species of claims.

New Kanaka Camp, Tuolumne County, allowed, in 1858, "creek-claims" of two hundred feet in width, and from bank to bank; also "gulch-claims," of one fourth that size; and "bar or flat" claims, of twenty feet in width and fifty feet in length. Work must be done "one full day in three, unless the owner is sick or on a jury." On this point the law of a little Trinity County camp in 1854 said with grim humor: "and a physician's certificate is needed"; there being at that time but one or two medical men in the county, and none at all in that particular camp. New Kanaka furthermore ordained that each miner might hold one claim by pre-emption, and one by purchase, but no more. The Chinaman was shut out; "not allowed to own, either by purchase or pre-emption." All disputes were left to three arbitrators, who "must be paid at the rate of three dollars per day for their time." One curious item was, that the elected recorder should number each claim registered, and himself attach to a claim-stake, in the presence of witnesses, a piece of tin bearing that number. The laws of Copper Cañon District, Calaveras County, were similarly exact on this point, requiring the recorder to visit each claim and examine its bounds.

One of the most remarkable instances of definite regulation of the "legal representation" of miners at all meetings was that afforded by Brown's Valley Camp, Yuba County. The miners of this place appear to have been sufficiently energetic; for we find them, early in 1853, assembling, and repealing a "previous arbitrary and oppressive set of laws to-day revoked by common consent." They met again August 8 and resolved:

"That each claim shall be entitled to a vote in the miners' meetings of this district by the proper owner, or may be represented by a power-of-attorney from the proper owner, specifying the object of that power, and its limitation."

These meetings were semi-annual, and claims not represented were declared to be forfeited. This code was in full force until 1864, and many of its provisions lasted until a few years ago.

Examples of kindred regulations might easily be quoted from the laws of placer camps in California. We have before us notes from pioneers upon the codes of Cherokee, Nimshew, Bangor, and Forbestown camps, in Butte County; of La Porte, Hungarian Hill, and Grizzly Creek, in Plumas County; of Port Wine, Forest City, Monte Cristo, and Downieville, in Sierra; of Slabtown, Tiddletown, and Volcano, in Amador; of Mount Ophir, Blue Gulch, Peñon Blanco, and Horseshoe Bend, in Mariposa; and of many other camps once famous, but now lost in oblivion. None of them present important variations from those already described. The laws of Mud Springs, El Dorado County, as late as 1863 provided for the use of arbitrators; and Georgetown Camp in 1866 clung to many of the primitive forms. In 1868 each district in Placer County had its own rules, and little uniformity was manifest.

A claim-notice posted in San Andreas District, Calaveras County, in 1862, was as follows:

NOTICE. — The Undersigned claims this ground for mining-purposes, known as the Robert McCall Claim, being a deep or shaft claim, and bounded on the northwest by the Gilchrist & Cornwell Claim, & on the southeast by the Plug-Ugly Claim, and he intends to work it according to the laws of the San Andreas Mining District.

(Signed)   WILLIAM IRVINE.
JOHN SKOWALTER, *Recorder,* Aug. 18.

Another notice found by the writer over a deserted claim in Shasta County a few years ago was of a much more primitive type, and read after this fashion:

NOTIS: To all and everybody. This is my claim, fifty feet on the gulch, cordin' to Clear Creek District Law, backed up by shotgun amendments.

(Signed)   THOMAS HALL.

A few quotations from other claim-notices that were in their time accepted as "good and sufficient" may perhaps be pardoned. One man wrote: "TAKEN. — This is my Honest Claim of Ten feet each way." Another: "To MINERS. — Look further. Respect my claim stakes driven by the rules of Douglas Bar." Still another grew combative with his "CLAME NOTISE. — Jim Brown of Missoury takes this ground; jumpers will be shot." Some camps prescribed the proper size for the "notice," and that it "should be written in ink"; others required it to be "painted or cut on wood"; and it was often boxed, or otherwise protected from the weather. One camp described the legal claim-stake as four feet high and five inches square. There was evidently a great deal of honest attention paid to details of this sort.

All the laws we have hitherto described are those of placer districts where mines were worked at comparatively little cost, except when tunneling was required. But the first quartz-mining began in 1850–1, near Oroville; and the necessity of having laws by which to regulate the size of quartz-claims, and their tenure, was at once manifest. The miners soon took steps to enlarge their code and extend it to county jurisdiction. Late in 1852 the miners of the various districts of Nevada County held a meeting at which there was a full discussion of the subject and a free interchange of opinion. A committee was appointed to report at another meeting,

called for December 20, at which time a convention of
the quartz-miners from all the districts of the county
was held at Nevada City. The laws they adopted at this
meeting were still in force in 1881, and have served as
the regulations of all the quartz-mining of that region.
They carry the force of law, and have sustained various
judicial decisions. The jurisdiction of these laws was
declared to be "over all quartz mines and claims in Nevada County." The extent allowed to a claim was "one
hundred feet on the ledge," including "all dips, angles,
and variations," or, as later laws read, "all dips, spurs,
and angles." The discoverer was entitled to two hundred feet. The marking and staking of a claim must be
done within three days, and the recording within ten
days; and within thirty days, work to the cost of one
hundred dollars, or twenty full days' labor, must be
done, and the same repeated each year to hold the
claim, until a company is fully organized, and has a
mill worth five thousand dollars "contracted for in good
faith." The recorder may then give the company a title-
deed to the mining property, guaranteeing possession
and proprietorship forever. Failure to comply with this
provision about the quartz-mill ultimately works forfeiture. Any citizen of the United States can take up one
quartz-claim, and may also hold "all that he purchases
in good faith." The regular county recorder of Nevada
County was to serve as mining-recorder in the matter
of quartz-claims. His deputy was to be elected by the
district.

The Sacramento County miners assembled in 1857
and passed laws that were in force until after 1868.
They required twenty days of work per year on each
quartz-claim; the work when done "to be examined by
the recorder of the local district," and a certificate
given. Whenever a quartz-mill worth five thousand dol-

lars has been contracted for in good faith, the company is entitled to receive a permanent title-deed to the lands from the county recorder. Only citizens, or "those who have declared their intentions of becoming so," are entitled to hold claims. About 1855 the miners of Sierra County formed a code, requiring work to the value of a hundred dollars per year, allowing "foreigners who pay their miners' tax" to hold claims, and limiting the size to two hundred feet on the lode, by a total width of five hundred feet. In 1858 the miners of Tuolumne County assembled, and made uniform laws for the quartz interests.

At the present time most of the counties in the state have held "miners' meetings," at one time or another, to regulate the interests of the owners of quartz-lodes. There was a plan suggested some time before 1860 for a state convention of delegates from all the mining districts of California, to formulate a general mining code; but the need was not sufficiently felt at that time, and Congressional action a few years later rendered such a convention useless. No student of the life of the camps, however, can deny that the full possibility of a state-wide organization existed.

Enough has been said to show how exact and definite were the California camp laws which regulated property rights. They dealt in a practical manner with river and placer mine-rights, with cement and deep-gravel rights, with tunnel and water-ditch rights, and with leads, ledges, and lodes of every description. These laws thus created became the common heritage of the entire body of American miners, and were in a few years adopted by camps in far-distant regions.

In the Territory (now the State) of Nevada, Virginia City District adopted its first code September 14, 1859. Quartz-claims were to be two hundred feet on the

lead, including "dips, spurs, and angles." Three days of
work were required each month. Each quartz-claim was
to receive a name, and to be recorded within ten days.
"Hill and surface" claims might be a hundred feet
square. "Ravine and gulch" claims were to be a hundred feet wide, and extend "from bank to bank." Claims
of every sort were forfeited if not worked. The recorder, elected for one year, should hold his book "subject to inspection," and should post copies of the district laws in two conspicuous places within the camp.
Reese River District in 1864 extended twenty miles
north and south. Its laws were numerous and definite.
A written notice signed by fifty claim-owners could at
any time be called to depose the recorder. That officer's
fees were one dollar; and he could appoint deputies,
since the district was so large. The written application
of twenty miners would at any time call a special district meeting.

The regulations of the famous Alder Gulch in Montana, the richest for its size that has ever been found,
were adopted in miners' meeting, September 16, 1864,
and consisted of two articles in thirty-one sections. They
were drafted by a select committee chosen by the miners in open "folk-moot"; and were approved in like
manner, clause by clause, after free discussion. The officers of the district were president and secretary. We
have now passed beyond the utmost limits of the alcalde
and the "government by committee" systems. A written
application of five claim-owners was sufficient to call a
special meeting. Much space is devoted to riparian
rights, laws of trespass, and flume ownership. Tailings
must not be permitted to accumulate on another miner's land. Bar-claims, creek-claims, hill-claims, and other
classifications are mentioned. Three days per week is
the work-requirement. All in all, it is a highly organized

and definite code, and shows the influence of experienced miners from Idaho, Colorado, and California. The growth of Montana was marvelous. Before 1867 twenty-five hundred mineral lodes were prospected and recorded in the territory. In Confederate Gulch, in 1866, three miners are said to have taken out four hundred and forty-one thousand dollars from a claim three rods square. Montana miners in 1865–70 founded dozens of new camps, even as far north as the Saskatchewan.

We must turn to the later manifestations of law in single mountain camps, organized by Americans. In the autumn of 1883, away up in the northern corner of Idaho, the Cœur d'Alene placers were discovered, south of Lake Pend d'Oreille, in fastnesses of the North Rockies that romance and tragedy have made their own. The mining excitement that followed was enough to revive the most vivid memories of 1849. From New Mexico, Arizona, Colorado, California, hardy prospectors by the hundred started for Spokane and Rathrum, the gateways of the region. They surged in from Minnesota, from Puget Sound, from Winnipeg and the Assiniboine, from British Columbia, and the wheat-plains of Dakota. Mining papers devoted columns to the new mineral belt. Some doubted, some warned, some condemned; but still the gold rush continued.

On Pritchard and Eagle creeks, Shoshone County, Idaho, the first local laws of the new mines were adopted. It was early in March 1884, in Cœur d'Alene mining district; and the "by-laws," as the code is termed, show clearly how the ideas of the earliest camp laws have since been modified.

The greatest of changes is in regard to size. All locations on lodes of quartz, conforming with the United States mining laws of 1872, are to be fifteen hundred feet in length by six hundred feet in width. Placer-mine

claimants are allowed twenty acres, so located that neither length nor breadth shall exceed eighty rods.

Section three of the thirteen sections of this code in-
troduces a new factor. It provides that authorized agents
for capitalists may locate and record claims for them.
Such a thing was seldom or never heard of in old California days; but, as all the world knows, the professional prospector and locator for others is one of the
most prominent figures in Western camps. "Give me a
grub-stake, an' I'll locate ye a dozen good mines," is the
appeal made to each "tenderfoot," as a greenhorn is af-
fectionately termed.

Section four allows persons to locate one claim on
each gulch where mineral is found, and also to hold
other claims by purchase. This also marks the growth of
the interests of capital and large moneyed enterprises.

Section five regards assessments and claim-work. The
first year after location, one hundred dollars of work
must be done; and twenty dollars each month between
June and November of subsequent years. Necessary
work, such as making roads or trails, building cabins or
other improvements, is allowed to count on the assessment at the rate of five dollars per day. Between November and May — the winter season in that trying
climate — all claims are "laid over"; that is, no work is
needed to retain their ownership.

The section relating to claims being recorded allows
fifteen days from the date of location, evidently because
the district is so large, and the mountain trails so steep
and difficult to travel over, that a shorter time would in-
convenience prospectors who wish to make long tours
before returning to camp.

Riparian rights, as always, receive careful attention.
The oldest locations have first privilege of water; but
cannot control the surplus, nor waste the water, which

is in every case to be returned to the channel of the stream for the use and benefit of those below.

The regulation regarding company organization permits miners to unite their claims for purposes of working them better, and to perform "all their assessments on one claim." This is extremely similar to the usage in the early California mines.

The principle of arbitration is still preserved in almost its pristine exactitude. All difficulties are to be settled thus: "Each disputant to be allowed an equal number of arbitrators; and, in case of a tie on the decision, said arbitrators shall have power to call in an assistant."

Claims located prior to the adoption of these laws are endorsed. Changes in the district laws require the written application of at least twelve miners, and ten days' notice of a meeting posted in three or more conspicuous places in the district. Changes between the 1st of November and the 1st of June are illegal and void. Previous unwritten laws are repealed. The officers are a claim-recorder, and a chairman, who has power to call miners' meetings.

Now, these rules made for the government of the Idaho camp of 1884 have many resemblances to the laws of the California camps of 1848. The thirty-six years between have only caused those inevitable changes that come from the increased capital invested in the business, and from the more definite state and national legislation upon the subject. The generic relationship of the earlier and the later codes is manifest. American frontiersmen are ruling in Idaho, as once they ruled in California.

In October 1884 a New York gentleman who had been present at a miners' meeting, Eagle Creek Camp, in the Cœur d'Alene, only a few months before, told the writer that the impression he received from it was that it was the true descendant of the New England town meeting, and illustrated local self-government of the highest order. Another gentleman recently returned from a journey to the head-waters of the Peace River, the Frazer, and the Saskatchewan, about the gigantic precipices of Mount Hooker, says that the prospectors there were forming camps, and adopting their local codes concerning "claims," their primitive land law. The process is going on at this hour in the narrowing realm of the pioneer, to the north and to the south, along the ridge of the continent; and the close of this century will not see its completion.

Chapter XXII. THE EARLY RELATIONSHIPS OF MINING AND AGRICULTURAL INTERESTS

THE student of mining camps and their local customs and enactments soon becomes interested in a class of problems peculiar to those districts of the West that are situated upon government lands. He finds that class-difficulties have arisen between farmer and miner; and that not merely camp law but the decisions of the state courts have taken abundant cognizance of this fact. These interests, naturally helpers, he finds at times opposed to each other; and he can trace the sources of many recent lawsuits to early local legislation.[1]

Several of the district laws quoted in the preceding chapter recognize the duty of "restoring roads destroyed in mining operations," and protect a few feet about a building so that it shall not fall, nor slide into the gulch. At this point these local rules stop: arbitrators must decide the amount of loss in each individual case.

As a matter of fact, the mining-interests were in those days held to be altogether predominant in importance

---

[1] Among the important decisions of early state courts which deal with the relations of miner and agriculturist are the following: Hicks *vs.* Bell, 3 Cal., 227; Irwin *vs.* Philips, 5 Cal., 145; Stoakes *vs.* Barrett, 5 Cal., 39; McClintock *vs.* Bryden, 5 Cal., 97; Tartar *vs.* Spring Creek Mining Company, 5 Cal., 398; Conger *vs.* Weaver, 6 Cal., 556; Burdge *vs.* Underwood, 6 Cal., 45; Nims *vs.* Johnson, 7 Cal., 110; Martin *vs.* Brown, 11 Cal., 12; Burdge *vs.* Smith, 14 Cal., 380; Henshaw *vs.* Clark, 14 Cal., 460; Smith *vs.* Doe, 15 Cal., 100; Gillam *vs.* Hutchinson, 16 Cal., 153; Coryell *vs.* Cain, 16 Cal., 573; Lentz *vs.* Victor, 17 Cal., 271; Fremont *vs.* Seals, 18 Cal., 433; Rogers *vs.* Soggs, 22 Cal., 444; Ripley *vs.* Welch, 23 Cal., 452. For mining-debris cases, Woodruff *vs.* North Bloomfield Mining Company, opinions of Judges Sawyer and Deady, printed in San Francisco journals of second week in January 1884.

over the agricultural interests, over the entire gold-bearing area. Law was made by the miners, for the miners; and this meant in practice a disregard of agricultural interests that seems unjust and short-sighted, until we have analyzed its causes and comprehended its reasons. Nominally, we may remark, the district rule in early days, and the decision of state courts afterwards, was, that full damages must be paid; in practice the obtaining of a fair compensation was often difficult.

At an early date the state courts of California decided that "agricultural lands, though in possession of others, may be worked for gold"; that "the right belongs to the miner to enter on public mineral lands, although used for agricultural purposes by others, and whether enclosed, or taken up and entered under the Possessory Act." "All persons," it is held, "who settle for agricultural purposes upon any mining-lands in California, so settle at their own risk"; they do it "subject to the rights of the miner, who may at any time proceed to extract any valuable metals which he finds in such lands." At a later date, some cases of great hardship and loss having occurred, it was decided that "the enclosure about the house and outbuildings of a farmer is protected against entry." The burden of proof was thrown upon the miner, who was required to justify his right to enter upon and work a farmer's land by showing that the land was public land, that it contained mineral, and that he proposed to occupy it for the *bona-fide* purpose of mining; and he must pay for the growing crops destroyed by his operations.

The state passed an act, April 20, 1852, providing that persons using public lands for pasturage or agriculture might bring action for damages against miners who enter upon said lands, but must not interfere with their operations. An act of April 25, 1855 protected "growing

crops, buildings, and other improvements" in the mining districts; but closes with: "Nothing in this Act shall
prevent miners from working any mineral lands in the
State after the growing crops on the same are har-
vested." Decisions under these acts were numerous. In
every case the right of the agriculturist to use and enjoy
public lands was considered inferior to the right of the
miner when gold was discovered in the land. The government would issue no patent to a pre-emption claimant upon mineral lands who claimed it for agricultural
purposes. Mere entry and possession gave no right to
the exclusive enjoyment of public mineral lands. "The
mines of gold and silver are as much the property of the
State, by virtue of her sovereignty, as are similar mines
in the hands of private proprietors"; and the state has,
therefore, the "sole right to regulate and govern these
mines." Growing wood and timber on public lands "belong to the prior appropriator." No person, under pre-
tense of holding land as a town lot, can take up and enclose a tract of mineral land in a mining district, as
against persons who afterwards enter on the land in
good faith to dig gold, and who do no injury to the use
of the premises as a residence or for business purposes.
Decisions like these, and many of a similar nature, help
us to understand the completeness of the early mining
rights.

The license granted by the state to each and every
miner allowing entry upon land for mining-purposes,
as we have amply shown, was restricted to the public
lands. No person could enter upon agricultural lands
held by a United States patent, and most of the farms
in the mining counties of California are at present so
held.[2] In cases where the land has never been "with-

---

[2] See the famous case of Boggs *vs.* Merced Mining Company, 14
Cal. Rep., 279, in which Chief Justice Fields gave the decision.

drawn as mineral land," but, on the contrary, has been
classed by the Surveyor-General as "agricultural public
lands," the burden of proof rests on the mineral claimant. Within the last year the Secretary of the Interior
has rendered a number of decisions upon controversies
of this character, in some cases overruling the decision
of the commissioner of the Land Office. He has decided,
in regard to placer mining on small, unnavigable
streams, that it is well settled that such places "may be
appropriated; and that, as to the water, the locator ob-
tains only a usufruct in it"; and granted a patent to a
claim in the bed of Bear River, California. Local laws
are allowed great weight in such decisions in the territories.

The foregoing illustrations only serve to emphasize
the predominance of the mining interests during the
gold era, when all the lands of the Sierra region were
unsurveyed; when there was no farm in the mining
counties that miners could not condemn and mine out,
paying for only the actual damages done. The fairest of
gardens, the thriftiest of vineyards, the most fruitful of
orchards, one and all were liable to be destroyed without remedy by the early placer-miners. The gold-seekers
could, and often did, sluice away roads, or cut them
across by channels impassable for years, undermine
houses, wash away fertile land, move towns to new sites,
and tear the old location down to bed-rock with torrents
of water. There are towns in the mining region that
have been twice or thrice thus removed; there are others that have been "tunneled," and "coyoted," and
"drifted," until "caves" and "breaks" are of not infrequent occurrence in the midst of streets or town lots.

But it has not been destructive always, this endless
onslaught of the miners upon rock and hillside, vale and
cliff. Lands have as often been created as others have

been ruined; barren beds of rock have often been filled up to the very brim with rich hillside soil, the alluvial deposit of ages, and so turned into gardens of magnificent beauty and exhaustless fertility. Farmers on mountain streams in the early days have more than once found that the mud-laden waters from mines above them brought added fruitfulness to their soil. Many persons have occupied adjoining tracts for mining and for agriculture, and have used water first for gold-washing and then for irrigation. Though the pre-eminent rights of the miner over all public lands sometimes worked hardship, yet the full recognition of these rights was the only logical conclusion of early California society; and the only wonder is that so few serious difficulties occurred in the gold period, over this difficult problem.

The earliest authenticated case of forcible entry upon fenced-in property used for agricultural purposes of which we have an account occurred in Grass Valley in the spring of 1850. There was in all the mountain land no more lovely and fertile spot than this valley when the placer-miners began work there and stripped its soil to the bed-rock along the wonderfully rich ravines; there is no lovelier spot today, when the restoring hand of time and the labor of loyal home-builders have embowered it in gardens of unsurpassed beauty; it is one of the fairest and most prosperous of the long array of mining towns, once mining camps, that nestle in the Sierra foothills, or rest in its pine-clad canyons.

But in 1850, when Grass Valley was the "camp," two men fenced in a natural meadow. Here they could annually cut two heavy crops of hay, which was worth eighty dollars per ton; they counted upon receiving at least four hundred dollars per acre that year. However, before a month had elapsed, a prospector climbed the brush fence, sunk a shaft through the soil, struck "pay gravel," and in less than twenty-four hours the whole hay-ranch was staked out in claims of fifty feet square; and, as tradition reports, the ravaged proprietors, through neglect or inability, did not obtain a single claim. The tract was not property, in the miners' definition. The possessors had fenced it, subject to the risk that there might be mineral there. They ought to have prospected it for themselves first, and whispered the secret thereof to their intimate friends: so the sturdy, red-shirted, blue-overalled miners said.

In 1851, it is said that two miners began to sink an exploration shaft in Main Street, Nevada City, nearly in front of the office of the South Yuba Canal Company and in the business center of the town. A sturdy merchant came out and expostulated with them, but was promptly told that nobody had made any law against digging down to bed-rock and drifting out the streets, and they proposed to try it. "Then, I'll make a law to suit the case," said the irate and energetic citizen, himself an ex-miner. Walking into his store, he came out with an army revolver and by its persuasive presence established the precedent that Main Street, at least, was not mining ground. Of course, this was an extreme case. A jury, or a miners' court, would probably have decided to exempt Main Street from exploration, as more valuable for business uses. But in the lesser towns of the mining region permanence did not exist. Nothing was sacred: all rights were subject to the claims of the miner. Many a case occurred where the entire town was moved to an adjacent spot, and every inch of the soil on which it stood was sluiced away from grass-roots to bed-rock. In many other cases the miners thought it better to tunnel underneath and work out the layers of rich gravel as best they could; though this sometimes

caused disasters, and buildings slid from their foundations with the crumbling soil during winter rains.

As regards the destroying of roads by miners, an instance which came under the writer's observation may
serve to illustrate the custom. Nine miles of well-built
mountain road connected a village of two hundred inhabitants with the county-seat. Though there was no
district organization remaining (in 1878), its influence
was still strong. Along the river-bed, filled twenty feet
deep with the wash and debris of the mines of 1850,
were rich spots, neglected by those careless, hasty pioneers. About a dozen men spent their illy-paid days in
making experiments here and there, trying to find one
of these unspoiled, unrifled bits of a placer. Two of
these prospectors sank a shaft at the edge of the gravel,
five or ten feet from the county road, and "struck it
rich." They worked a few days and found the pay-streak
extended into the hill; they cut a rough and barely
passable wagon-road through the dense thicket, a hundred feet higher up the slope, and in a week had torn
out fifty feet of the road, leaving a chasm twenty feet
deep. Farmers, merchants, county officials, passed by,
swore at the climb, told them to hurry with their work,
and asked how much they meant to clean up, but never
hinted that the proceeding was illegal or unjustifiable.
A few weeks passed, and the small, irregular piece of
virgin ground overlooked by the early miners was swept
clean, yielding enough, it is said, to pay for a well-
stocked farm in the Sacramento Valley. The two miners tapped a ditch that passed by on the hillside, far
above them, hired the use of the water, and sluiced
earth, rock, and bushes down into the chasm until it
was full to the brim, ready, when fairly settled down, to
form a good foundation for the county road again.

Countless stories might be told to exemplify the supreme position of the miner in early California. But there was little abuse of that supremacy. Once admit that the highest use of the soil was to yield gold, and the rest follows as a matter of course. The great majority of the early farms and orchards were planted on soil that was guiltless of containing gold in paying quantities, and so remained undisturbed. In one case a miners' court decided, when a small orchard of four-year-old apple-trees had been mined out, that the land was worthless; but that the trees, which had been brought overland from Oregon, were worth fifty dollars apiece, fruit being then excessively high-priced in the mines. They had not yet borne fruit, but the owner received twenty-five hundred dollars for them. We have heard of several instances where men who paid high prices for possessory claims to agricultural lands made extensive improvements; and, the lands being entered upon for mining-purposes, no equivalent damages could ever be obtained. In Placerville we were shown a bit of meadow which in 1881 had been mined out five or six times, as it receives the rich wash from mines above and the soil from the hillsides. Pieces of waste and worthless bed-rock, swept clean by the pioneers, have often been restored and made into beautiful and profitable vegetable-gardens, clover-fields, and fruit-orchards, simply by the process of washing the rich surface soil of the hillside down into the hollows, by using the hydraulic method.

As a rule, in the mines, agriculturists and miners lived together in harmony in those early days. The profits of vegetable-growing, hay-raising, etc., were so great that the man who tilled the soil often made more than did the man who washed out gravel; and their unity of interests has been so well recognized that in the long struggle between the valley farmers and the miners, over the debris question, which has now passed into history, the farmers of the mining region often helped to support the miners through their thoroughly welded-together organizations.

Of that great struggle, which has been to all intents and purposes a suit between valley counties and mining counties, it is yet too soon to speak, for a generation must pass away before its results are manifest. But it will always rank as one of the most important judicial decisions ever made in an American state. The calculations of engineers were that since 1876 a hundred million cubic yards of gravel, sand, and clay had been washed into the Yuba and its tributaries; that in 1880 some 15,220 acres had been seriously injured by these "slickens" deposits; and that six hundred million cubic yards yet remained to be removed. The steady shoaling of navigable rivers and bays was also charged to the mining detritus. It was testified that prior to 1862 at least thirty thousand miners worked the Yuba and its branches. The citizens of the valleys brought many suits of a representative character; and between 1877 and 1884 the issue was fought with the best legal weapons, and funds were raised on both sides by means of associations. The question was *sui generis:* the agricultural interests of the lowlands were pitted against the hydraulic-mining interests. The state supreme-court decision of January 7, 1884 was that private rights could not be encroached upon under guise of "miners' customs," even in districts where the statutes recognize the validity of such local laws. The maxims of the common law in reference to water-rights were fully sustained, and a perpetual injunction granted against the miners "unless they can so mine as not to injure the valleys." The rights of miners to use places of deposit for "tailings" and other mining debris, substantially supported by earlier decisions, were thus subordinated to agricultural interests; and only the alternatives of "drifting" out the rich gravel, or of impounding, satisfactorily to the courts, the hydraulic debris, have been left the miners. The hidden wealth of the pliocene river-channels is so great that many portions of them will pay for working, even by these more expensive methods; but the early predominance of mining over agricultural interests, granted by local law, is now a thing of the past.

The time is not far off when the varied agricultural possibilities of the old mining region will be recognized as second to that of no territory of equal size on the Pacific coast; and when the population supported by agricultural and horticultural pursuits within those famous mining districts whose laws we have studied, and whose early organizations we have described in the previous chapters, will be greater than that of those camps in their "flush times." The land, every acre of it, will pass under full private ownership, held by government patent; and the mineral in the land will belong to the dweller thereon. Indeed, the railroads and various large corporations now hold a great part of the lands in this mineral belt, once entirely public lands. The timber is being removed, the iron is being smelted, the valuable stone-quarries worked; in some places colonies of settlers are planting orchards and vineyards, orange-groves and olivariums, using for irrigation the water of mining-ditches cut by the labor of the energetic pioneers of '49, enlarged and extended by the vast associated capital of later years. The future of the mining region used to be a favorite subject of conversation with the late Mr. B. B. Redding, one of the foremost nature-students on the Pacific coast, one of the noblest and most generous of men, the friend and associate, all his life, of the pioneers, founders, and leaders of the state. He used to say that Italy, Spain, and southern France, all combined, would some day seem poor in comparison with eight or ten counties of the mineral belt of California, whose resources in horticultural directions were simply incalculable. The work done in that region during the past five years has gone far towards justifying Mr. Redding's bold prediction.

Chapter XXIII. DECISIONS OF CALIFORNIA AND OTHER COURTS RESPECTING LOCAL LAWS AND CUSTOMS

THE miners' local land laws, as we have heretofore seen, rested on the proposition that the soil was all government property, and that the nation allowed them the use thereof, under a possessory title, even though they should never wish to purchase it. Digging gold was early declared to be "a franchise from the government, and free to all." In this faith American miners developed the system we have been studying in notes from the laws of different camps. But the hundreds of important mining-litigations that occurred during the gold era of California preserve in their dreary wastes some precious bits of local history, like diamonds in the sea-sands. Law is the great shrine-builder, after all. The wrecks of old systems, the superstitions of forgotten races, the customs of perished kingdoms, are frozen in this iceberg of law, sealed forever in its translucent prison-walls, like mammoths in the ice of the Siberian tundras; or, if we choose, we may use a gentler simile, and call law the amber of the Baltic, making precious each bit of ancient life entrusted to its care.[1]

---

[1] Among the important cases in the California Reports referring to "local laws and customs" are the following, besides many others: People *vs.* Naglee, 1, 238; Hicks *vs.* Bell, 3, 219; Mitchell *vs.* Hagood, 6, 148; Davis *vs.* Butler, 6, 511; Fairbank *vs.* Woodhouse, 6, 433; Sims *vs.* Smith, 7, 148; McKeon *vs.* Bisbee, 9, 137; Packer *vs.* Heaton, 9, 568; Jones *vs.* Jackson, 9, 237; O'Keiffe *vs.* Cunningham, 9, 589; Clark *vs.* McElvy, 11, 154; Waring *vs.* Crow, 11, 366; California *vs.* Moore, 12, 56; McGarrity *vs.* Byington, 12, 426; Jackson *vs.* F. R. & G. W. Co., 14, 22; Merritt *vs.* Judd, 14, 64; Brown *vs.* '49 and '56 M. Co., 15, 160 and 20, 198; Clark *vs.* Duval, 15, 85; Edmond *vs.* Chew, 15, 142; Roach *vs.*

We find that because the early miners of California, in their plain, effective, and untechnical system, had made use the only basis of ownership, they also ordained that the same piece of ground could be occupied and owned by different persons at the same time, providing it was required and held for different purposes. If one man held a placer-claim for placer-uses, and another miner discovered a quartz-ledge on the same tract, it could be recorded and held without any interference from the placer-miner. If there was also an unclaimed spring or stream of water on the same tract, it could be taken up, or claimed, for mining-purposes, by still a third prospector; and these three men might long continue to use and enjoy the profits of their separate interests in the same small tract. Ground taken up for mining could be again taken up for fluming purposes. Riparian rights were possessory, and subject to much the same rules that governed the holdings of mineral lands; neither party claiming absolute ownership.[2]

The state courts recognized as legal mining claims those held by local law and customs, and also those held by actual occupancy of government lands. But the size of claims must not be unreasonable: even where no local law exists to limit them, it must conform to the general usages of miners. The customs of miners in the definition of quartz ledges are entitled to great if not controlling weight. Proof of similar customs in other districts besides that in which a claim is located is not improper.

Gray, 16, 387; English vs. Johnson, 17, 107; Atwood vs. Fricot, 17, 37; Prosser vs. Parks, 18, 47; Gore vs. McBrayer, 18, 582; Logan vs. Driscoll, 19, 623; Table M. T. Co. vs. Stranchan, 20, 198; Copper Hill M. Co. vs. Spencer, 25, 18; Martin vs. Solambo, 26, 527; St. John vs. Kidd, 26, 263; Hess vs. Winder, 30, 349; Stone vs. Bumper, 46, 318; Shay vs. Ryan, 46, 33. Also California Legislature, Act of April 14, 1860; Act of May 17, 1861; and Act of April 4, 1864.

2 "Surveys, notices, stakes, and blazing of trees, followed by work, . . . give title to unclaimed water." Kimball vs. Gearheart, 12 Cal., 27.

Subsequent mining rules of a district have been accepted as valuable evidence to aid in determining prior rights. The entire mining code of a district must be considered, not merely a portion of it. The state courts waived the right of inquiry into the "regularity of the modes in which these local legislatures or primary assemblages act. They must be the judges of their own proceedings. It is sufficient that the miners agree, whether in public meeting, or after due notice, upon their local laws, and that these are recognized as the rules of the vicinage." [3] Consonant with this is the decision that the authority of "mining customs" is to be allowed to take precedence of written district laws which have been disregarded or long neglected. What gives district laws their authority is not their mere enactment, but the obedience and acquiescence of the miners following upon that enactment; and a custom in itself reasonable and generally observed ought certainly to take precedence over a generally ignored district written law. The moment a district law falls into disuse, it is void. This question has been held "one of mere fact, for the jury to determine"; and similar in nature, recognizing the will and intention of the miners' assembly, is a decision that "although mining laws were passed on a different day from that mentioned in the notice calling the meeting, they are not invalidated. It is sufficient that the miners agreed when they did meet. The regularity of their local meetings is not to be questioned."

Controversies must be settled by the customs and usages of the "bar" or "diggings" embracing the claim in question, whether such customs be written or unwritten. Miners have the right to prescribe rules governing acquisition and divesture of title to claims, and their ex-

---

[3] Gore *vs.* McBrayer, 18 Cal., 582.

tent, subject only to state laws. But mining rules must not limit the number of claims that a person may acquire by purchase, nor prevent prospectors from locating mines for others.

No acts are required of the miner other than use of his property in accordance with local laws. He need not live on his claim (though government land could not be held for agricultural purposes unless used as a homestead by the claimant), nor need he build upon it, nor cultivate it, nor enclose it. His title is fundamentally different from that of the agricultural settler. And it has also been decided, that the right the miner has possessed since 1848 to enter and mine upon government land carries with it the right to whatever else is needful, such as use of water and of wood. It includes the right to build, to make a home, to plant orchards and gardens. But fences are not necessary for the miner: the defining of his boundaries by district monuments is sufficient. He still keeps his homestead, not by agricultural pre-emption, but by a miner's possessory title, and as a privilege attached to the ownership of his claim.

It was decided by the Colorado courts that not until compliance with district rules had been attacked was any proof of such compliance required; that if the district, for instance, made "notices" and "prospect-stakes" sufficient without registry, it is taken for granted, without proof to the contrary, that the local law is obeyed.[4]

In Montana, as in California, it was decided that the rights of ownership vested in a person, under the rules of a given mining district, are not affected by a change in the district boundaries: the old rules still govern as regards size, but not as regards method of working.[5]

In the old California camps, as we have seen, the oral

4 Sears vs. Taylor, 4 Colorado Rep.
5 King vs. Edwards, 1 Montana, 236.

conveyance of a claim was sufficient. Until 1860 the validity of such oral sales was fully sustained by the state
courts, which had previously held that writing was not
necessary to vest or to divest the title; which title is in
the government, and the right to mine is in the local
custom. A transfer may as well be by simple possession
as by deed. All miners' claims, under local law, to public mineral lands are to be regarded as titles; but the
right passed by a bill of sale, without seal and without
warranty, is only a possession, and is subject to a superior right.

The penalty of forfeiture fixed by camp laws if a certain amount of work was not performed has been amply
sustained by the courts. A person who had abandoned
his claim was not allowed to reassert his former interest to the prejudice of others. In questions of "abandonment," the intention governs. The rule, custom, and
usage of the district must be open, plain, notorious, so
that the miner leaving his claim knows that his action
is tantamount to an intention of abandonment. If a
miner attempts to hold more than local custom permits,
any other miner can take possession of and work the
surplus portion, and the injured party cannot recover
damages. The term "forfeiture of rights," as used in
mining customs, has been decided to mean "the loss of
a right previously acquired to mine a particular piece
of ground, by reason of neglect or failure to comply
with local rules and customs." Forfeiture reopens a
claim to immediate location by a new owner. But in
the absence of any custom or local regulation of the
given district on the point, the right of property in a
claim is not nullified by lack of diligence in working it.
According to recent decisions of the Secretary of the Interior, it is not necessary to require miners relocating a
lode to furnish positive and complete proof of its aban-

donment by a former locator. The fact that such abandonment was alleged in the notice of location and published in the manner and for the time required by law
is thought sufficient, provided that no adverse claim is
presented. Full recognition of the force and authority of
local laws is nowhere more evident than in the state-
court decisions regarding abandonment of claims.

Those special rights granted to discoverers of, and
first locators upon, new placers receive encouragement
from state decisions, which ruled that "the owner of the
oldest location on a stream or cañon-bed may dam up
the cañon to work his claim, even though it floods other
claims the owners of which are *damnum absque in-
juria.*" Ordinarily each person mining in the same
stream is "entitled to use, in a proper and reasonable
manner," both the channel of the stream and the water
flowing therein. According to good law and reason, miners were forbidden to deposit the waste gravel, or "tailings," on other men's claims.

As regards actual work done upon a claim, the local
laws have been sustained and liberally interpreted by
state courts. Work on adjoining land to construct roads;
drains and improvements necessary to development of
the mines; efforts made to procure machinery, as the
hauling of the same; starting a tunnel, though at a considerable distance, to run into the lead or deep gravel-
bed — these and similar labors are termed "work" in
the eyes of the law; such acceptance being in fullest ac-
cord with miners' local legislation.

Mining claims having been recognized as property,
and the course of local enactments being to give their
ownership the permanence of real estate held under
United States laws, we find that in 1861 those provisions
of the law exempting mines from taxation were repealed. "The interest of the occupant of a mining-claim

is property liable to taxation, and to being taken and sold under execution."

We have previously seen how great a monthly tax was levied upon foreigners in the early mining days. By 1861 the tax, once thirty dollars per month, had been reduced by successive state enactments to four dollars. The tax-collector of the county was then authorized to sell at public auction, on one hour's notice by proclamation, the mining property of any person refusing to pay such tax. Americans connected in any way with foreigners in working mining ground were held liable for the amount of license of each such foreigner. This tax upon foreigners was held to be only a license-fee, and its imposition not contradictory to the powers of Congress. And "the State alone can enforce the law which prohibits foreigners from working mines without a license": other miners could not take the law into their own hands and trespass on such claims.

The mass of printed material relating to the decisions of district, county, territorial, or state courts upon mining subjects is so extensive that the illustrations already given form but a small part of the whole. Volume after volume of Western law reports deal with mining cases and contain laborious researches into Spanish archives and Californian provincial history, and the masterly deductions of unsurpassed judicial intellects. A book written by a lawyer, for lawyers, upon some of the great mining cases of California, from those of the early fifties in Tuolumne, Placer, and Butte, to the famous group of "mining-debris" cases of the last few years, would be a notable work, and one well worth the while of some fully equipped jurist.

From a lawyer's standpoint, the worst thing about the local laws of the early camps was their lack of uniformity; but from an institutional standpoint, this irregular and spontaneous element is their strongest claim to a place in Western history. A great need called them into existence: they grew in accordance with the nature of things, as simply and surely as pines grow in a forest. Yet we have previously shown many points of resemblance; and a still closer analysis of the hundreds of codes of old camps now obtainable — of camps from every mining county of California, Nevada, Oregon, and some of the territories — proves that the local laws and usages over this great region are based upon five principles: to have each claim of definite size; to enforce the law of use; to maintain "inclined locations" (*Gestreckfeld*) in case of quartz; to record all claims; and to insist on this record as final in case of dispute. All these appear to be Germanic ideas, now a part of our race-equipment for the world's battle, but none the less a heritage from Teutonic ancestors. German, English, American laws adopt the "inclined-location" idea — that a man takes up a piece of mineral land for the lode alone, and shall have the right to follow it downward indefinitely, including all dips, spurs, and angles. Spanish law insists upon "square locations," simply the surface, and all beneath it in a perpendicular direction. Some high authorities, such as Professor Raymond, prefer the latter system, as greatly lessening litigation. Commissioners, among whom were Clarence King, J. W. Powell, and Thomas Donaldson, recommended, in 1880, the abandonment of the "inclined-location" system. It is a question that should, of course, be decided upon practical grounds; but it is not likely that our present system will soon be discarded.

Chapter XXIV. THE EXTENSION AND PERMANENT INFLUENCE OF MINING-CAMP LAW

THE varied methods by which camps were governed and district law enforced, and the acceptance of their enactments by the early state courts, have probably received sufficient illustration; but the way in which these enactments spread over the surrounding territory and ultimately aided to form a national system of mining law deserves our attention, as added proof of its creative force.

Recognition by state legislatures began with California, in 1851, when senators and representatives, acknowledging the fact that the miners had perfected a practical working-system, provided that in all actions respecting such claims the proceedings of the miners' meetings should be regarded by the courts, "so far as they are not inconsistent with the laws and constitution of the State." It was this legislature that conferred jurisdiction in all cases of mining claims, whatever their value, upon the local justices of the peace.

A little before this time the very existence of the mining code had been in great danger. When John C. Frémont was United States Senator from California, he introduced a bill to establish police regulations throughout the mining region and levy a small tax upon the miners. At that time — the winter of 1850–1 — such a measure would have destroyed the institutions so rapidly developing in the camps of energetic gold-seekers. The discussion in the Senate was a tedious one. Many of the senators favored sale of all mineral lands to the

266]

highest bidders. But it is to those great but widely different leaders Seward and Benton that the full acceptance by the nation of the policy of free mining on government land was finally due. They vainly urged it, and at last insisted upon delay in legislation. A year later the local regulations of the mining camps were so satisfactory that Congress hesitated to change the system. Meanwhile the miners accepted this delay as a tacit recognition of their demands, a tacit promise to legalize their possessory rights. So they pushed forward their explorations of gravel-beds and rock ledges, of ravines and mountains; they increased their investments in machinery, water-ditches, costly tunnels, flumes, embankments, and other requisites of their gigantic undertakings.

By 1861 the miners' customs, usages, laws, and regulations had spread outward from California, whose court decisions were almost universally followed and were recognized in other states and territories of the West. In Colorado the miners made local laws long before the territorial legislature attempted to regulate such things. Illinois District, Gilpin County, allowed claims to be two hundred feet long by fifty feet wide, and prospectors were allowed to locate claims for others. In November 1861 the legislature of Colorado decided that valid mineral locations could only be made in full accordance with the local laws of the district in which the location was made.[1]

The laws of Nevada Territory, passed in November 1861, declare that —

"In actions respecting mining-claims, proof shall be admitted of the customs, usages, or regulations established and in force in the mining-district embracing such claim; and . . . [they] shall govern the decision of the action in

---

[1] Sullivan *vs.* Hense, Colorado Rep., vol. 2, p. 425.

regard to all questions of location, possession, and abandonment."

The laws of Nevada in 1862 provided that —

"All conveyances of mining-claims . . . shall be construed in accordance with the lawful local rules, regulations, and customs of the miners."

The "location and transfers of mining-claims . . . shall be established and proved before courts by the local rules, regulations, or customs of the miners in the several mining-districts." [2]

The Nevada statute of February 27, 1866 provided that —

"The extraction of gold or other metals from alluvial or diluvial deposits, generally called placer-mining, shall be subject to such regulations as the miners in the several mining-districts shall adopt."

Idaho, February 4, 1864, ordained that —

"The conveyance of quartz-claims shall be construed in accordance with the local mining rules, regulations, and customs in the several districts."

Arizona provided that the size of the mining claims, or *pertenencias,* should be regulated within given areas by the miners; and, further, that the records of mining districts "shall not be rejected for any defects in their form when their contents may be understood." Twelve or more persons were allowed to form a new district,

---

[2] The local laws of Reese River mining district, passed in 1862, and amended in 1864, provided for a mining-recorder, whose fees were one dollar for every location registered. The term of office of said recorder was one year, "unless sooner removed by an election called by fifty or more claim-holders." The size of a claim is fixed at two hundred feet on a ledge, "with all the dips, spurs, angles, offshoots, outcrops, depths, widths, and variations." An application of twenty-five miners is sufficient to call a miners' meeting.

"make laws therefor, and elect a recorder." Montana passed a Territorial Act allowing thirty or more miners to hold district meetings and "make all laws not conflicting with vested rights." Oregon, in a statute of 1867, ordained that "any person may hold one claim by location, and as many by purchase as the local laws of the district allow"; also, that the miners "shall be empowered to make local laws" in relation to the possession of water-rights, the possession and working of placers, and the survey and sale of town lots in mining camps, "subject to the laws of the United States."

Thus the local law of the miners had won recognition in state courts and had extended to other states and territories. It also gained a hearing in the Supreme Court of the United States. In 1865 Chief Justice Chase, in one of his decisions, said:

"A special kind of law, a sort of common law of the miners, the offspring of a nation's irrepressible march, — lawless in some senses, yet clothed with dignity by a conception of the immense social results mingled with the fortunes of these bold investigators, — has sprung up on the Pacific Coast, and presents in the value of a 'mining-right' a novel and peculiar question of jurisdiction for this court." [3]

Senator Stewart of Nevada, himself a miner of 1849, and one who helped to govern some of the early camps of northern California, speaks eloquently of the legislative work done by the pioneers. In a letter to Senator Ramsay, and in a speech delivered in the Senate in June 1866, he exclaims that the Argonauts "found no laws governing the possession and occupation of mines but the common laws of right which Americans alone are educated to administer. They were forced to make laws

[3] In Supreme Court U. S., December 1865, case of Sparrow *vs.* Strong; appeal from Story Co., Nev.: 3 Wallace, U. S. Sup. Ct., p. 100.

for themselves. The reason and justice of the laws they formed challenge the admiration of all who investigate them. Each mining-district in an area extending over not less than fifty thousand square miles formed its own rules, and adopted its own customs. The similarity of these rules and customs throughout the entire mining-region was so great as to attain all the beneficial results of well-digested general laws. These regulations were thoroughly democratic in their character, guarding against every form of monopoly, and requiring contin-ued work and occupation in good faith to constitute a valid possession." [4] About the same time the Conness Committee Report to the Senate of the United States said:

"The miners' rules and regulations are not only well un-derstood, but have been construed and adjudicated for now nearly a quarter of a century. . . . By this great system es-tablished by the people in their primary capacities, and ev-idencing by the highest possible testimony the peculiar gen-ius of the American people for founding empire and order, popular sovereignty is displayed in one of its grandest as-pects, and simply invites us, not to destroy, but to put upon it the stamp of national power and unquestioned author-ity."

In another place the same report says:

"The rules and regulations of the miners . . . form the basis of the present admirable system arising out of neces-sity; they become the means adopted by the people them-selves for establishing just protection to all. . . . The local courts, beginning with California, recognize those rules, the central idea of which was *priority of possession*." [5]

Congress passed an Act, July 26, 1866, which recog-

---

[4] Speech, reported in *Cong. Globe*, June 19, 1866.
[5] Report to Senate, May 28, 1866.

nized the "force of local mining-customs, or rules of miners wherever not conflicting with the laws of the United States." Subsequent Acts, principally the Act of 1872, have defined the entire subject of mining law; and decisions of the courts and of the heads of the departments have followed in the lines laid down by the Acts of 1866 and 1872. The manner in which a United States land-patent may be obtained for any land claimed and located for valuable mineral deposits is now fully set forth. The payment of five dollars per acre is required, and the smallest legal subdivision is ten acres. After a notice of "intention to purchase" a described tract of mineral land, sixty days are allowed for other parties to file their adverse claims, if any such exist; after the expiration of this time, no objection from third parties shall be heard except it be shown that the applicant has failed to comply with the law. Congress has required that placer-locations upon surveyed lands shall conform to public surveys in all cases except when this is made impossible by the previous appropriation of a portion of the ten or more acres desired (that is, by claims held under local law), or where it "is impracticable to so locate the claim." [6] "It is the evident intention of the mining-laws to allow persons to take a certain quantity of land fit for mining. Where the entire placer-deposit in a cañon within certain limits is claimed, and where the adjoining lands are unfit for any use whatever, the claimant need not conform to the survey-lines." [7]

The Revised Statutes of the United States relating to mineral lands and mining resources supersede and repeal many provisions of the Acts of 1866, 1870, and 1872; but mineral lands are still "free and open to exploration and purchase . . . under regulations pre-

---

[6] Act of July 9, 1870; modified by Act of May 10, 1872.
[7] Recent decision of Secretary Teller, February 1884.

scribed by law, and according to the local customs or
rules of miners in the several mining-districts, so far as
the same are applicable, and not inconsistent with the
laws of the United States." The sections referring to locators and their exclusive right of possession and enjoyment of their mining claims, to tunnel-rights, to
miners' regulations and improvements, to existing
rights, to vested rights in the use of water, to rights of
way for canals, and to titles of town lots as subject to
mineral rights are all of them distinct recognitions of
early local law and afford plain evidence of its widespread influence.

This liberal policy has filled the ravines of the Rockies with prospectors and miners. It has fostered freedom,
and aided the beginnings of law. Men still form mining
camps, still govern them under local forms; but as soon
as the district proves of permanent value, they usually
abandon this form of organization for township, county,
and territorial forms; for they are not only miners, but
also citizens of the Republic, and they look forward to
state life and national relationship.

In the course of the development we have endeavored
to trace, the most prominent fact appears to be the
widespread effect of these informal laws of frontiersmen. The best talent in the State of California was engaged at last in the task of codifying the scattered camp
laws, eliminating their manifold contradictions, and
remedying their shortcomings. Slowly, through a long
series of years, a multitude of wise judicial decisions
molded scattered customs, fragmentary camp laws, relics of the folk-moot era, survivals of the alcalde period,
usages of the time of the later hydraulic mining, into an
apt, terse, strong, useful, and comprehensive system of
common law, regulating not only the rights of miners
over mineral ground, but also their riparian rights.

Then the nation recognized its responsibility, and the work of creating a general system was begun. There is much yet to do; a National School of Mines must be established, and stricter legislation is required to prevent wasteful mining: but the great features of the present law are thoroughly consonant with the spirit of republican institutions. This we owe to the men of the mining camp.

Chapter XXV. EFFECTS, SOCIAL AND INTELLECTUAL, UPON WESTERN DEVELOPMENT

Conservation of energy is an axiom of science. Though every mining camp perished tomorrow, the impulse that gave them birth would still survive. The local life, strength, and energy of the early camps have already passed as a powerful force, not as a name, into the warp and woof of society. So far-reaching and powerful have been the influences of camp life and camp law upon the growing communities of the Far West that one might almost be justified in the belief that a new social order would thus be produced. Everywhere over the great region we have been studying, the spirit of the past abides in multitudinous forms.

It matters not that the elder camps have decayed; nor that the elder pioneers have departed, as the "poet of the Sierras" expressed it, "to prospect the stars"; nor that county officials sit where alcaldes sat, and schoolhouses stand where folk-moots met of old. The men and women whose childhood was passed in these camps are beginning to control the state. Each community, once welded together in camp life, possesses a unity of feeling that bids fair to be permanent. This is true of California, and may reasonably be expected to prove true of the later-settled mining regions. We observe in the newest camps of the British Columbia border the same spirit of swift, healthy camp life, the same return to primitive forms of jurisprudence, the same American determination that crime shall be punished, property and life made safe; therefore we may have faith that the same results will follow there as in California, that stable communities will be established and higher forms of society evolved.

The nature of the forces long ago set at work in new Western communities by the institutions of the typical camp can best be illustrated by a case which was but one of a thousand. It occurred in 1858, in California; and some of those concerned in the enterprise are still alive. The "surface diggins" of the camp were exhausted, but rich gravel was thought to lie beneath the mountain, to be reached only by a tunnel of great cost; and the men who owned the possessory right to tunnel were all poor. They met, and talked it over, counted their funds, and began work; blasted a hole forty feet in the rock — no more money in the treasury. They borrowed quite an amount in small sums, paying no interest, and drove the tunnel deeper. They appointed a number of men to continue the work, while the rest of the company hired themselves out at daily wages to support them and buy the necessary tools and blasting-powder. Economy was the order of the day, and fraternal co-operation was its watchword. At last they won: a company of poor and uneducated men, by reason of perfect faith in each other, and grim, tireless persistence, carried a load that capitalists would have refused, and walked at last into Nature's treasure-house, finding a bed of gravel rich enough to amply repay them all. It was not thought a remarkable thing in those days. All over California, groups of comparatively poor men were standing by each other in the same manly way. Now, that, in the last analysis, was and is the feeling fostered in true mining-camp life. In camps, too, we have something of the guild idea. The weavers and the goldsmiths of the Middle Ages had the fraternity feeling, and so have the miners of America. Sturdy self-reliance, mingled and tempered with a high appreciation of one's dependence upon others; the power to stand alone; the power to organize, if need be, with sudden energy and startling swiftness — these were traits fostered by the patient toil of the miners of America; and because of qualities such as these, the fame of the pioneers of California and the Rockies has gone wherever winds blow or waters run.

The physical spread of the mining-camp influence, through wandering prospectors and miners from deserted camps, assumes in this connection a greater importance than before. We have studied the growth of the miners' code from the rude regulations of the few camps of 1848. We have alluded to the nature of the frequent mining excitements that inevitably extended this code; but some of the features of this movement deserve especial prominence. In 1859, for instance, several thousand California miners went to Cariboo, British Columbia; in 1860 the first mining was done in Idaho, on the Clearwater and Salmon; and hundreds of Californians hastened thither. The same year, also, the Washoe rush began; and within two years the sagebrush deserts and treeless mountains of Nevada were explored, the treasures of Coso, Pioche, Tuscarora, Esmeralda, Potosí, Humboldt, Reese, and other districts had been unveiled; while Bodie in California was also discovered. The year 1862 also witnessed the rush to Boise, and to the John Day region in Oregon, in which state the Powder and Burnt River placers had been found the previous year. The Owyhee mines drew prospectors in 1863, the quartz of Alturas in 1864, the placers of the Big Bend of the Columbia in 1865, White Pine in 1866. California sent out thirty thousand or forty thousand stalwart and well-trained miners in these three or four years.

The reasons for such an exodus are not hard to find. When the surface wealth of California became so nearly exhausted that men could no longer make the wages to which they had been accustomed, they became restless; when surface miners could no longer make living wages, their occupation was clearly gone. The game was "played out"; so was the camp. There were then a few, more fortunate or more frugal than the majority, who were able to unite in companies to purchase machinery, build forty-mile flumes, explore the deeper auriferous channels of blue gravel, tunnel solid rock and walls of lava, turn the course of rivers, sink deep shafts — to hold their own, in brief, throughout the new era of capital and monopoly. The weak men sank into laborers for the new companies, or became searchers for precarious finds in the gravel-heaps of the past. Hundreds of energetic men of small means were still able to hold and work mining property on a moderate scale, but the one resource of the strong was to find a new camp. The great majority of those to whom the mines were no longer liberal swarmed out of the busy hive, as has ever been the custom of the pioneers of our race. When the smallest coin used for change in California sank from a twenty-five-cent piece to ten cents, the emigration began; when it sank still farther to five cents, the disgust and despair of the genuine forty-niner can hardly be described. He felt the earth slipping away from under his feet. Even as late as 1878, in Trinity County, five-cent pieces were very rarely seen and were sometimes refused. The smallest coin expected for a service was a quarter. Nickels were particularly obnoxious to the miners. Everything smaller than half a dollar was rather disrespectfully denominated "chicken-feed."

Under these conditions, hundreds of miners became tillers of the soil; but other hundreds swarmed out into the unexplored spaces, searching the ranges that loom higher and higher northward into British Columbia and Alaska, crowned with eternal snows, and dreadful with arctic dangers. Perhaps some of them sailed up the Yukon, the "Amazon of the North," long before Carl Ritter had heard its name or knew its vastness. Indeed, in 1874 a San Luis Obispo (California) miner told the writer that he spent a summer prospecting in Alaska for gold long before 1856. Miners once of California, but now of the world at large, prospected the chief districts of the new Southwest and of the new Northwest, becoming leading citizens in Arizona, New Mexico, Utah, Montana, Idaho, Wyoming; names familiar as household words to old Californians appear and reappear in the records of Tombstone, Candelaria, Leadville, San Carlos, the Black Hills. They followed the Rockies across the lines, northward, southward. American prospectors drifted into the French-Canadian settlements on the Saskatchewan, bringing lumps of silver and nuggets of gold from the then unexplored regions which the Canadian Pacific Railroad is entering from east and west with giant strides. American prospectors drifted into Mexico; adopted sombreros and tortillas; creviced for gold with Spanish machetes, instead of with Tuolumne County butcher-knives; built rockers, long-toms, and sluice-boxes, of Mexic cedar, instead of California sugar-pine; affiliated with the people, fought Indians for them, taught them better methods of mining, and prepared the way for closer international relations.

But the migratory impulse circling outward from Sutter's ruined mill had a meaning for lands outside of North America. It ultimately became of world-wide influence. E. H. Hargreaves, for a time a California miner, returned to his home in Australia, leaving good diggings. He went to the government, received an appointment to search for gold, and in a short time discovered the placers of that mighty island-continent. Many Californians followed his footsteps, leaving a strong impress upon the local mining-legislation and "miners' councils" of Australia, particularly of Victoria. In 1860 thousands of miners went to Barbacoas, New Granada; but the mines proved a failure. Large companies were, however, organized at times in the placer camps of California, and went to Central America, to Peru, Chili, Ecuador, Brazil, and Patagonia. They spent vast sums of money, endured extreme hardships, and surmounted enormous difficulties. Some of them acquired fortunes; others lost all their gains of toilsome years in California. Even within the past year (1884), many old and experienced miners have gone to the Transvaal Republic, to Australia, to Chili, to the United States of Colombia, and to Venezuela; some in the employ of capitalists, others on prospecting tours of their own, but all of them spreading abroad the spirit of American mining law. Wherever, since the brave days of '49, these miners went, they "stood by each other"; they had "pards," and local government; they could not forget the hard but sweet discipline of their loved and lost camps once nestling beneath the Sierra snow-peaks; they clung fast to the ethics of that stormy world whose stern code, it was once said, "is the creation of the American miner; and he loves, trusts, and obeys it." As, of old, Greece was wherever Greeks dwelt; so the spirit of the typical camp is with all American miners, wherever they wander. Some have toiled in Tibet and Assam, in Siberia and South Africa, in the mountains of Abyssinia, and in the rivers of Guinea. The rich mines rumored to exist in Korea and in Madagascar have long attracted the hungry gaze of these bronzed and audacious prospectors. A party of them built a steamboat, and explored the Yukon two summers ago; another party has visited southern Arabia; more than one expedition of miners has gone gold-hunting in the South Seas, among the isles of the Indian Ocean. Last summer a number of California prospectors, after explorations in Alaska, met with a fearful storm; and their schooner went down with all on board. Everywhere it is the same type — unconquerable kindliness, persistence, and simplicity, unwavering enthusiasm, unblenching courage.

The writer met a prospector in 1876, in Shasta County, California; age forty-five, health perfect, great fund of humor, keen observation, grammar-school education supplemented by much study. He rode a mule, total impedimenta were less than thirty pounds; had journeyed from northern Montana, was on his way to Mexico, staked his mule out by the roadside, and the total cost of the entire trip was expected to fall within twenty dollars. In 1881 we again met the same prospector near Calico Camp, San Bernardino County. He was riding a pinto horse, but otherwise appeared unchanged for better or for worse. When asked to give an account of himself, he replied that he had been in Lower California, had crossed northern Mexico, spent some months in Sonora, then in New Mexico; sold several good "prospects," and made money. He then went to western Colorado to take a hand in the expected invasion of the Indian country; hunted for silver in "the Mormon country," for nitrates in southern Nevada; tried his fortune in one of the old mining camps of Mono; and had gone on steadily in a similar round, seldom staying more than a few weeks at a place. But he had helped to start Calico, and it was a "pretty good camp," well-organized and prosperous: so he should probably stay there. Such a man is the individual prospector, a person who, though often solitary for days and weeks, can readily join others and create a society, found a camp, establish a town.

Out of the camps of old, powerful currents have flowed into the remotest valley of the western third of the American continent. A central fact of early New England is the town meeting; of early Virginia, the plantation; of the Pacific coast and Rocky Mountain region, the mining camp. It has taken hold of popular fancy, has become enshrined in tradition, and looms up across the gateways of the history of new states. We walk the streets of San Francisco: leaders in business here, who once were citizens of a camp, and swingers of picks in the beds of mountain torrents. We enter the political field: giants of debate and caucus here, whose first efforts to control their fellow men were under the Mariposa oaks, or beneath the dome of Shasta. We traverse the pastoral regions of the West, prairies dotted for miles with cattle, herds upon a thousand hills: sun-browned patriarchal princes here, a hundred herdsmen at their command, five hundred horses in their *manadas;* and under the starlight, as we ride homeward, our host will tell stories of "how we druv' the Sydney Ducks outen Pine Flat," and "the hanging of the man what killed Steve Truegood's pard." We visit the prosperous and beautiful colonies of southern California, fair as a garden of the Lord — realms of cherry and apple, olive and orange, grape and pomegranate, fig and guava, loquat and passiflora, fruits and flowers of two broad zones, mingled in rapturous profusion underneath azure skies as of Capri and Sicily; and here also, in the midst of colonists from all parts of the world, is some man of pre-eminent force and dignity of character, trained in the school of the early mines, transmuting by earth's subtle alchemy his golden nuggets of '49 to yet more golden apples of Hesperides, and planting golden-

banded lilies of Osaka in the place of golden leaves
from Proserpine's subterranean gardens. We may even
seek the great cities, whither all currents flow — New
York, London, Paris, Berlin, St. Petersburg — the marts
of commerce, the counting-houses of Barings and Roth-
schilds, the courts of tsar and emperor, the wonderful
Broadways of many a metropolis, flowing like Amazonian rivers day and night without pause: and we shall
find men long trained in the lessons of the mining
camps walking as calm conquerors through the midst of
this world of tumult, action, and desperate struggle, ruling railroad systems, laying ocean cables, planning for
isthmus canals, aiding in a thousand enterprises that require energy, capital, knowledge of men, and prestige
of former success; yet faithful in heart, cosmopolites
though they are, to the memories of their young manhood, the companions of their Argonautic quest, the
"pards" of their pick-and-shovel days in Sierra or Rocky.
Upon facts like these rest the social results of the mining-camp training.

But what of things intellectual? What new forces,
strong to shape the future, passed into the life of the nation because of the mining era? Again we must turn to
California as the first of the mining commonwealths.
Here the era of the camps is already ancient, and forever of the past. Its influence extends unconsciously
along the channels of daily existence and colors the
opinions of thousands who never heard of a mining
camp; but its fundamental importance consists in its
place as a classical and heroic background for modern
life. To all intents and purposes, the true mining era
now lies a century or two behind the California of today. The system of compulsory arbitration, and the ruling committee of seven elders, adopted in 1640 by the
pioneers of Portsmouth, marked no greater difference

from the Rhode Island commonwealth of today, than did the arbitrators and alcaldes of the mining camps represent a different California from that of the present time. Institutionally, the mining camp underlies these Western commonwealths, but intellectually it represents a colonial era; while the Spanish period lies behind it, a realm of romance and mystery. Some day all this must pass into literature, not from the standpoint of outside observation, but from the wiser standpoint of men and women of home training.

Of California's hoped-for poet, it has been said by one of her younger writers:

"He could not be among those mighty men,
The Argonauts, — their poem was the State;
Their hands were wed to pick and pan, and fate
Gave not to them to wield the slender pen.

.   .   .   .

But from her children one shall rise ere long
To give her mystic legends fitting lays,
To make her birds and flowers known to fame,
And match her mountains with his lofty song." [1]

There is a faith held by many that the mingling of civilizations, the crossing and tangling of varied eras, in California affords an increasing opportunity for art and literature; that the best thoughts of the dwellers in this sunny land will some day be equal to the best the green earth affords. The same sort of influences are at work throughout the mineral region, from the ancient pueblo realm of New Mexico to the shining "land of the silver bow," as the Indians called Montana. Laws change, systems decay; but the test of all that is highest and best in the life of a community is its literary expression, its poetry, its novels, its world-philosophies. The greatest

---

[1] Charles S. Greene, in *Overland* for January 1883.

value to the states of the Far West, of an environment so different from that of merely agricultural communities, and of institutional beginnings of such diverse origins, is in the precious materials thus being accumulated for art and song and tale, for literature in its world-wide illumination, and for the patient use of coming genius.

AUTHORITIES CONSULTED

[*A complete bibliography of works relating to the subject-matter
of this book, if extended to pamphlets and periodicals, would probably be quite sufficient to fill another volume. We must refer to the
lists of books and manuscripts relating to Mexico and California in
Mr. H. H. Bancroft's History of the Pacific States of North America, and in the Catalogue of the Mercantile Library of San Francisco; also to notes and references throughout the foregoing pages.*]

MINING IN ASIA AND EUROPE

ASIA: *Compendium of Geography and Travel*. Stanford.
London, 1882.

BOECKH: *Public Economy of Athens*. 2 vols.

BURTON, R. F.: *Gold-Mines of Midian* (1878) ; also his *Explorations of the Highlands of Brazil* (1869), chapter
on Mining Systems.

CAMDEN: *Britannia*. ("Old Authors," 1870 edition.)

CHEVALIER: *Remarks on Production of Precious Metals*. Tr.
London, 1851.

COMSTOCK: *History of the Precious Metals*. New York, 1849.

Cornwall: Its Mines and Miners. London, 1857. Also
Hunt's *Romances of Cornwall*.

ENGLISH MINING CASES, in King's Bench Reports: especially
Rowe *vs.* Brenton, Concannen's Special Report; Smirke's
Report; Rogers *vs.* Brenton; Ivimey *vs.* Stocker; Ark-
wright *vs.* Cantrell.

GMELIN: *Reisen durch Sibirien*. 4 vols. Göttingen, 1751.

HEEREN: *Historical Researches into the Politics and Trade
of Africa and Asia*. 4 vols. London, tr., 1860. Also his
Ancient History (published in 1833, translated by Mr.
George Bancroft in 1842).

HERODOTUS: Sayce's edition. Vol. I and appendices. London,
1883.

HODGSON: *History of Northumberland*. 6 vols. 1857.

HUNT, ROBERT: *Mineral Statistics of the United Kingdom.* 1865. (Notes on local customs.)

JACOBS: *Historical Inquiry into the Production of Metals,* etc. London, 1851.

LALOR: *Cyclopædia of Political Science;* article "Mining." Professor R. W. Raymond. (Also, Professor Raymond's historical article on "Relation of Government to Mining," in the *United States Report for 1879 on Mineral Resources.*)

LODGE, HENRY CABOT: *The Anglo-Saxon Land-Law* (1876).

Mining Customs and Mineral Courts Act (*High Peak District*), English Parliament. 1851.

POLLOCK, FREDERICK: *The Land Laws.* English Citizen series, 1883.

REITEMEIER, Dr. J. F.: *Geschichte des Bergbaues und Hüttenwesens bei den alten Völkern.* Göttingen, 1785. (Received prize of Royal Society of Sciences; contains fragments of ancient literature on mines and mining organization.)

SCHÖMAN: *Antiquities of Greece.* London, 1826.

SEEBOHM, FREDERIC: *English Village Community* (1883).

SPRENGER: *Alte Geographie.*

TRAVELS IN ASIA: Atkinson (*Siberia*); Curzon (*Armenia,* 1855); Hexthausen (*Transcaucasia*); Mouhot (*Indo-China*); Palmer (*Desert of the Exodus*); Pumpelly (*Across America and Asia*); Travels of Porter, Palgrave, Rawlinson, Richthofen, and Stanley; Yule's *Marco Polo;* Gill's *River of Golden Sand* (Tibet, etc.); Colquhoun's *Across Chryse* (Chinese borderlands).

WILSON, ERASMUS: *Egypt of the Past.* London, 1882.

WYLD: *Notes on the Discovery of Gold.* London, 1851.

MINING IN AMERICA

ACOSTA, FATHER JOSEPH: *Naturall and Morall History of the Indies* (Hakluyt Society Publications).

ALCEDO, ANTONIO DE: *Diccionario Geográphico Histórico de las Indias Occidentales.* Edition of 1812.

ALSOPP, ROBERT: *California and its Gold-mines*. London, 1853.

ANDERSON: *Silver and Gold of the South-west*. St. Louis, 1877.

ARIZONA: Territorial Laws and Reports.

AUBERTIN, J. J.: *Flight to Mexico*. London, 1882.

AVERY, B. P.: *California Pictures*. New York, 1878.

BANCROFT, H. H.: *History of the Pacific States of North America*. 13 vols. (Particularly *Mexico*, Vol. VI, and *California*, Vol. I; 1542–1800).

BATES, MRS. D. B.: *Four Years on the Pacific Coast*. Boston, 1860.

BARRY, and PATTEN: *Men and Memories of San Francisco*. 1873.

BARTLETT: *Personal Narrative*. 1854.

BAUSMAN, WILLIAM: *Early California*. San Francisco, 1872.

BENTON, J. A.: *California Pilgrim*, 1853.

BERRY: *Gold of California*. London, 1849.

BONWICK, J.: *Mormons and the Silver-mines of the West*. 1872.

BORTHWICK, J. D.: *Three Years in California*. Edinburgh, 1857.

BOWIE, AUGUST J.: *Hydraulic Mining in California*. San Francisco, 1878.

BROCKLEHURST: *Mexico To-day*. London, 1883.

BROOKS, B. S.: "Alcalde-grants in San Francisco." *Pioneer Monthly*, Vol. I.

BROOKS, J. T.: *Four Months among the Gold-seekers*. London, 1849.

BRYANT: *What I Saw in California*.

BUFFUM, E. G.: *Six Months in the Gold-mines*. Philadelphia, 1850.

BURNETT, GOV. PETER H.: *Recollections of an Old Pioneer*. New York, 1880.

BURTON: *Across the Rocky Mountains*. 1862.

CALIFORNIA DOCUMENTS: 1850. (Correspondence with alcaldes, and reports to the successive military governors.)

CALIFORNIA: Journals of the Senate and Assembly, 1849–55;

Debates in Convention of 1849, J. R. Browne; Law
Reports and Digest (40 vols.); Statutes of, 1854–6;
Speeches of Gwin, Latham, and Rhodes; Professor
Trask's Senate Report (Sacramento, 1853–4).

CALIFORNIA: County Histories and Directories; Amador
(1881); Alameda (1878); Calaveras (1880); Tuolumne
(1856); Nevada (1867 and 1878); also Shasta and Trinity (1879).

CALIFORNIA PIONEERS (Society of) : Addresses of Messrs. Van
Voorhies, Dwinelle, Clark, Clay, Freelon, Kewen, Ran-
dolph, Holmes, Browne, and others.

CALIFORNIA: Works of Travel and Observation not sepa-
rately noted; Writings of Bowles, Bushnell, Evans,
Loviat, Linen, M'Clellan, Nordhoff, Ord, Parke, Parry,
Prime, Rae, Revere, Roberts, Saxon, Seemann, Simp-
son, Soares, Todd, Vassar, Warren, Wilkes, Wilkinson,
Winthrop, Wise, Wogan.

California: Its Gold and Inhabitants. London, 1856. 2 vols.

CALDERÓN DE LA BARCA, MADAME: *Life in Mexico.* London,
1852.

CARSON: *Early Recollections of the Mines.* Stockton, 1852.

CASTANARES: *Discovery of Gold in 1844.*

CHAMISSO: *Californien* (1816).

CHEVALIER: *Le Mexique, ancien et moderne;* 2 vols. 1864.

CLAVIGERO: *Historia México.* 1787.

COKE: *Ride over the Rocky Mountains.* London, 1851.

COLLIER: *Pictorial Dictionary.* London, 1721.

COLORADO Territorial Enactments; also, Law Reports. Also
Fossett's descriptive work on early Colorado. New York,
1879.

COLTON: *Three Years in California.* 1856.

CONGDON: *Mining Laws and Forms.* San Francisco, 1864.

COULTER: *Adventures in California.*

DANA, R. H.: *Two Years before the Mast.*

DELANO: *Life among the Diggings.* New York, 1854.

EMORY: *Military Reconnoissance.* 1846.

Engineering and Mining Journal. New York. 38 vols.

Engineering and Mining Magazine. New York, 1869–74.

FARNHAM, E. W.: *California In Doors and Out*. New York, 1856.

FITZGERALD, REV. O. P.: *California Sketches*. Nashville, Tenn., 1879.

FISHER, WALTER M.: *The Californians*. San Francisco, 1876.

FORBES: *History of Upper and Lower California*. London, 1839.

FOSTER, G. G.: *Gold Regions of California*. New York, 1848-9.

FREMONT, and EMORY: *California Guide-book*. New York, 1849.

FROEBEL: *Seven Years' View in Northern Mexico*. London, 1859.

GERSTACKER: *Kalifornien Gold*. Leipzig, 1856.

GLEASON: *History of Catholic Church in California*. Also, for missions, Reports of Padres Piccola (1702) and Serra (1773) ; Governor Figuero's Manifesto to Mexican Government; Report of Father Serra Centennial at Monterey, Cal., Aug. 28, 1884, in San Francisco dailies.

GRAY, WILLIAM: *Pioneer Times in California*. San Francisco, 1881.

HALL: *History of San José* (California). 1871.

HAWES, HORACE: *Missions in California* (pamphlet). 1856. Also, his arguments in Mexican land-cases.

HELPER, H. R.: *Land of Gold*. Baltimore, 1856.

HELPS, SIR ARTHUR: *Spanish Conquest*. 4 vols. London, 1861.

HITTELL, JOHN S.: *Resources of California*. San Francisco, 1874. Also, his *History of San Francisco*.

HUGHES, ELIZABETH: *The California of the Padres*. San Francisco, 1871.

HUMBOLDT, ALEXANDER VON: *Essai politique sur la Nouvelle Éspagne*.

JONES, WILLIAM C.: *Report on Land-titles in California*. Washington, 1850. Also, *Pueblo Question solved*. San Francisco, 1860.

KING, CLARENCE: *Mountaineering in the Sierra*. Boston, 1872.

KING, THOMAS B.: *California, Wonder of the Age*. New York, 1850.

LETTS, J. M.: *California Illustrated.* New York, 1853.

MARRYAT, FRANK: *Mountains and Molehills.* London, 1855.

MAYER, BRANTZ: *Mexico, Aztec, Spanish, Republican;* also *Mexico, New Mexico, and California.* Baltimore, 1850.

MEXICAN LAW: Gamboa's *Commentaries* of 1761; *Ordenanzas de Minería* of 1783; *Recopilación de las Leyes de las Indias,* 1781; *Constituciones de Méjico y de los Estados Mejicanos.* Chapters in H. H. Bancroft, Vol. VI, and Woolsey's *Political Science,* Vol. II, chap. vii. Decisions in California courts relating to Mexican land-grants and mineral claims.

Mining and Scientific Press. San Francisco (49 vols.).

Mining Record. New York (16 vols.).

NEVADA: Territorial Acts and State Reports.

NICOLAY: *The Oregon Territory.* London, 1846.

OBER: *Travels in Mexico.* Boston, 1884.

Overland Monthly, the: First and second series. Articles on Indians, Missions, Spanish Period, Mexico, Pueblos, Mining camps, Pioneer days, Early government, etc. San Francisco, 1868–84. The interregnum between the two series was occupied by the *Californian.*

PALMER: *New and Old California.* New York, 1852.

PARRY: *Mineral Products of the South-west.*

PATTERSON: *Twelve Years in the Mines of California.* Cambridge, Mass., 1862.

PERIODICALS, etc.: Articles in *New Englander,* 1850; *British Quarterly,* 1850; *Edinburgh Review,* 1858; *Blackwood's,* 1857; *Quarterly Review,* 1850; *Macmillan's,* 1867; *Blackwood's,* 1851; *Scribner's Monthly,* 1878; *Hesperian Magazine,* San Francisco, 1856–64; *Hutchings's Magazine,* San Francisco.

PLUMMER: *Vigilantes of Montana.* Helena, M. T., 1866.

PHILIPS and DARLINGTON: *Records of Mining.* 1862.

PRINCE: *History of New Mexico.* 1882.

RAYMOND, R. W.: *Statistics of Mines.* 1869–73.

RÉMOND: Report on Northern Mexico, in *Proceedings of California Academy of Sciences,* Vol. III.

ROCKWELL: *Compilation of Spanish and Mexican Laws Relating to Mines.* New York, 1851.

RYAN: *Personal Adventures in California.* 2 vols. London, 1851.

SHUCK: *Representative Men of the Pacific.* San Francisco, 1876.

SOULÉ: *Annals of San Francisco.*

TAYLOR, BAYARD: *Eldorado.* New York, 1850.

TUTHILL: *History of California.* Also, works of Frost, Norman, Capron, Greenhow, Thornton, and others.

TYSON: *Geology and Industrial Resources of California* (including official reports). Baltimore, 1851.

UNITED STATES MINING LAWS, 1866–72; also Revised Codes now in force.

UNITED STATES (mining before Californian discoveries): Bainbridge (*Law of Mines*) ; Law Reports of Louisiana, Missouri, Georgia, North Carolina; scattered articles in periodicals and journals elsewhere referred to; also the United States Mineral Reports.

VENEGAS: *Natural and Civil History of California;* also *Noticia de la Californie* (1757).

VIGNOTTI, A.: *Coup d'œil sur les richesses métallurgiques du Mexique.* 1868.

WEEKS: *Laws of Mines, Minerals, and Water-rights.* San Francisco, 1877.

WESTGARTH: *Victoria, late Australia Felix.* Edinburgh, 1851. (Notes on organization of early Australian miners as compared with those of California.)

WILSON, HON. R. A.: Alcalde System of California. *California Reports,* Vol. I, Appendix.

WHITNEY, PROFESSOR: *Mineral Wealth of the United States.* Philadelphia, 1851. Also, California Geological Reports.

YALE, GREGORY: *Legal Titles to Mining-claims and Water-rights in California.* San Francisco, 1867.

Index

Missions, the, economic features, management, and secularization, 59–64; appearance of California during mission era, 66–7; lands of Buenos Aires missions, 73 n

Monopoly in mines, its failure at Rough and Ready, 162–3

Montezuma Camp, laws of, 235

Mormon Diggings, the first mines there, 108

Nevada City, its early days, 200–1

"New Helvetia," and Captain Sutter, 101

New Kanaka camp, laws of, 237

North San Juan, laws of, 236

Occupation, evidence of, 164, 165, 234

Oglesby, Governor R. J., of Illinois, notes from his pioneer days, 152–3

Orchard paid for by miners' court, 254

Oregon, camps of, 181–2; local mining laws, 269

Ownership of same ground for different purposes, 259

Parsons, George F., graphic picture of gold-fever, 149–50

Partnership a sacred bond in the mines, 105

Patterson, Lawson B., views in the mines, 154

Phoenicians as miners and traders, 12

Pilot Hill, laws of, 236–7

Pioneers, American, their fitness for self-government, 5, 220; their contribution the mining camp, 5; views of a Senate committee, 10; their settlement of the West, 99–100; tendency to maltreat the Mexican, 208; their world-wide influence, 278–82

Placers, definition of, 7 n; early Italian, 18; ancient miners in, 18; in British Isles, 25; Cornish tin-placers, 25, 35; French

Placers (continued)
Broad, the, 38; Santa María del Darien, the, 46; California, 111 (See also Mining camps, Claims, Districts.)

Population, statistics of, 125, 128

Possessory rights, 7, 223, 258

Poverty Hill, laws of, 231–2

Prices in the mines, 131–2, 153

Prospectors, Grecian, 16; Thracian and Gaulish, 19; German, 20; Cornish, 27, 34; in the Southern states, 38, 39; in Spanish Mexico, 52; American, 132–3, 135–6, 276–81; professional, 244

Public lands, state decisions regarding miners upon, 248–9

Pueblos, or free towns, 63; Indian pueblos of New Mexico, 68; early California pueblos, 69–70; town council, 70; lands, and how granted, 72–3

Quarrels in the camps, 119–20

Quartz of ancient Nubia, 12

Quartz-claims, California laws of, 239, 241; laws of, in Nevada, 241–2; according to United States mining laws, 243; "inclined" and "square" locations, 265

Quartz-mining, beginning of, in California, 239

Ramona, its realism, 71–2

Recorder of claims, 160; fees of, 228, 234, 242; to examine work done, 240; time allowed prospector, 244

Redding, B. B., 256–7

Reese River, district of, laws of, 268 n

Registry, book of, 227

"Revolution of February," the, 100

Rights of miners to enter on agricultural lands, 229; local laws upon, 247; state acts and decisions concerning, 248–50; illustrations of, 250–7; the famous "Slickens" suits, 255–6; state decisions concerning rights, 261

A NOTE ON THE TYPE USED IN THIS BOOK

The text of this book has been set on the Linotype in a type-face called "Baskerville." The face is a facsimile reproduction of types cast from molds made for John Baskerville (1706–1775) from his designs. The punches for the revived Linotype Baskerville were cut under the supervision of the English printer George W. Jones.

John Baskerville's original face was one of the forerunners of the type-style known as "modern face" to printers: a "modern" of the period A.D. *1800.*

The book was composed, printed, and bound by The Plimpton Press, Norwood, Massachusetts. The binding is based on original designs by W. A. Dwiggins.